The Mitchell Beazley pocket guide to

Drawing

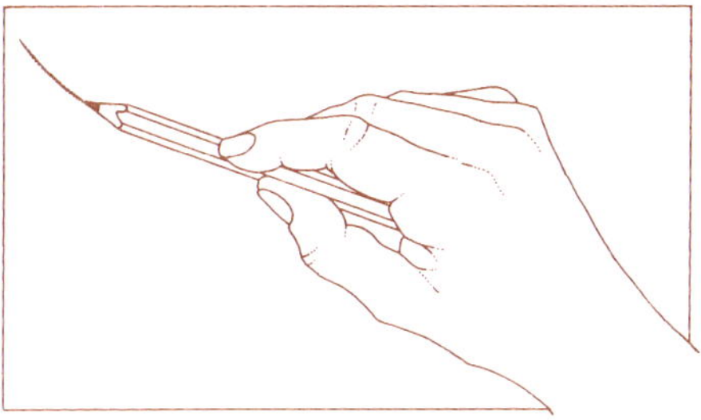

Series Consultant

Diana Armfield MSIA, NEAC, RWA, ARWS

Mitchell Beazley

Series consultant	**Diana Armfield MSIA, NEAC, RWA, ARWS** Painter, Visiting Lecturer at the Byam Shaw School of Art, London, and Editorial Consultant for *Leisure Painter* magazine
Consultants	**Peter John Garrard VPRBA, RP, NEAC** Painter, Editorial Consultant for *Artist* magazine and Head of the Painting Department, Mary Ward Centre, London
	Philip Matthews RWA Painter and Head of the Fine Art Department (Painting), Camberwell School of Art, London
	Ian Simpson ARCA Painter and Principal, St Martin's School of Art, London
	Marc Winer BA, Ed M, CAS Visiting artist, Ruskin School of Drawing and Fine Art, Oxford University

Acknowledgements

The publishers would like to thank Winsor and Newton Ltd for their advice and for the materials they supplied. We would also like to thank the following for their assistance: Falkiner Fine Papers Ltd, Janel Minors and David Morris.

Step-by-step illustrations by Candida Amsten, Clare Belfield, Christine Donnelly, David Humphreys, Albert Jackson, Elaine Keenan, Rachel Peacock, Lorraine Spiro, Lawrence Weaver, Marc Winer.

Line illustrations by Coral Mula, with additional illustrations by Russell Barnett and Elaine Keenan.

Picture credits are listed on page 144.

Chief Contributing Editor Carolyn King
Art Editor Linda Cole
Contributing Editors Susanne Haines, Paul Holberton, John Roberts
Editor Susanne Haines
Picture Researcher Brigitte Arora
Editor in Chief Susannah Read
Executive Art Editor Douglas Wilson
Production Sarah Goodden

Edited and designed by
Mitchell Beazley International Limited
87–89 Shaftesbury Avenue, London W1V 7AD

ISBN 0 85533 371 5

Typeset by Tradespools Ltd, Frome
Colour reproduction by Reprocolor Llovet S.A., Barcelona, Spain
Printed in Hong Kong by Mandarin Offset International Ltd

Introduction

This book aims to teach you to draw. The only qualification you need is to be sufficiently interested to spend some time in experiencing for yourself the information given in each chapter.

This information has been compiled from a series of discussions on drawing involving a number of practising artists who are all experienced teachers. Each artist has a different approach to his or her own work and to teaching but we all agree on the principle underlying the teaching in this book: that to learn to draw it is first necessary to learn to see. Of course, most people think they can see very well but seeing in general terms is not the same as seeing in the specific way which is necessary for drawing.

The Pocket Guide to Drawing shows you how you can begin to see in this specific way.

This is a practical book with information to stimulate you to make drawings yourself and with a wide variety of illustrations by distinguished draughtsmen to demonstrate that there is no single way of drawing.

Ian Simpson

Contents

How to use this book

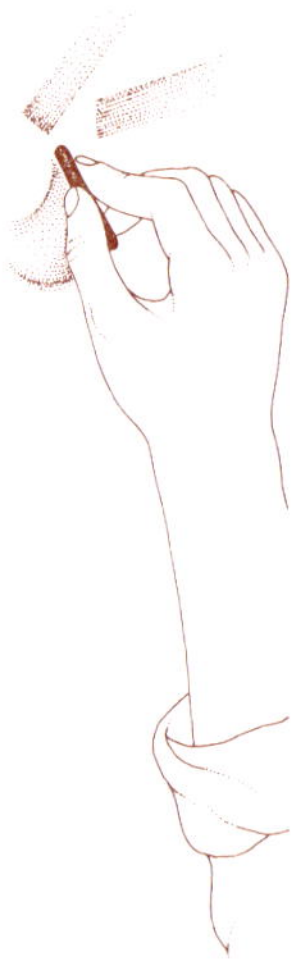

Whatever kind of drawing you want to do, this *Pocket Guide* should prove extremely useful. It can be followed from start to finish as a complete drawing course, introducing you to the full range of techniques and mediums, and it can be referred to again and again when you need solutions to specific problems.

The book is divided into three sections covering materials, techniques and useful reference. A glossary explains the technical terms and cross-references at the head of the page will enable you to turn quickly to pages containing additional information. Some of the illustrations are included as step-by-step examples of the techniques, others are diagrams. There are also examples of drawings by great artists.

Use the *Pocket Guide* to increase the range of subjects you can handle confidently. It should also encourage you to try new materials. But use it as a means of developing your personal style.

Materials

Drawing involves putting marks (usually dark) on paper (usually light). This simple process can be very different according to the materials used – as can the appearance of the resulting drawings. This section looks at the various types of paper on which you can work, together with the substances and implements you will use to make the lines and areas of tone from which a drawing is made up. Finally, it looks at the surface on which the paper will be supported and the materials most suitable for working outdoors.

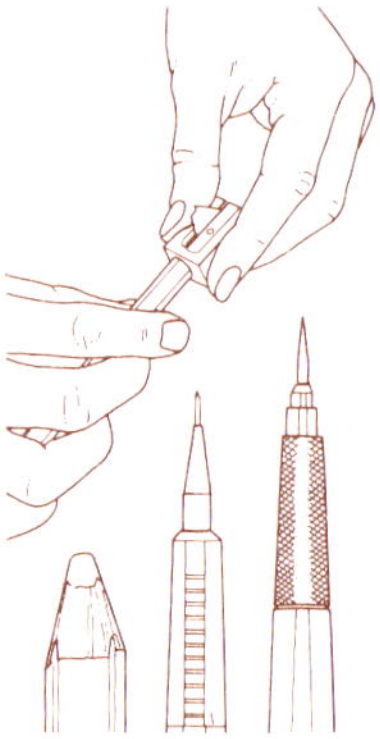

Techniques

Drawing should be spontaneous and imaginative, but an understanding of the techniques and the special aids to handling factors such as perspective will give you greater freedom to put down your ideas. The section also covers the particular problems of drawing subjects such as the human figure and animals. Landscape and buildings are included, together with the techniques for making complex compositions from quick sketches done in the field. Practising the exercises is an excellent way to increase your confidence in each subject area.

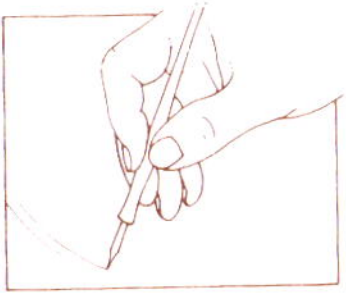

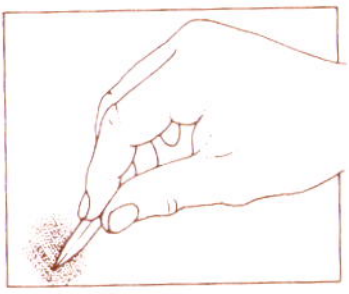

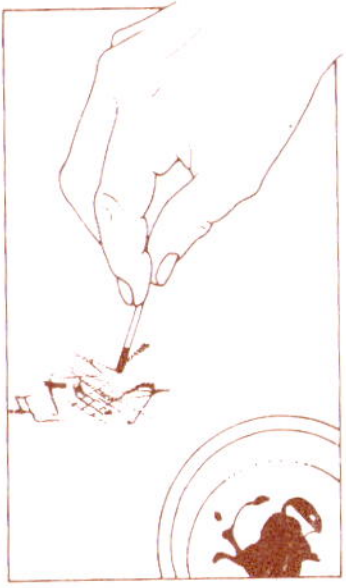

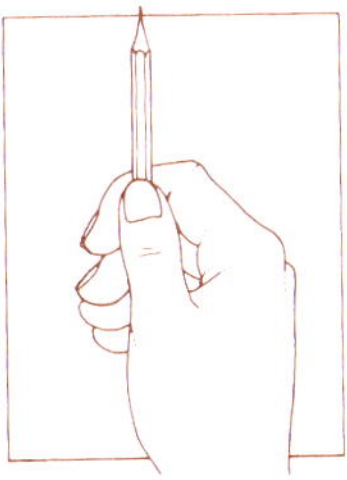

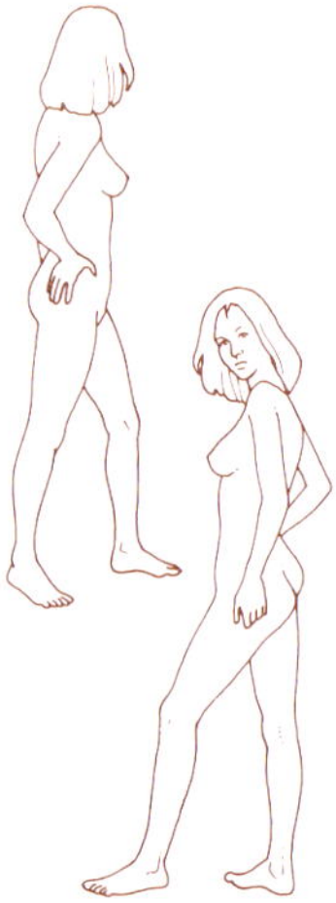

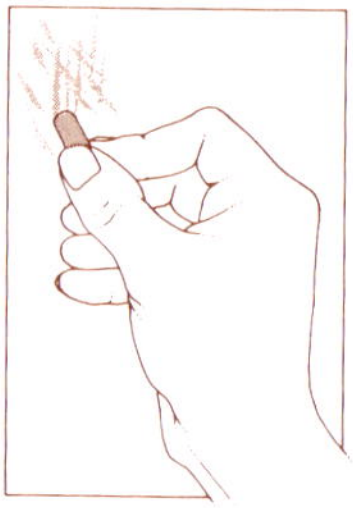

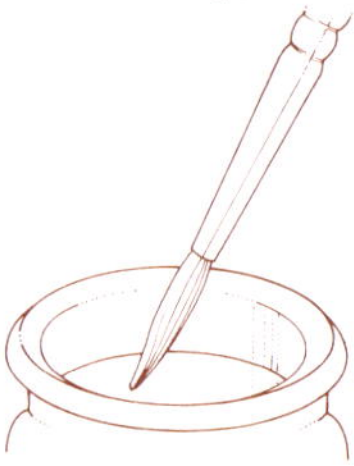

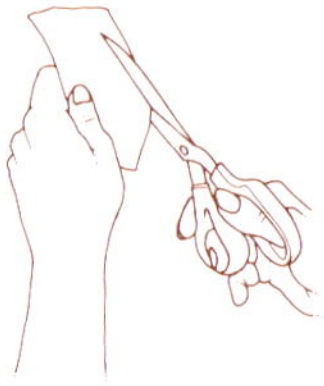

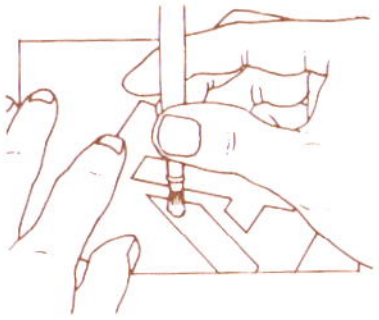

Reference

This section includes useful miscellaneous information for the artist. The processes involved in making drawing implements and preparing the paper surface are described. Finishing can also be very important – certainly if you wish to keep or display your drawings – so framing and mounting are also covered. Finally, the best ways to store drawings for their lasting protection, and the addresses of leading suppliers are given.

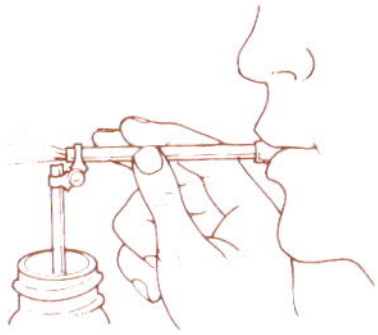

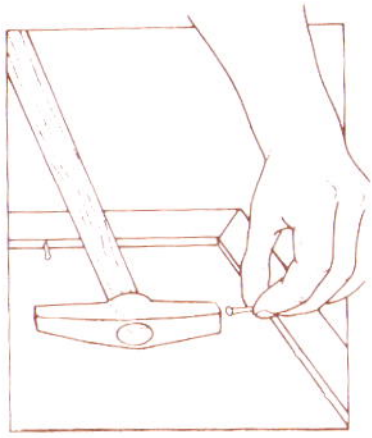

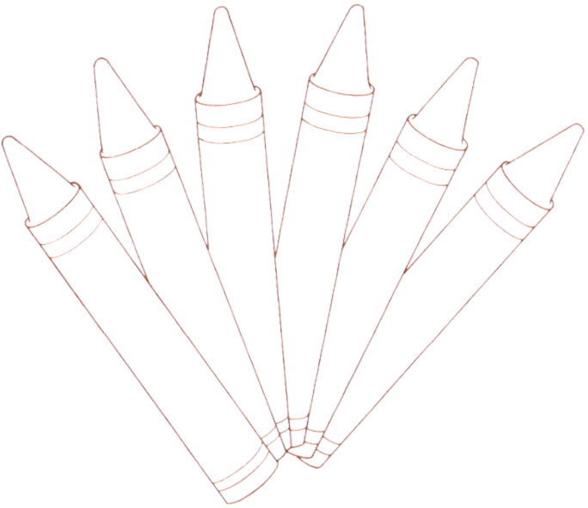

Materials

A random selection of materials illustrated and described on the following pages, all available at any good art supply shop.

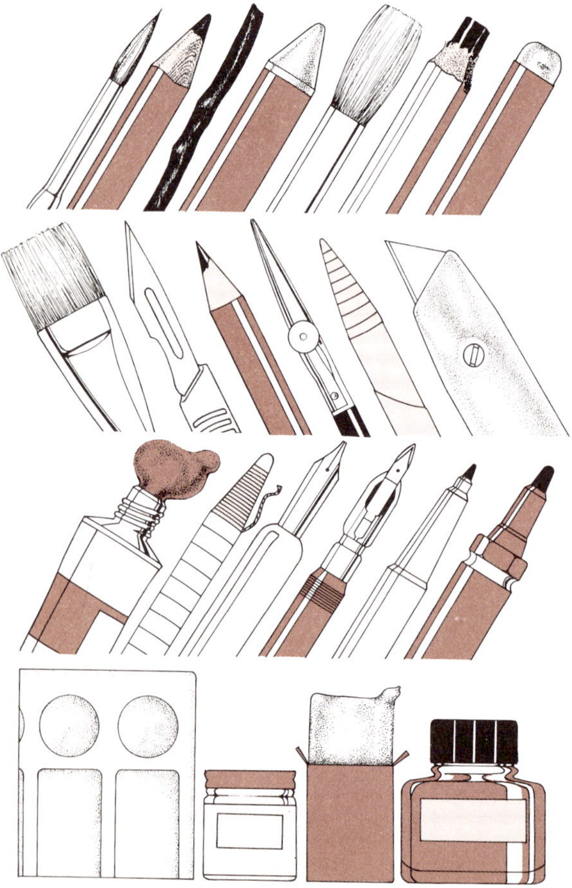

Choosing materials that are compatible with the subject you are drawing will widen the scope of your expression and should be explored. A selection of drawing tools and paper, with suggestions on how they may be used, has been given on the following pages, but keep up to date by visiting artists' suppliers to stay in touch with what is new on the market and by going to exhibitions and looking at what other people are using. Experiment with everything you see, and remember that there are no rules in your choice of material. To convey the character of the same subject one person may choose to explore the textural qualities on a piece of tinted rough paper using chalk, another may prefer pen and ink on smooth white paper.

Have a large assortment of materials to hand and use them all. If you cannot get along with one, move on and try another.

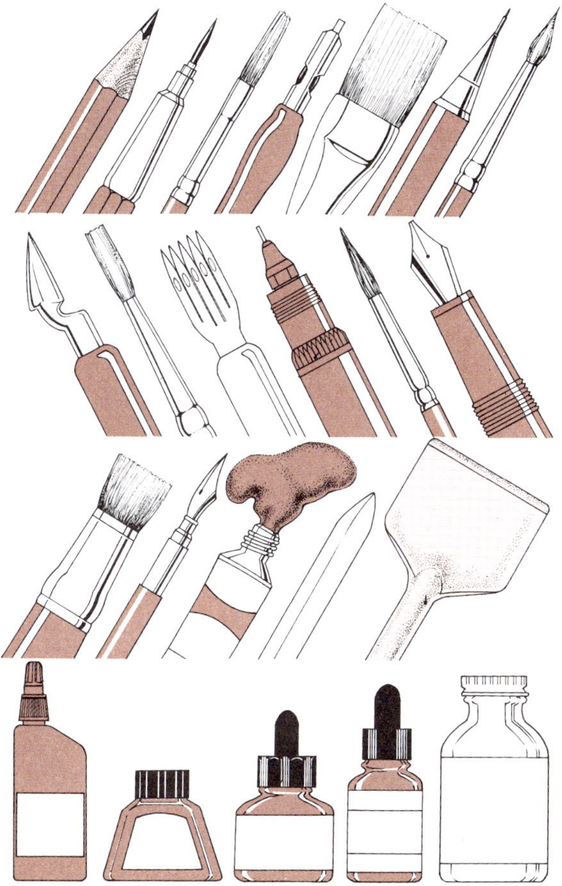

Paper

The character of a paper can totally change the effect of a drawing so it is very important to be aware of the wide variety available. Certain papers are generally recommended for certain materials and this is useful as a guide but should not necessarily be adhered to; the most interesting and surprising results can come from using what might conventionally be regarded as a totally unsuitable paper. Before buying paper consider exactly what you want from it. The information on these pages will help you to de-code such mysterious descriptions as mould made, double elephant, 175gsm and Not.

Paper is made by three different methods. Handmade is the best quality and most expensive; it is hard-wearing and long-lasting and both sides of the sheet can be used. Mould made is a good quality machine-made paper that imitates handmade but has a right and wrong side. Machine made is produced by a continuous web process; it is the least expensive type of paper and does not have the character of handmade.

Surface

Hot pressed (HP): pressed to give a smooth, hard surface. **Not pressed:** ie not hot pressed; lightly pressed to give a slightly textured surface. A useful all-purpose paper. **Rough:** dried naturally without being pressed to give a rough, toothed surface. **1 Wove:** paper with a continuous, even texture, produced by the woven wire mesh of the mould in which the paper is formed. **2 Laid:** paper that shows the impression of the chain lines of the mould at regular intervals across the sheet (such as Ingres).

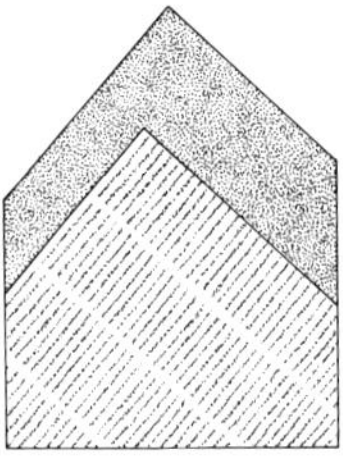

Right and wrong side

Handmade papers have the same surface on both sides. To distinguish the wrong side of a machine- or mould-made paper look for the impression of the fine mesh of the machine web. The watermark should not be used as a guide.

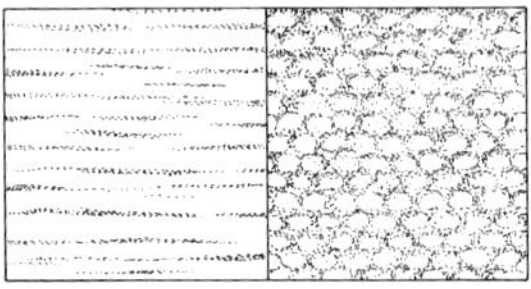

Grain or direction

Handmade paper does not have a grain. The grain of a machine-made paper follows the direction of the web, the way the fibres have been pulled, making it easier to tear and fold in that direction.

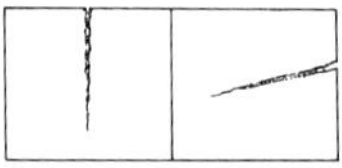

Quality

The quality of paper determines its longevity. The best quality is made from cotton rag. It is the acidity (measured on a pH scale – 7.0 is neutral) that affects the quality; an acidic paper will fade, discolour and disintegrate. See p136 for test for paper fading.

Quantity and form

It is cheaper to buy paper in bulk, by the quire (25 sheets) or by the ream (500 sheets). Machine-made paper is sometimes available in a roll. Paper can be bought mounted on board or in blocks (a pad glued at the edges), and also, of course, in sketchbooks, either case or spiral bound.

see also pages 18, 96–97, 130–133, 136

Weights and measures

Paper sizes and weights are going over to metrication but some papers are still measured in Imperial. Weight is measured in pounds per ream (eg 72 pounds – light, 300 pounds – heavy) or in grams per square metre (gsm or gm^2; eg 100gsm – light, 640gsm – heavy).

Metric	Imperial
A0	Antiquarian 53 × 31in
841 × 1189mm	(1346 × 787mm)
A1	Double Elephant 40 × 26¼in
594 × 841mm	(1016 × 679mm)
A2	Imperial 30½ × 22½in
420 × 594mm	(775 × 572mm)
A3	Double Crown 30 × 20in
297 × 420mm	(762 × 508mm)
A4	Royal 24 × 19in
210 × 297mm	(610 × 483mm)
A5	Medium 22 × 17½in
148 × 210mm	(559 × 444mm)

Choosing a paper

Compare the marks made by various media on a smooth Bristol Board and on rough watercolour paper. Judge their suitability for yourself.

Pencil		
Charcoal		
Pen and ink		
Soft pastel		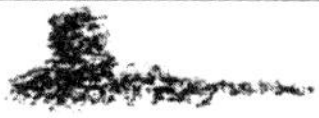
Watercolour wash		

Choose a paper that will enhance the quality of the medium and add to the mood of your drawing. The brilliance of a white paper varies greatly, and there is a large range of coloured papers to choose from. How absorbent do you want your paper to be? The amount of glue sizing determines this and varies from paper to paper. Do you want a rough or smooth paper?

Smooth paper Hot pressed, smooth paper is generally recommended for detailed work in line or tone, particularly suitable for pencil and pen and ink and also for crayon.

Textured paper Not or rough papers give an interesting texture, and provide a tooth for charcoal and pastel to grip.

Some good quality papers generally available in the UK and US are: R.W.S., a cotton handmade watercolour paper (HP, Not and Rough); Saunders, cotton rag mould-made watercolour paper (HP, Not and Rough); Bockingford, acid-free wood pulp machine-made artists' paper (Not); Aquarelle Arches, cotton mould-made paper (HP, Not, Rough); Fabriano, cotton hand- and mould-made paper (HP, Not and Rough). Strathmore produce good artists' papers in the US. There are many cartridge papers of various qualities and weights; Bristol Board, detail and tracing paper all have a smooth finish; Ingres paper (made by Fabriano, Canson and Mi Teintes) is a tinted, laid paper which sometimes has a fleck, and is suitable for charcoal and pastel.

Charcoal

Charcoal is a universal drawing material, used since earliest times. It has great versatility, expressed in the widest range of marks, from light to very black, and from simple line to gradated tone. Textured, tinted and ordinary cartridge paper – even brown wrapping paper – are all suitable for charcoal drawings, though shiny surfaces are not. The inexperienced may find this medium rather messy at first and will need practice to gauge the brittleness of willow charcoal but, once mastered, it has great freedom and energy.

Because of its dusty quality, you will have to learn to draw with your hand raised off the paper so as not to obliterate the marks. To keep the lines sharp, a fixative is sprayed on at intervals as areas of the drawing you like are completed (p 132). This fixing is particularly necessary on the blacker areas where the depth of tone has to be built up.

Different forms of charcoal

1,2,3 Charcoal made from willow comes in fine, medium and thick sticks. This is charcoal in its natural state. **4** Scene painter's charcoal makes a less precise line but is good for large tonal areas. **5** Compressed charcoal can be set in wood like a pencil (in soft, medium and hard). It has a harder texture than a stick but wears down quickly. If dropped it breaks and becomes useless. **6** A *porte-crayon* holds a short piece of charcoal and keeps fingers clean.

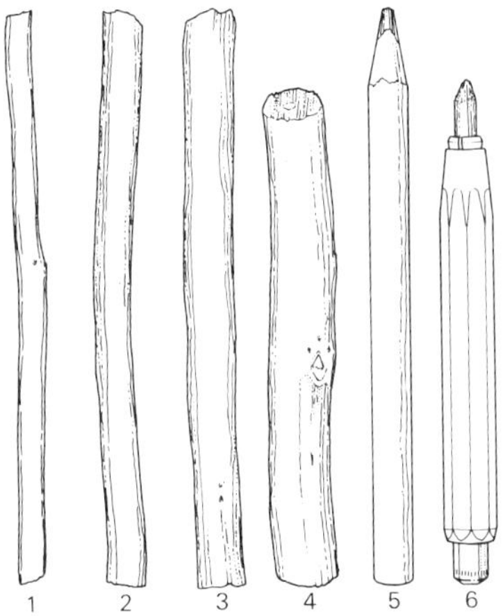

Highlights

A kneadable putty rubber can be used to pick out the highlights in toned areas. Tear off a small piece and shape to a point. Dab on and pick off the charcoal gradually, turning to a clean side of the eraser each time. White chalk can be used for more dramatic highlights when drawn on tinted paper.

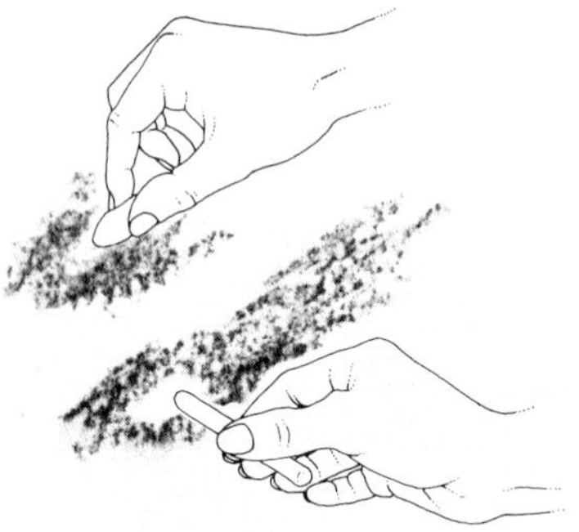

see also pages 28, 132, 136

Drawing with charcoal

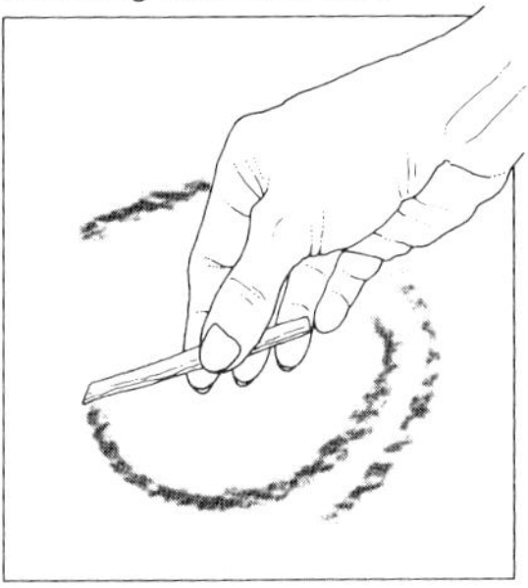

Charcoal used in line has a speed and boldness, a spontaneity which is more appropriate to large, free drawings than to precision work.

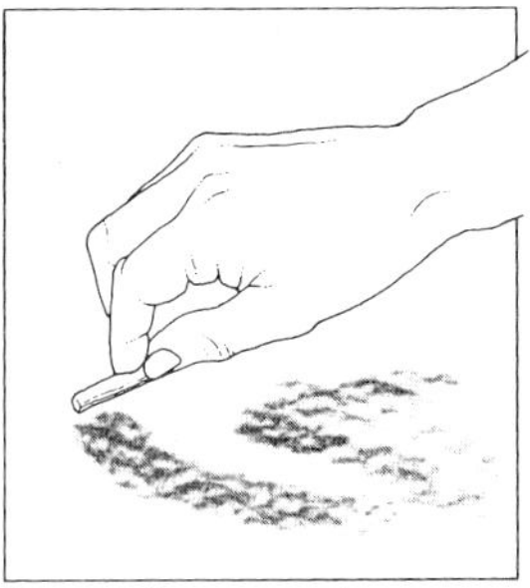

When laid flat on textured paper, scene-painter's charcoal, or a short piece of willow charcoal, is ideal for drawing contrasting areas.

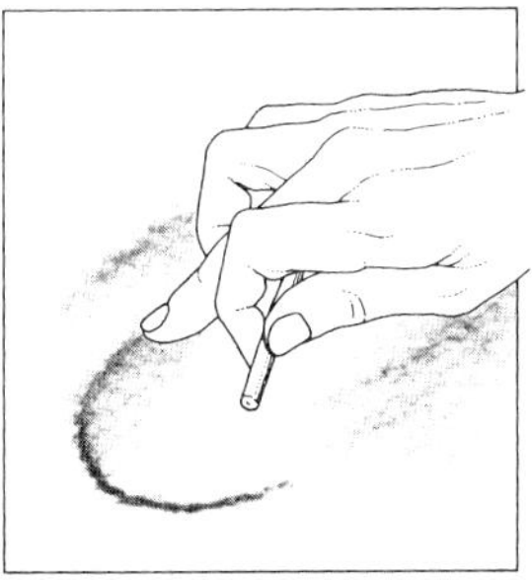

Fingers or a stump will smudge and soften lines. Powdered charcoal from the chemist, or crumbled short pieces, can be used to gain effects.

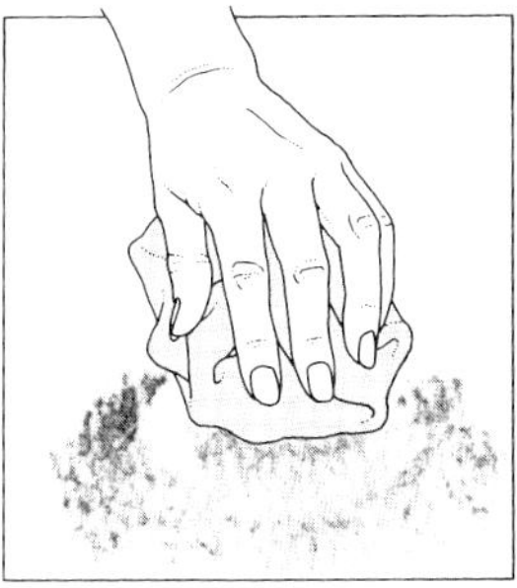

To dust off charcoal a fine, soft cloth (even a feather duster) can be gently flicked at the mark. A putty rubber will then rub out most lines.

Sharpening willow charcoal

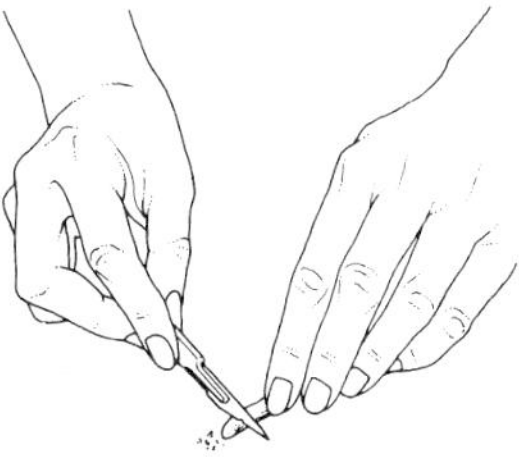

1 By turning the charcoal frequently when drawing, it will remain pointed. It can be given an edge with a knife, or simply by breaking it.

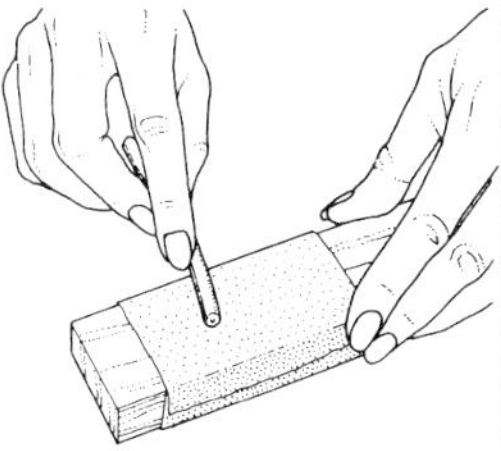

2 The best way to achieve a precise point is to use fine emery paper or to rub it to a chisel shape on a scrap of coarsely textured paper.

Pencils

A lead pencil is a misleading name as the 'lead' is actually graphite, a form of carbon. In fact, to add to the confusion, the term 'pencil' was used in the past to describe a finely pointed brush. It was Nicolas-Jacques Conté who patented the process of varying the degree of hardness in graphite at the end of the eighteenth century, thereby boosting its popularity as a medium for permanent drawing.

The great attraction of the pencil, familiar though it is, lies in its immediacy, its versatility and its sensitivity. The ease with which it can be erased should not be ignored either. Although made in grades of softness and hardness, the pressure on the pencil and the texture or grain of the paper also lend variety. The pencil is equally capable of producing a quick study or a finely detailed drawing.

Grades of pencil

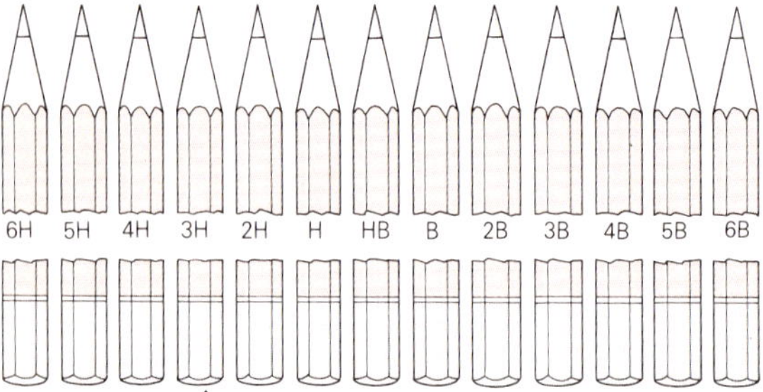

Hard pencils Leads vary from 9H (the hardest) to HB. They make fine, pale grey lines and precise, hard marks and are appropriate for highly detailed or technical work.

Soft pencils These range downwards in blackness to 8B. For general use a B or 2B is sufficient. B pencils give more varied lines and tones, particularly on textured paper.

Other forms of pencil

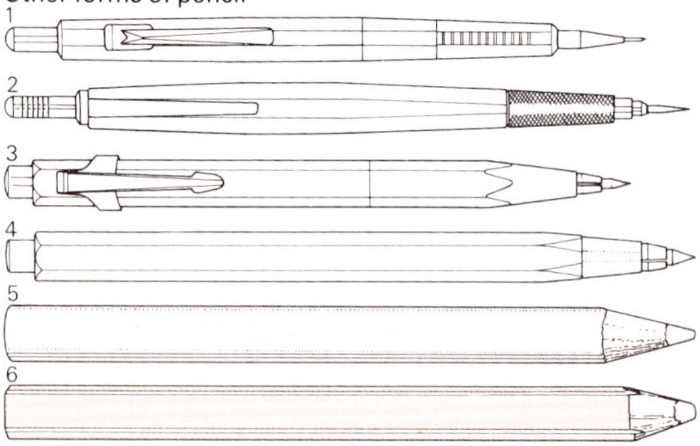

1,2 Clutch pencils take replacement leads just like those in the various grades of wooden pencils. They do not need sharpening as the lead is advanced automatically and can be kept at a constant length, nor do they wear down to stumps. **3,4** Some clutch pencils take coloured leads. **5** A Black Beauty makes a thick mark. **6** The flat carpenter's pencil can be sharpened to a chisel shape.

see also pages 28, 43, 59, 132

How to hold the pencil

The pencil in drawing is a linear tool and by its response to pressure will make a variety of lines. To some people it is a writing instrument and to control it sufficiently means holding the pencil close to the lead. Writing is concerned with making small marks of similar size, essentially a finger/wrist movement. Resting the hand on the paper in the conventional manner is the correct way for detailed drawing. This method may be extended if you want to achieve a broader range of marks, in which case hold the pencil nearer the blunt end, leaving you free to draw from the elbow or even the shoulder if you want to make a more sweeping line. Grasp the pencil comfortably with the hand relaxed. The fingers should support rather than grip it.

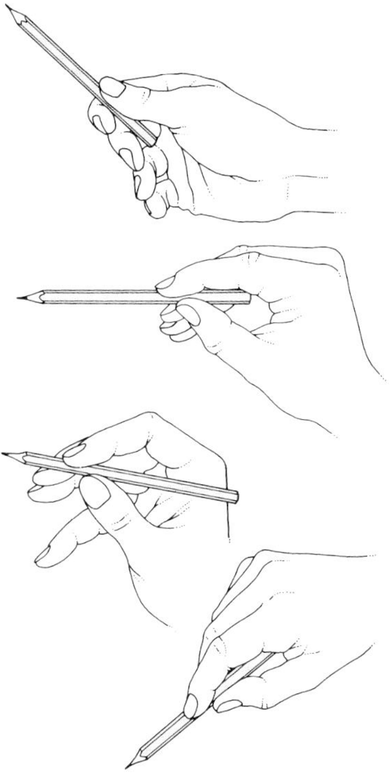

Sharpening pencils

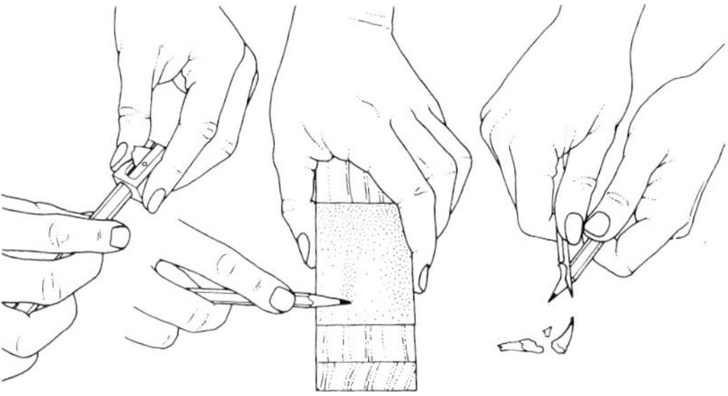

In constant use B pencils will wear down very quickly. Although pencil sharpeners are convenient, they tend to eat up too much wood before coming to a point, and give too short a lead. If a knife is used, the wood can be left for strength and a long point produced, sanded to needle fineness.

Crayons

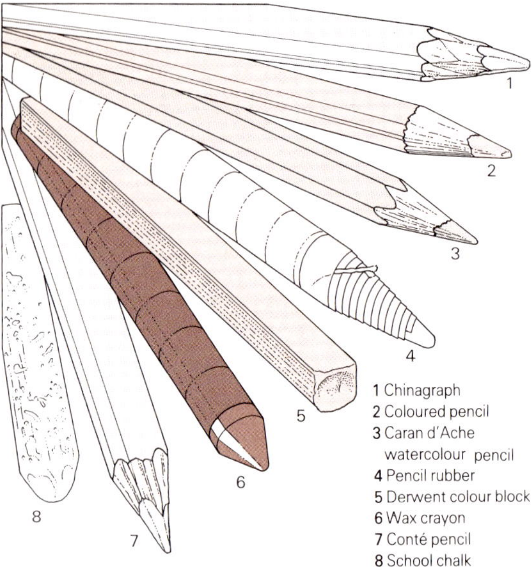

1 Chinagraph
2 Coloured pencil
3 Caran d'Ache watercolour pencil
4 Pencil rubber
5 Derwent colour block
6 Wax crayon
7 Conté pencil
8 School chalk

Everyone is familiar with the crayon boxes and colouring books of childhood yet may have little opportunity in adulthood to reacquaint themselves with the delights of making coloured drawings. There is an extensive range of pencils, crayons and chalks on the market, loosely grouped under the heading of crayons, in a wide variety of prices. Their use is by no means restricted to children, as many artists find great satisfaction in being able to enjoy the essential simplicity of a pencil but with the added fillip of working in colour.

The permanence of crayon drawings is not their strong point. They are fragile and impossible to clean. However, their main appeal is in their spontaneity rather than their durability.

Conté crayons

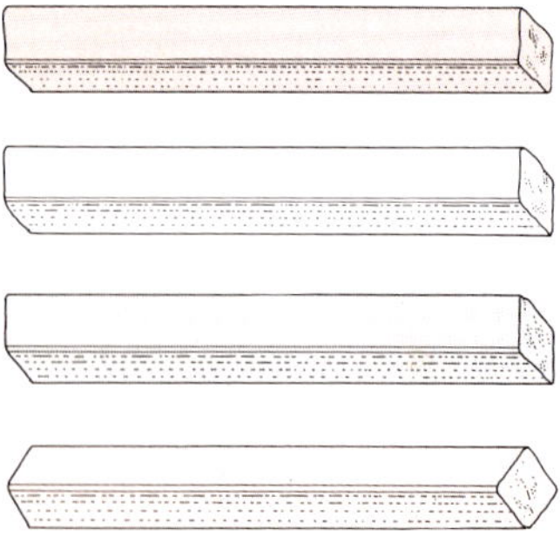

Conté crayons do not break or smudge easily as they are slightly greasy and more finely textured than charcoal. They are limited to sepia (brown), white, three degrees of black, and sanguine (terracotta). Pencils (above) and sticks respond sensitively to any type of surface and look particularly well on tinted paper.

see also pages 29, 84, 112

Wax crayons

Wax crayons are the most vigorous of them all, produced in a large series of strong, luscious colours. What they lack in discretion they make up for in full-blown vitality. They can be mixed by careful cross-hatching, building up the dark colours over the light ones, but this should be done with a judicious touch to keep the colours fresh.

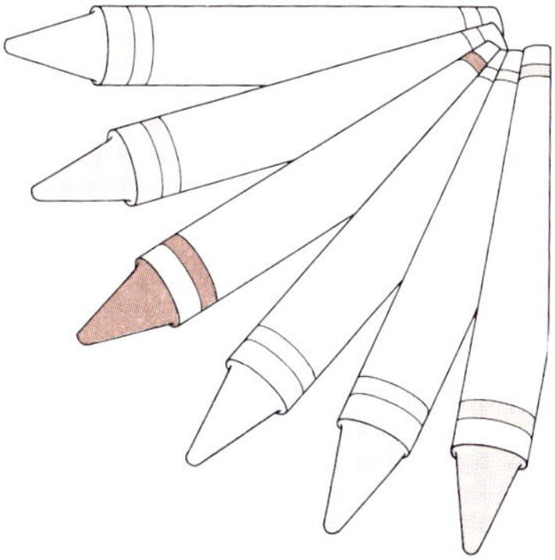

Using crayons

Luminous drawings by Georges Seurat in conté on textured paper fully realized the beauty of these crayons. Watteau combined conté with chalk on tinted papers. Artists such as David Hockney have drawn with coloured crayons that are cleverly blended and mixed by means of dense little lines, and handled rather like paint (see p34).

Some crayons such as conté pencils and coloured pencils can be sharpened to a point but the distinguishing characteristic of most crayons is a soft, sensuous line that can be either strongly defined or gently broken, and in part is dependent on the surface on which it is drawn. Whether used on their own, with a watercolour wash, or in conjunction with other media, crayons seem to have an irresistible charm.

Water-soluble crayons

Some crayons, such as those made by Caran d'Ache, are water soluble, which means that a straightforward line can be transformed into a wash of colour by the application of a sable brushload of plain water, leaving behind a faint shadow of the crayon outline.

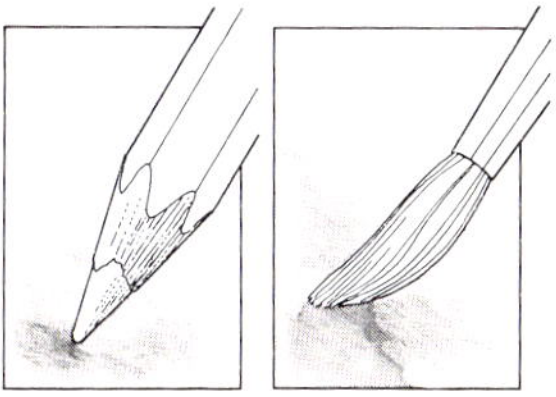

Crayons combined with other media

Wax crayons and wash

Draw in the highlights with white wax crayon (a candle will do) and lay watercolour over it. This rolls off the wax, leaving the white paper.

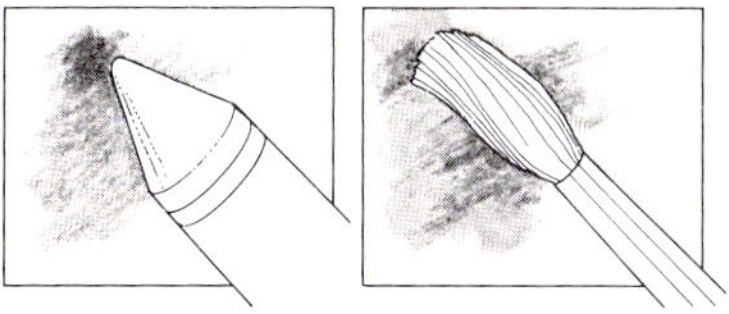

Wax crayons and coloured pencils

Draw with the pencils over wax crayon marks. The wax will resist the pencil, making an interrupted or random pattern.

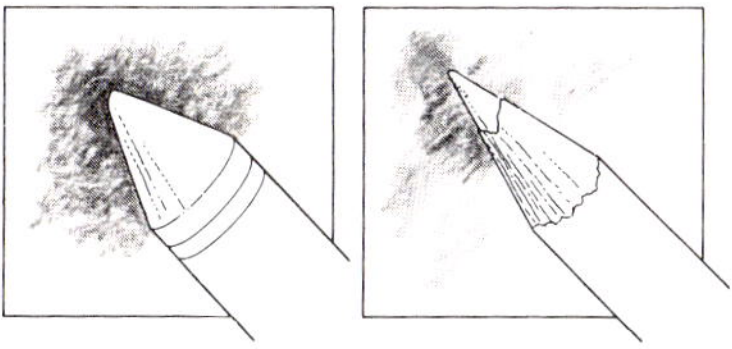

Pastels

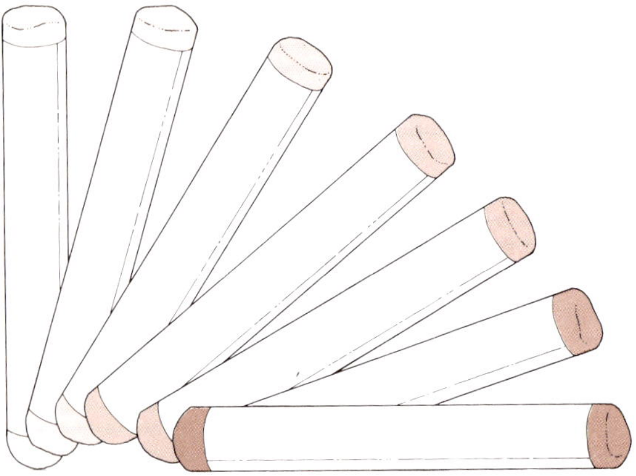

There are three types of pastel: the soft pastel stick, the oil pastel and the pencil. Unlike oils and watercolours, soft pastels, the most popular form, have maintained their true colour values and freshness over the centuries because they contain no additives and are not varnished. They are made from pigment, chalk and gum in more than 600 tints. Unlike mixing a vast range of colours from a limited palette, soft pastels cannot be mixed as you go along, so you will need about 40 as a basic collection.

Pastel pencils

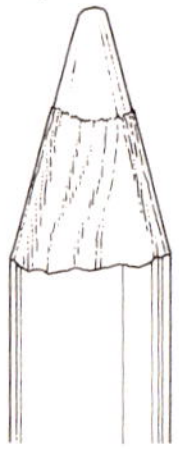

These are not as crumbly as soft pastels; they have a narrow colour range and make a precise mark.

Grades of pastel

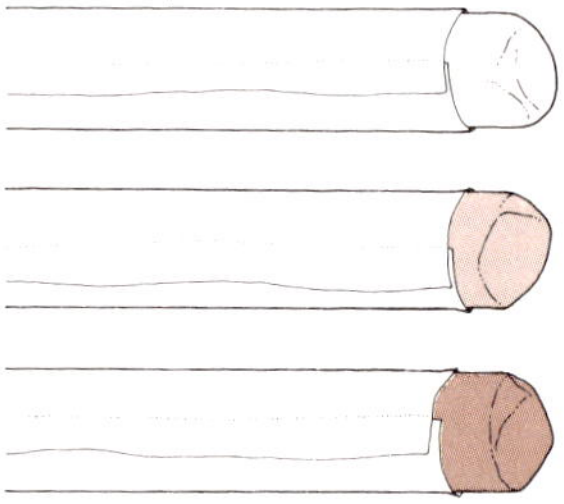

Pastels are graded from 0 to 8, from lightest to darkest. Very light tones are softer and contain more chalk, while the darker colours are made up of a greater percentage of pigment and are generally harder in consistency. Some pigments are harder than others despite their grading (eg yellow ochre 4 is not nearly as fragile as cobalt blue 4).

Pastel papers

The best surface for pastels is paper. It is also considered the most durable. The paper should have a 'tooth' (a textured surface to which the particles of chalk cling) and soft colour: Bockingford, Saunders, Ingres and coloured wrapping papers are all suitable, although the striations of 'laid' paper may be distracting. White paper is a poor substitute in comparison with the deliciously tinted grey, fawn or smoky blue papers which can be incorporated into the composition and left exposed in places to add a subtle extra dimension.

see also pages 29, 86, 92, 95, 129, 132

Pastel strokes

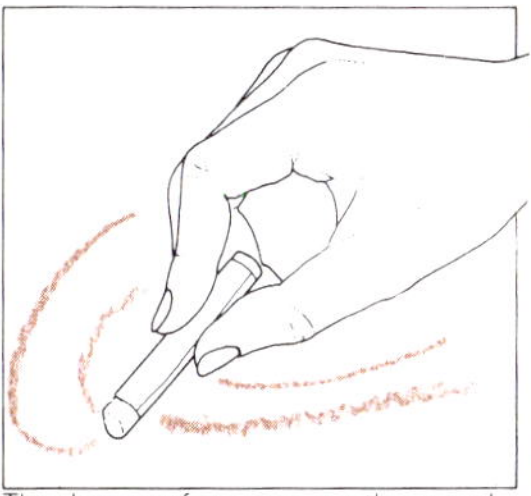

The degree of pressure on the pastel helps to determine different effects. Cross-hatching, or alternating thick and thin strokes made with the end of the pastel and a broken edge, are ways of achieving tone and shading.

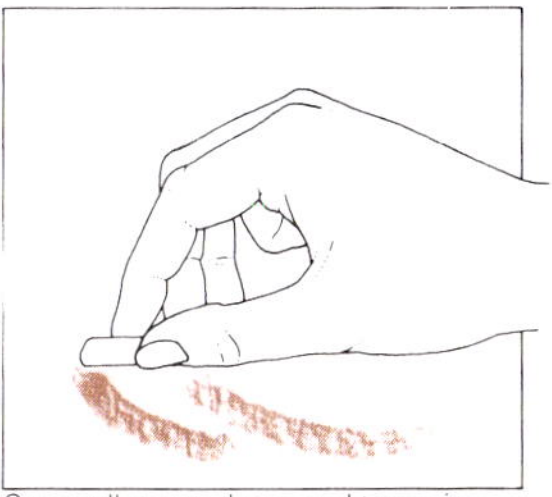

Group all your colours and tones in families on corrugated paper so that they are easily to hand. For an area of colour or texture use a short piece of chalk on its side. Keep the wrapper for future identification.

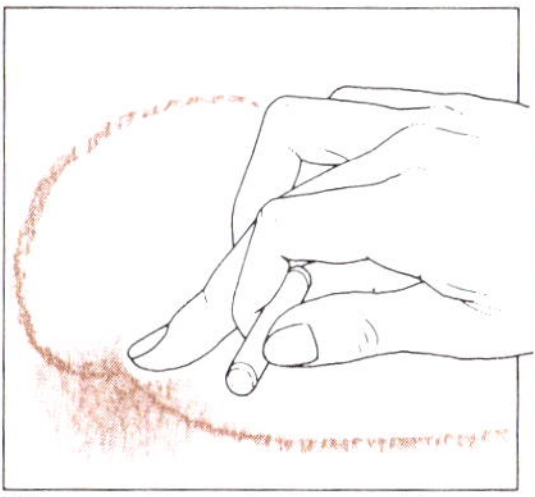

When pastels are built up, making thick marks, the effect has much in common with oil painting. Honoré Fragonard, the 18C artist, used his fingers to imitate this richness. A finger can also soften an edge.

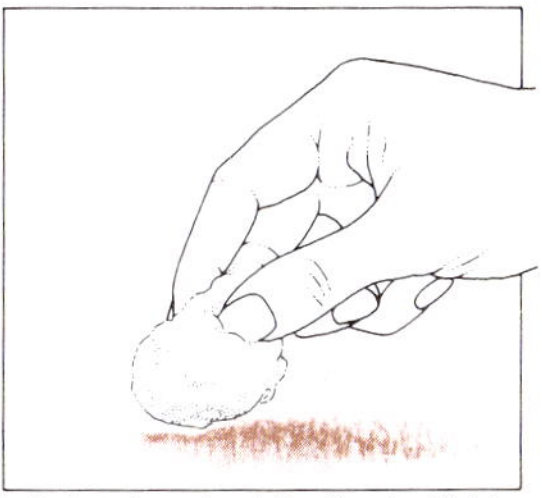

Initial strokes should be firm but light to avoid clogging the grain of the paper. If making alterations, dust off first with cotton wool before adjusting. This prevents a sticky build-up on the surface.

Oil pastels

Although oil pastels can be confused with soft pastels, they are not interchangeable and should not be mixed together in a drawing. The colours are limited and rather bright. Oil pastels are considered a painting medium; they can be used on canvas or board as well as paper, and are sometimes mixed with turpentine to make a wash which is applied with a brush.

Rubbing out

This is not easy. A putty rubber will spoil the glow of the paper, which is important if you intend to leave some of the paper exposed in places. A hog brush, as used for painting in oils, can be more effective. The bristles remove most of the chalk from the grain of the paper without destroying the tooth.

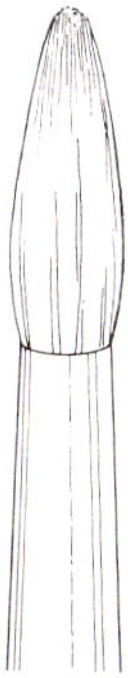

Pens and inks

Any pointed instrument can be dipped into ink to make a mark – a sharpened twig, a matchstick, the end of a brush, a piece of trimmed bamboo, or a dried cow parsley stalk.

Ink is a line medium so that various techniques such as hatching, stippling and combinations of marks must be employed to convey tone. Alternatively, a wash of diluted ink or watercolour may be applied with a brush. The other effects that can be achieved with a little experimentation are interesting, including laying a wash over a wax resist, spattering ink with a stiff brush, blowing blots, and working with a sponge or the fingers to represent textures or fine details.

Almost any paper is suitable except soft or textured papers that will catch in the nib and make it splutter. A smooth cartridge or watercolour paper, which does not have to be limited to white, is most common. The paper should have a hard surface if a precise line, drawn with a technical pen for instance, is required. The heavier the paper, the less chance of spoiling it if there has been much correction. This is important because, when a wash is to be part of the drawing, it will not roll on smoothly if the surface has been roughened by erasing.

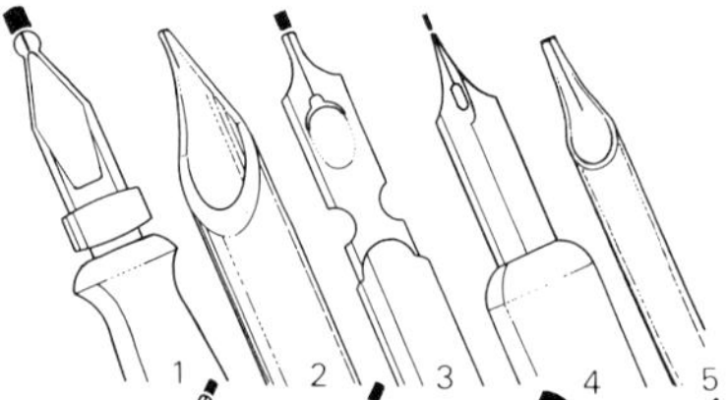

Dip pens 1, 3 The steel pen (usually with a reservoir) and range of nibs, **2** the reed pen and **5** the goose quill make a variety of marks possible. **4** The mapping pen takes some skill.

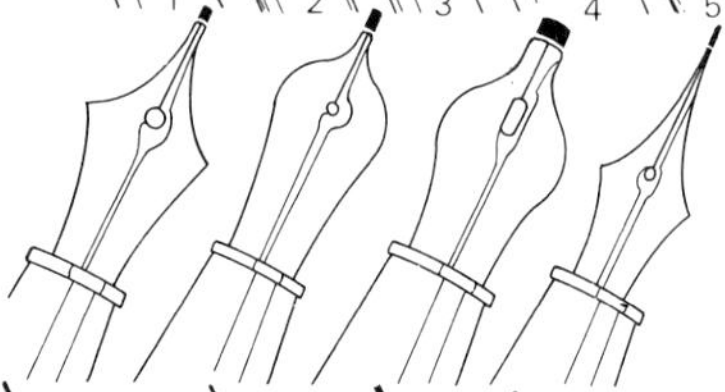

Fountain pens The best ones for drawing have flexible nibs and are convenient for sketching. Some take permanent ink, others non-waterproof ink. The range of nibs is small.

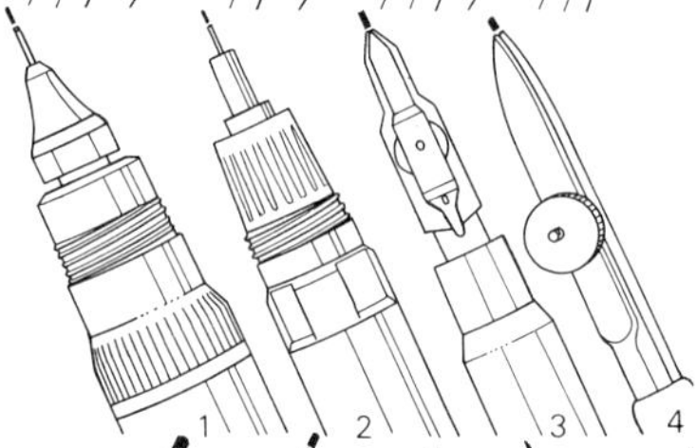

Technical pens draw consistently even lines. **1** The Rapidograph and **2** Isograph move in any direction. **3** The Graphos takes various nibs. **4** A ruling pen draws fine lines on mounts (p 134).

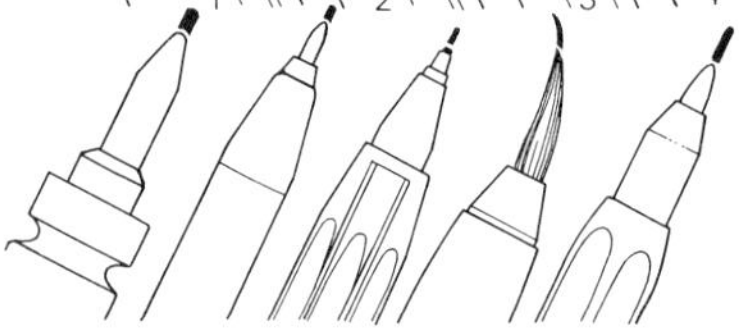

Ball points and fibre tips These familiar instruments are the antithesis of the precise technical pen. They are made in several colours and make lively marks, difficult to control.

see also pages 30, 37, 88, 128, 134

Various pen marks

Those who have little experience with a pen will need to practise on some smooth paper to get the ink to flow evenly from the nib.

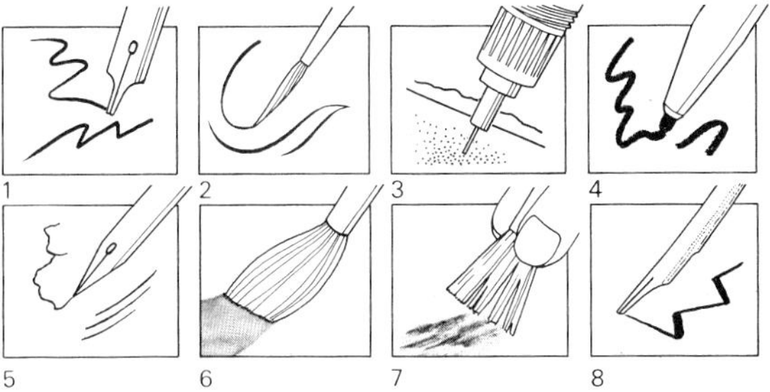

1 A dip pen; **2** a fine sable brush, producing an expressive line; **3** a stylo-tip pen, giving a controlled line or stippling; **4** a fibre tip, which results in an energetic line.

5 The thin, scratchy line of a mapping pen; **6** a wash applied with a large sable; **7** dry brush technique, the bristles splayed out with the fingers; **8** the quill's crisp line.

Inks

1 Chinese inkstick: long-lasting; creates any density of black. Dries matt; is excellent on all surfaces. **2** Indian ink leaves a strong, glossy line. Dilute with distilled water. **3** Filler bottles for stylo-tip pens. **4** Coloured inks are water-resistant but not colour-fast (may take 15 years to fade away). **5** Non-waterproof inks can be diluted with tap water and are produced in limited colours. Drawing on wet paper will give soft lines. **6** Chinese white is for tinted papers. **7** Watercolour for laying washes.

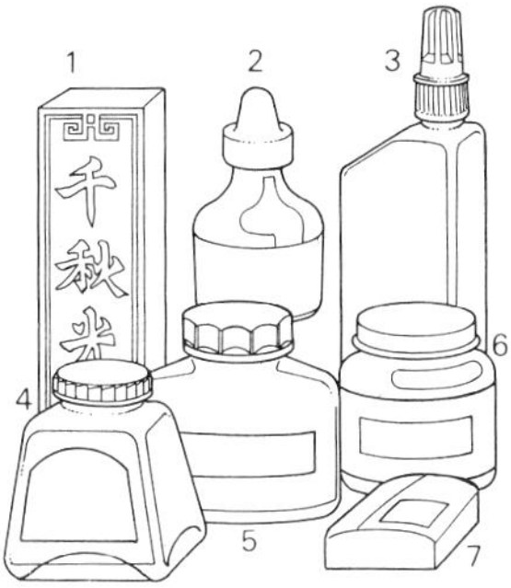

Removing blots and errors

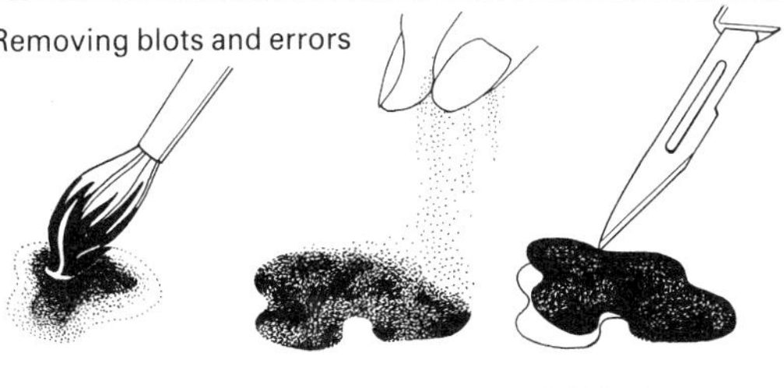

Blotting paper or a small sable absorbs spilt ink. Dry ink is scratched off hard surfaces with a blade.

Sand or salt will dry up blots and can then be shaken off. Erase remaining stain with an India rubber.

With fresh paper underneath, cut around a mistake with a knife. Tape the clean piece on from the back.

The work area

It is a straightforward matter to make a drawing board from softwood, or composition board which can be cut with a craft knife. The wood will take drawing pins and does not chip or warp. Hardboard is an adequate material to use and is inexpensive but masking tape or clips will be needed to fasten the paper to a hardwood board. It will require a pad of several thicknesses of paper to cushion the drawing surface, rather than a single sheet of card, all that is needed with composition board.

If you intend to buy a drawing board, do not economize on quality. Cheap boards tend to warp. Heavy duty ones are usually metal edged or are battened at the back. Table-top models are adjustable from a horizontal to a nearly vertical position.

Attaching the paper to the board

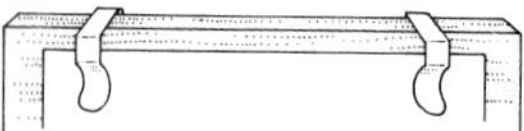
Drawing-board clips

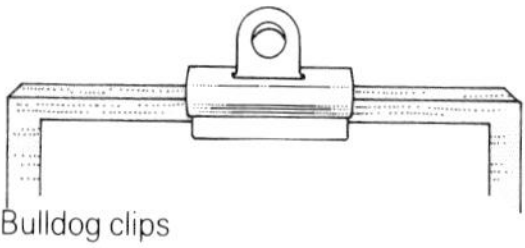
Bulldog clips

Drawing pins
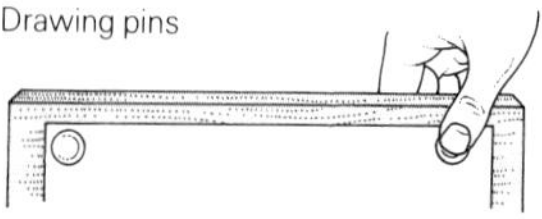

Masking tape
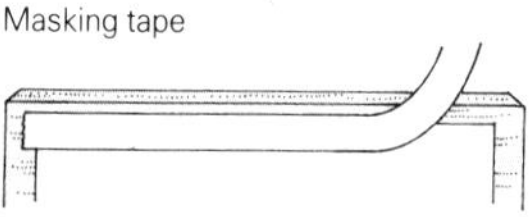

The light by which you draw is of fundamental importance. Artificial light will cast deep shadows, and even natural light can be an impediment if the shadow cast by your drawing hand falls across the paper. The drawing board should be vertical to avoid distorting the perspective. When you are setting up your subject make sure you leave enough space to view it from every angle.

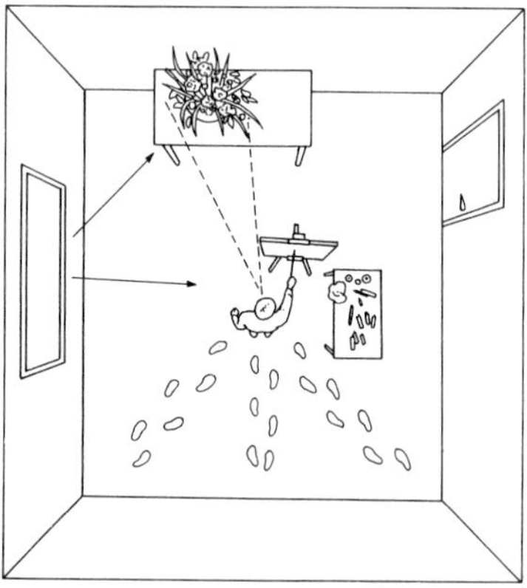

Cleaning erasers

Erasers collect a great deal of grime if left loose in a drawer. Hard rubbers should be cleaned on the corner of the paper from time to time. Putty rubbers can be cut into smaller pieces or the frayed threads removed as you go.

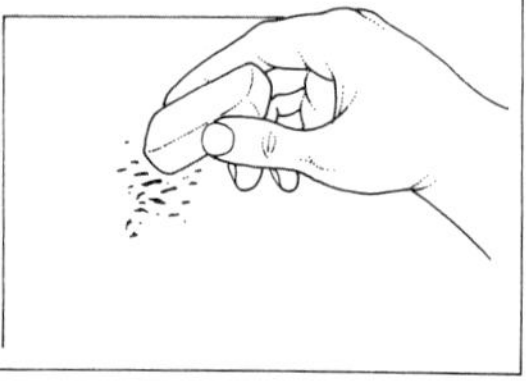

Organizing the work area

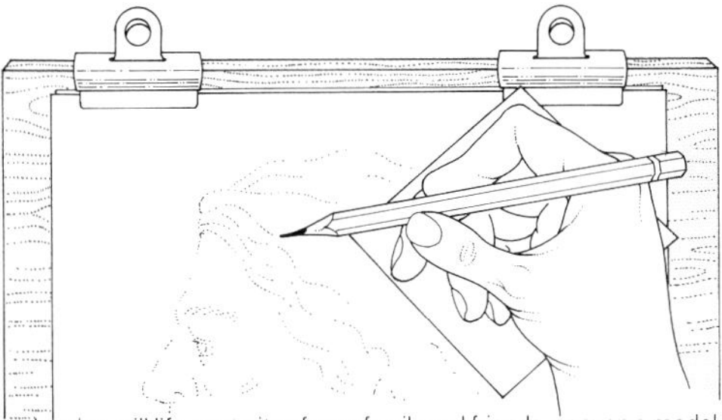

When drawing still life, portraits of your family and friends, or even a model in a life class, one definite advantage is that of being able to view the subject from all angles. It is impossible to walk around behind a landscape or a row of buildings as if it were a film set. A still life neither moves nor breathes so it can be inspected closely and at leisure.

Place the board vertically so that what you see in front of you will be interpreted on the paper without any distortion. If the board is sloping away from you, then every plane or curved shape will assume new and unreal proportions. Your line of view should strike the paper at right angles. Position yourself so that your arm extends comfortably, neither cramped not rigid, or your back will quickly begin to ache. When working close up on small or highly detailed drawings, a piece of acetate or clean cartridge paper under your hand will keep the surface free from marks.

Protecting your work

Eraser rubbings can be whisked off the drawing surface with a large, soft-bristled brush. Water pots or ink bottles should stand well clear of any drawings or sketchbooks and kitchen paper or cotton buds should be within reach to mop up spills. Keep a jar of water clean for dabbing on any ink spills with a soft brush, then when dry rub out the stain.

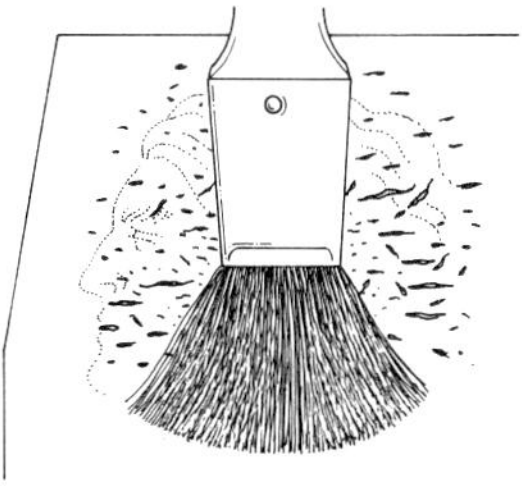

How to erase

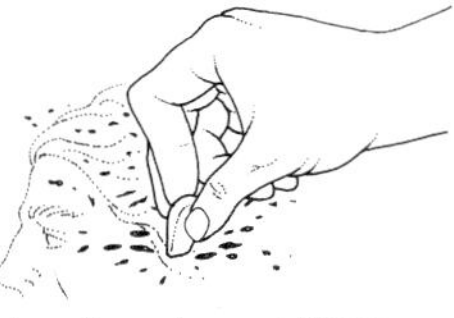

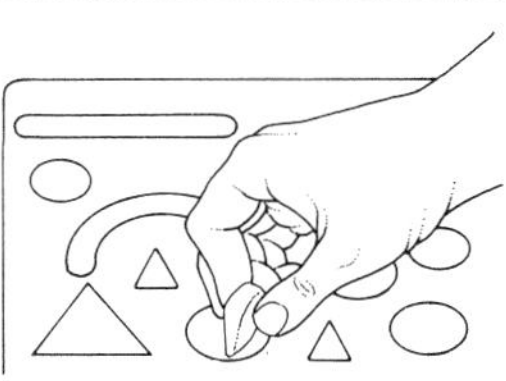

Most media can be erased if you know which tool will do the most effective job. Pencil is removed effortlessly with an India rubber but it may smudge. Cut it into a triangular shape to produce a fine edge. Charcoal responds to fresh white bread rolled into a ball, or a kneadable putty rubber which does not damage the paper. Special shields or acetate will protect the rest of the drawing from smudging.

Outdoor materials

One of the secrets of successful drawing on the spot is to minimize your materials so that they are well organized and therefore portable. A primary consideration is that almost everything you will want to tackle out-of-doors will be in motion – people, foliage, clouds, etc. This means working under pressure, and all your equipment must function and be close at hand. One distinct difference between drawing at home and working outside in the street or at a café table, for instance, is that you are bound to attract an audience. It may be just an inquisitive child but you will probably have to learn to resist conversation as well as endure the scrutiny and curiosity of passers-by.

Setting up

A light drawing board can be put up on a metal or wooden sketching easel, or held vertically in the lap, although this position is tiring over long periods. Masking tape or bulldog clips are convenient outside; drawing pins are easily lost. A brush holder formed from cardboard tubing or corrugated paper will protect sable brushes carried in the sketching bag. Drawing books should be at least 15×25cm; anything smaller will be too restrictive for worthwhile sketches. For tonal drawings and sketches (such as those by Turner, p81), washes in gradated ink dilutions or watercolour can be mixed up before going out, and carried in separate watertight bottles. Glycerine or a drop or two of liquid detergent in the container of clear water will prevent it freezing in cold weather. You will also need water for cleaning brushes, washing your hands and quenching thirst.

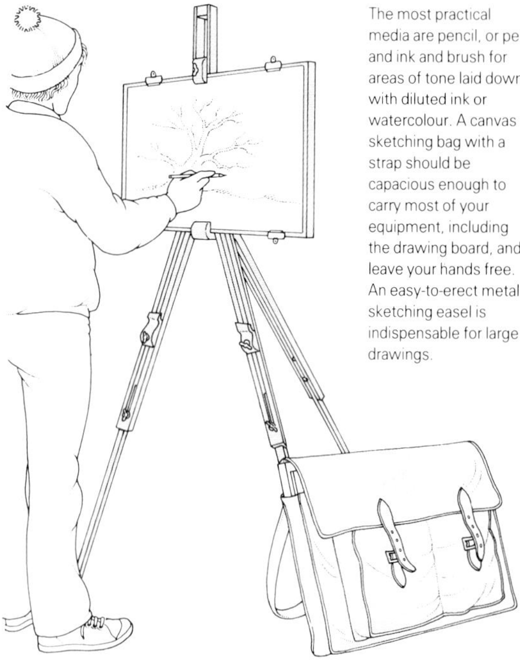

The most practical media are pencil, or pen and ink and brush for areas of tone laid down with diluted ink or watercolour. A canvas sketching bag with a strap should be capacious enough to carry most of your equipment, including the drawing board, and leave your hands free. An easy-to-erect metal sketching easel is indispensable for large drawings.

Drawing in the landscape

Unforeseen hazards such as marauding insects or animals in the country and obstructive traffic in the town are often unavoidable. However, do not run the risk of neglecting your personal comfort as this will make it difficult to concentrate. Fishing tackle shops are a fertile source for items such as large umbrellas which afford generous protection from the weather, folding canvas chairs (and even lead weights for making plumb lines).

The far horizons are distracting when working outside and many hours can be spent pleasurably, but not very profitably, wandering about searching for an appropriate or pleasing view. Isolate an area by cupping your hands or using a rectangular cardboard viewfinder (p82). Drawing in direct sun, the glare reflecting off the white paper, can be most uncomfortable; take advantage of the shade of a tree if at all possible. In bad weather get under cover in a barn or doorway.

Other equipment

Distilled water for diluting ink. Buy in bulk and decant it. **Gummed strip** used in stretching paper. **Fixative** comes in an aerosol can or as a liquid blown through a **Spray diffuser** (nickel-plated brass with a plastic mouthpiece) for fixing charcoal, pencil and conté drawings.

Putty rubber moulded to a fine point picks out highlights in charcoal. **Blotting paper** for ink spills. **Kitchen paper** or J-cloths for every other spillage. **Porcelain saucers,** in all shapes and sizes, for mixing colours. (Or an enamel plate.) **Plastic palettes** are light to carry.

Plastic water bottle with separate unbreakable containers. **Golf umbrella,** and brimmed hat or sun visor for rain or glaring sun; woolly hat and fingerless gloves for the cold. **String and a plastic bag,** to be filled with stones, for weighing down the easel.

Knives

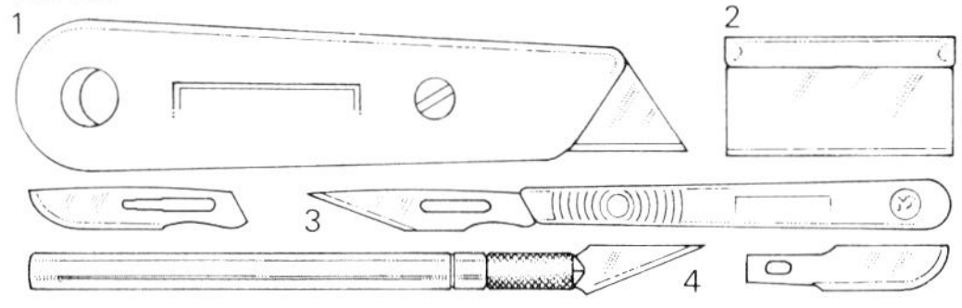

1 A craft knife with interchangeable blades will trim card, cut mounts and composition board. **2** A safety razor blade is used for scratching out ink marks or removing wax when used as a resist. **3** A scalpel and **4**, an X-acto knife cut paper and card. All these knives should be handled with respect.

Sharpening a knife

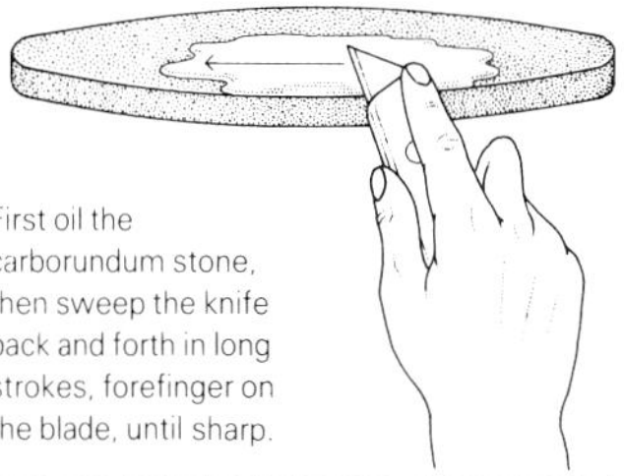

First oil the carborundum stone, then sweep the knife back and forth in long strokes, forefinger on the blade, until sharp.

Techniques

These four sequences show the development of the drawings step-by-step. From top to bottom: a pencil drawing of a still life with flowers; a portrait done in conté; a landscape sketch in charcoal and chalk; townscape in pen and ink over wash.

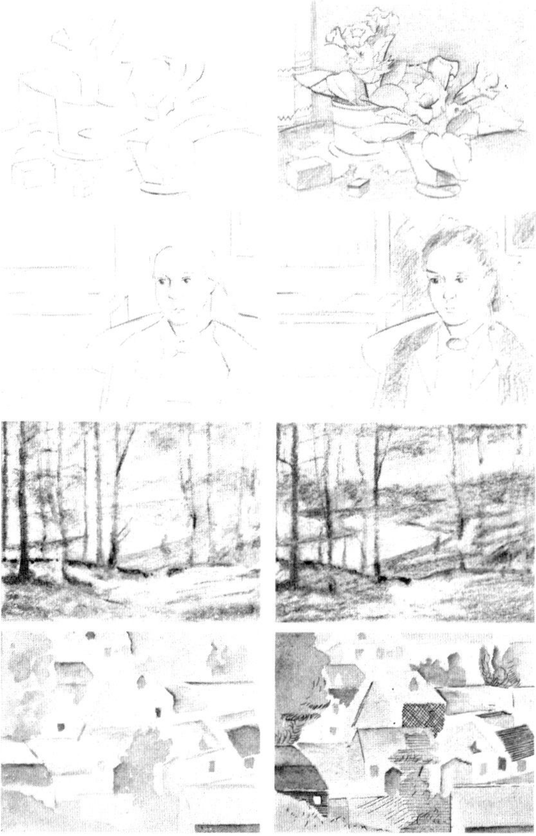

Drawing is the most immediate way of representing something visually in two dimensions. The choice of subject, the view, the emphasis, mood and the materials used all help reveal the artist's experience of the world. Enjoyment is most important, and it will show in your drawing. The examples of drawings by famous artists (among them old masters) show how they retain a freshness and timelessness that can be lost in a painting.

Develop your awareness by drawing and sketching constantly to record observations you have made. Try different approaches, whether in terms of scale, materials, or subject matter – this will develop your ability to see and your confidence.

The exercises, examples and tips in this section will guide you through any problems you may encounter, giving simple ways of understanding them. Suggestions are made for methods and approaches – use those that appeal to you.

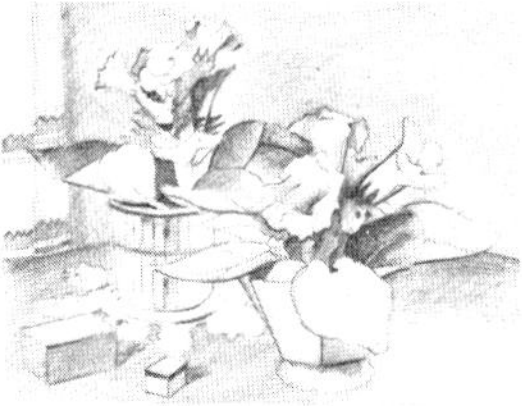
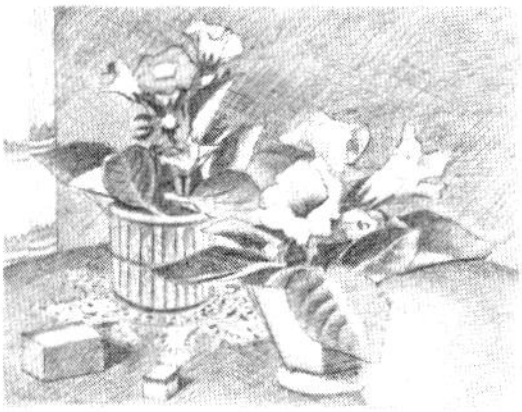
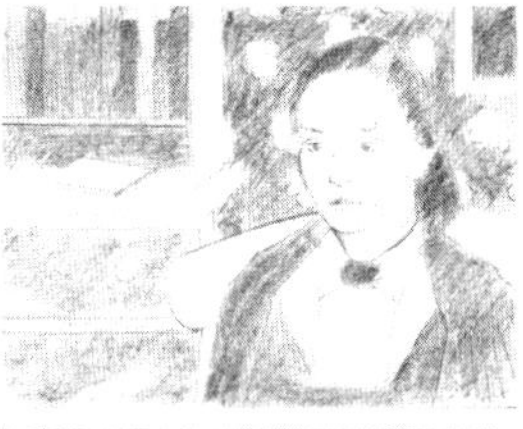
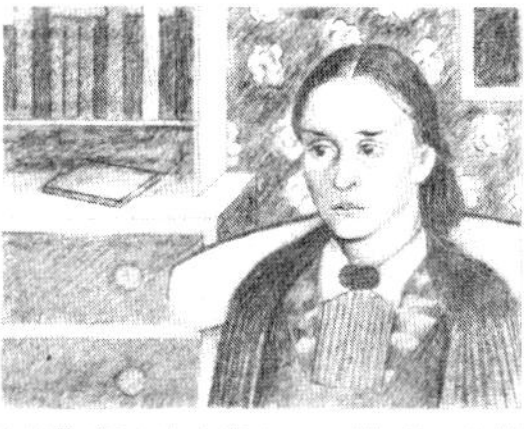
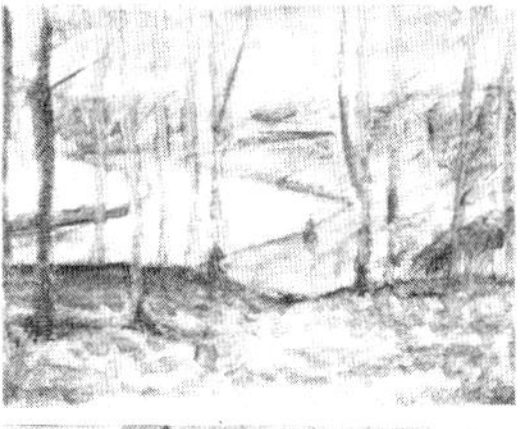
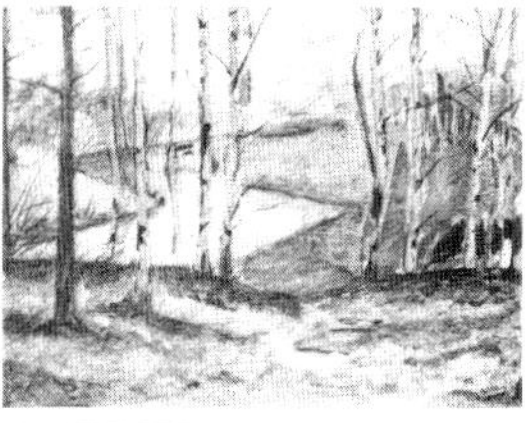
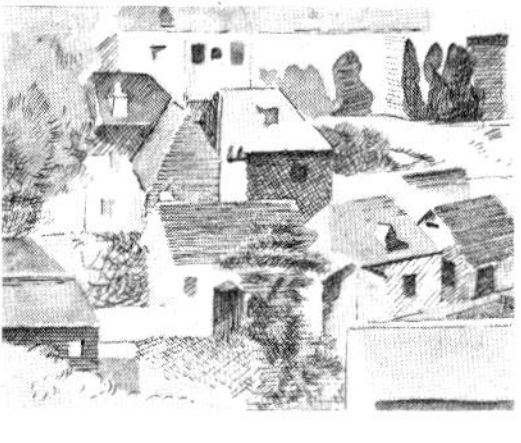
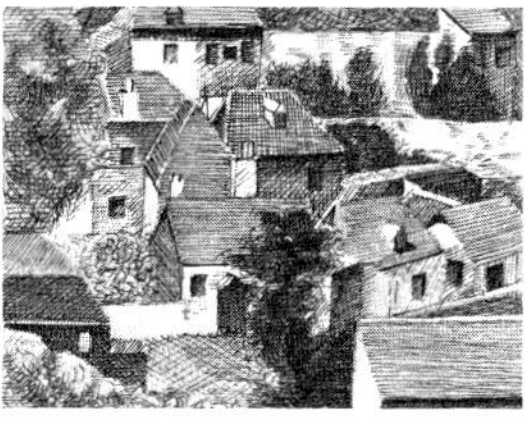

Approaches to drawing

Make the most of the particular characteristics of a medium and let it help you get the results you want with the minimum of effort. Discover, by drawing the same subject with different media, which is most suitable, which encourages rapid strokes, which is good for detailed work, which for line, which for tone.

Charcoal

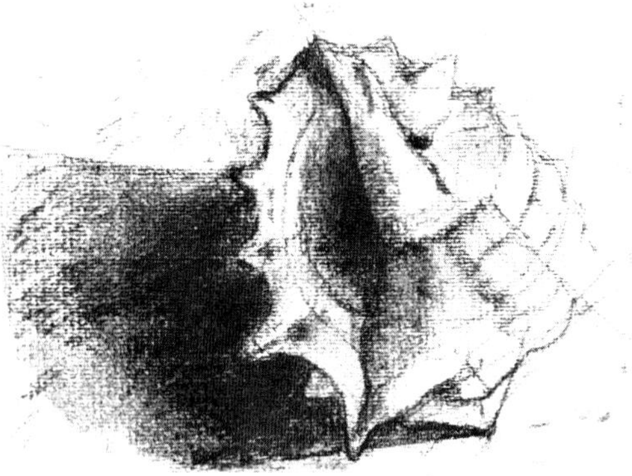

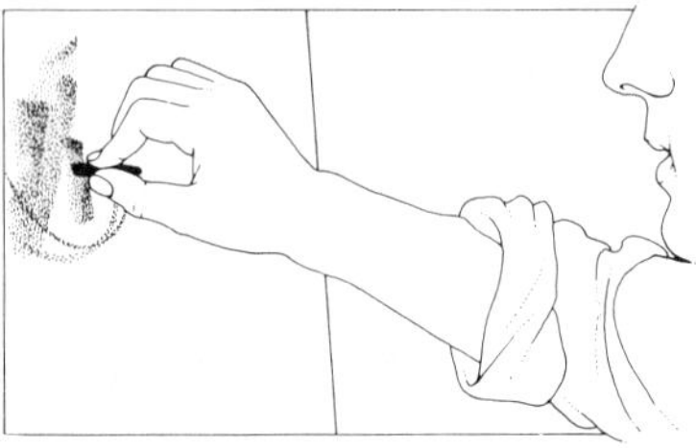

Charcoal is an ideal medium for broadly worked sketches. It is soft and easy to rub out, giving the freedom to develop an evocative tonal drawing. Hold the arm outstretched to make bold, fluid, large-scale drawings.

Pencil

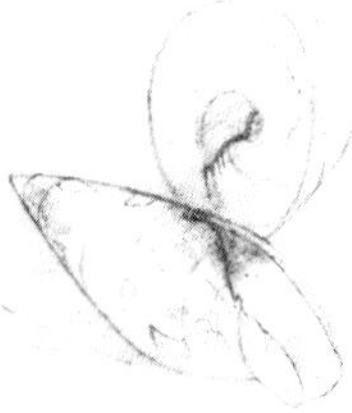

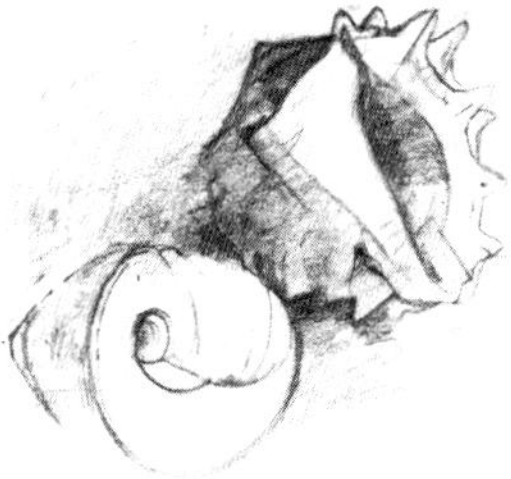

Hard pencil is good for precision work if sharpened to a fine point, but once a mark has been made it can be difficult to rub out. It will give a limited range of fairly light tones, which can take on a smooth, almost glassy look if handled subtly.

Soft pencil can give a lot of tonal variation, from a subtle light tone to a deep grey, depending on the pressure applied or the degree of tonal build-up. Vary the line by sharpening the pencil for more precision; leave it blunt for a broader line.

Conté

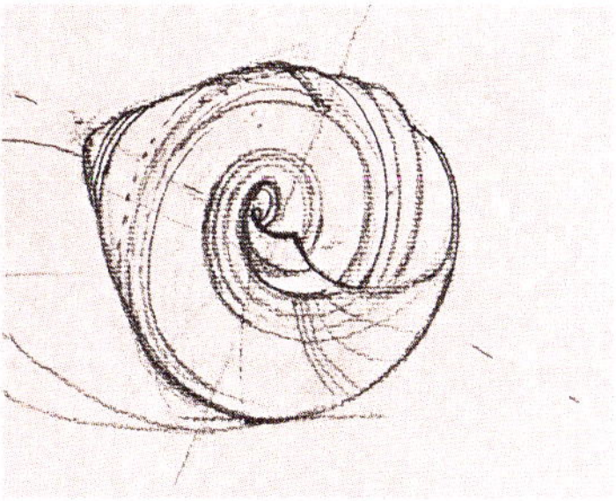

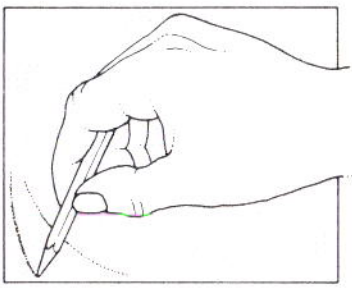

Conté gives little tonal variation when sharpened to a point for use as a linear tool. It can make a line just as dark as a charcoal line.

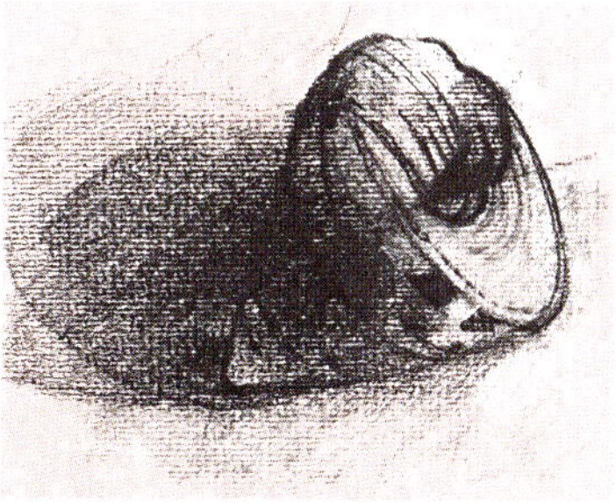

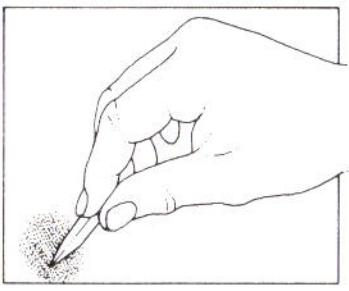

Use the side, or the edge of the point for tonal drawing. It will accentuate the grain of the paper; light tones can be heightened with white conté.

Soft pastel

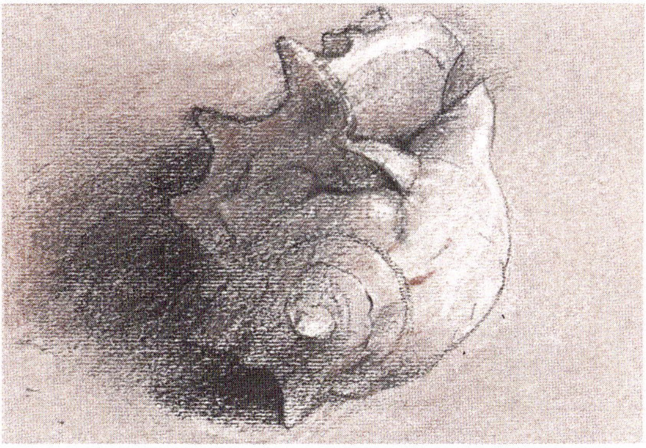

This versatile medium can be used to suggest line, tone and colour and is most effective when used on tinted paper, which can take the place of tone or colour. The grain of the paper can be brought out by the pastel to imply texture. Edges can be defined with the point of the pastel or with a pastel pencil. In this drawing the grey-tinted paper sets the mid-tone, black was used for the dark tones merging into shadow and to define the edges in light areas, while white gives highlights and red ochre adds a tint.

Pen and ink

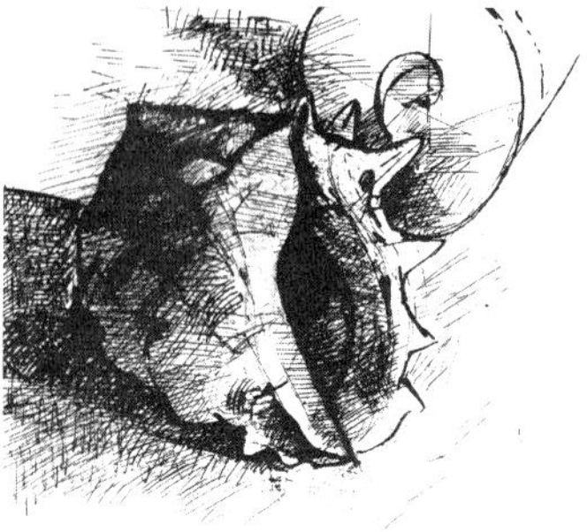

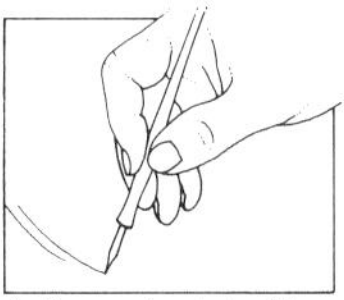

A dip pen loaded with ink can be used quite freely. Do not be afraid to emphasize or even correct lines with firm strokes, and build up dark areas with cross-hatching.

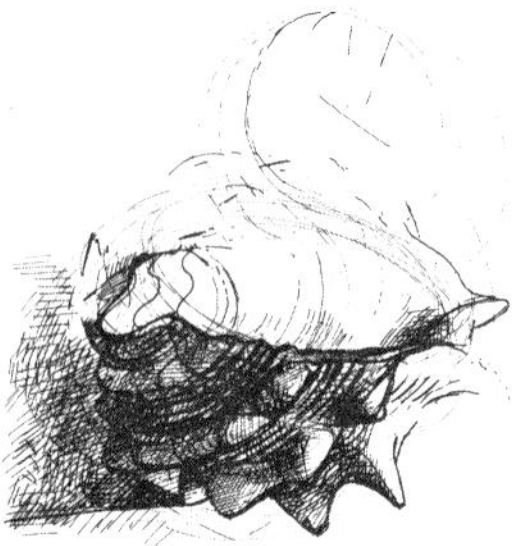

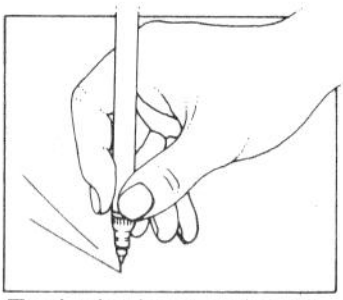

Technical pens should be used on hard paper. They are good for slow, controlled drawing (as the diagram above) but can also build up freer drawings (left). Hold the pen upright.

Fibre-tip pen

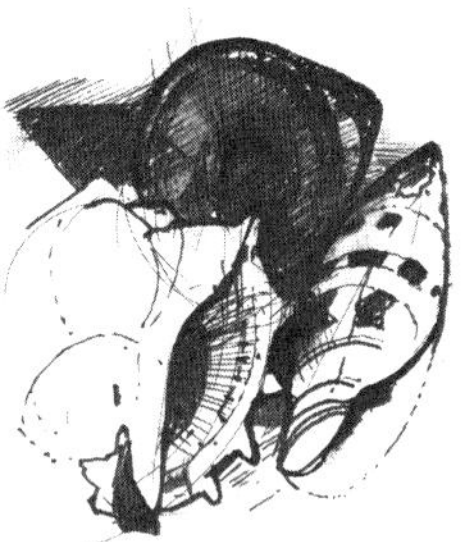

This relatively insensitive medium produces a consistent line that is difficult to vary (particularly in small-scale drawings), although this depends on the type. Lines can be softened if moistened with a slightly damp brush. Transparent tones can be achieved with the use of light hatching.

Ball-point

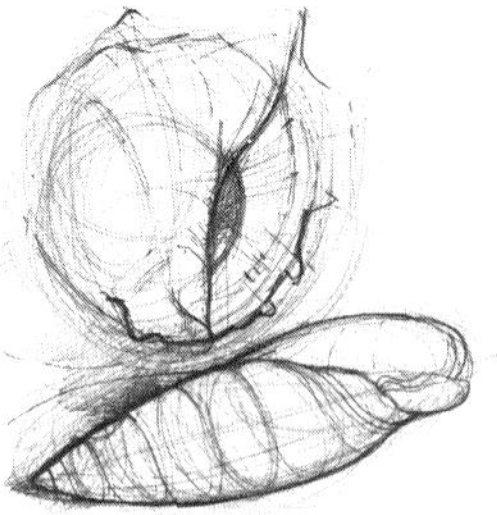

Ball-point can produce some surprisingly effective results, although drawings will tend to fade in time. The weight of the line can be easily controlled to build up from light, spidery lines to darker tonal areas. It flows well and can be used to explore volume in a series of repetitive contour lines.

see also pages 20–21, 87–88, 128

Brush and ink

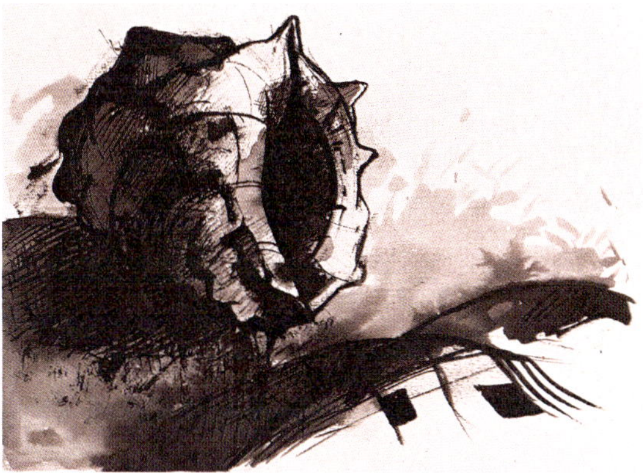

This direct medium encourages you to work quickly, laying in tonal areas to capture the general shapes. Pre-mix washes of varying dilutions or different colours of watercolour or ink. Dry-brush technique requires a little more precision.

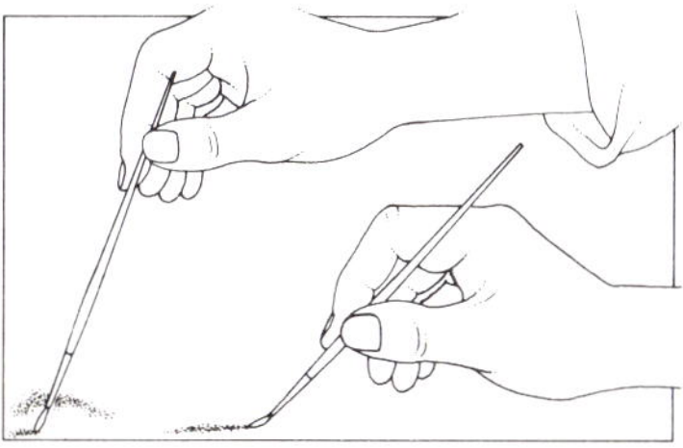

Improvised media

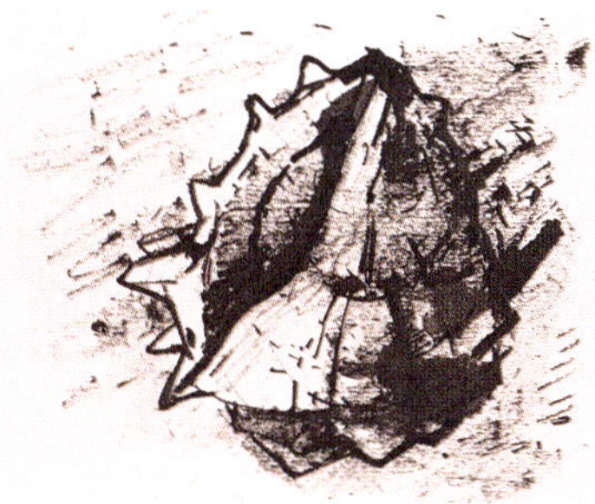

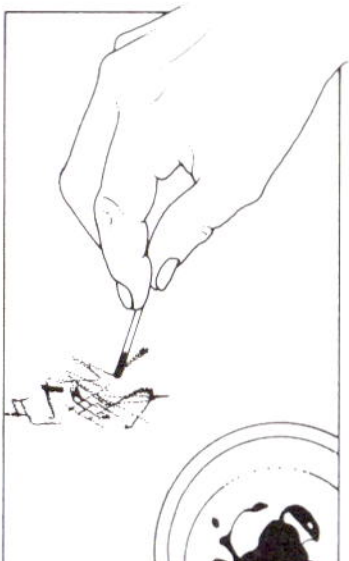

It is interesting to discover the different marks that can be made on paper by tools other than those that are commercially available. A matchstick was used for this drawing. It has none of the flow of a pen drawing since the match had to be continually dipped into ink as it dries so quickly. This has given the line a stop-start quality and an idiosyncratic tonal effect. Any kind of stick could be used in this way. For bolder lines – with even greater difficulties of control – try dipping a sponge or a piece of cloth into the ink and drawing with it. A small lino-printing roller can be used to draw on a large scale, giving a very broad 'line' – almost an area of tone in its own right.

Drawing with a grid

Drawing is about observation and training your eye to send a message to your hand to transpose and represent the three-dimensional on a two-dimensional surface. Unless the eye is properly trained, no amount of deft pencil strokes will convey the true form of an object and its relation to the space around it. To sharpen your powers of observation and to really *see* what you are drawing, start off by limiting what you put to paper by considering only the outline shape. With the aid of a grid you will be able to plot shapes in relation to one another within a framework. By limiting your expectations of the finished drawing you will intensify your concentration, begin to understand the problems of proportion and shape and you will get a feel for the materials you are using and the marks you can make.

Drawing a grid

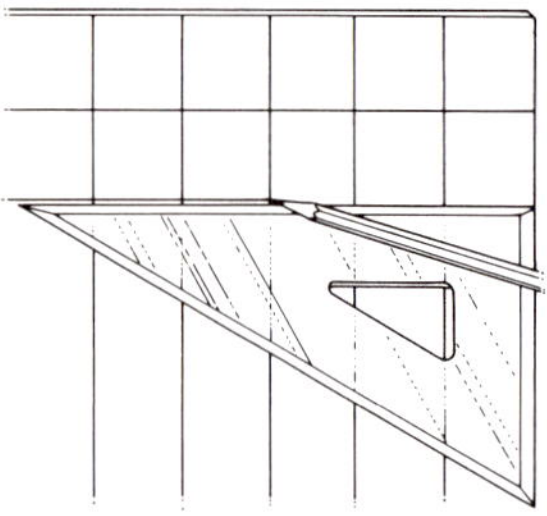

Rule up a sheet of paper that is larger than the subject you have chosen. Using a ruler and set square or a T square divide up the sheet into 5cm squares with a soft pencil (a 2B or 3B) so that the lines are dark and clearly visible.

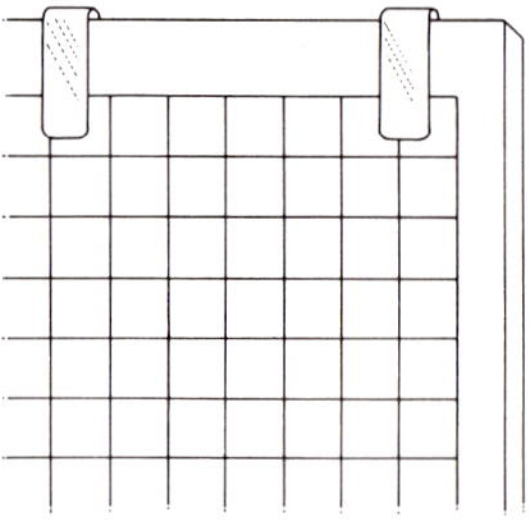

Select a sheet of paper for your drawing. Smooth cartridge paper is suitable for this kind of detailed work. Divide up the paper using the same measurements, but with a harder pencil (an HB) to contrast the grid lines with the drawing.

Setting up the subject

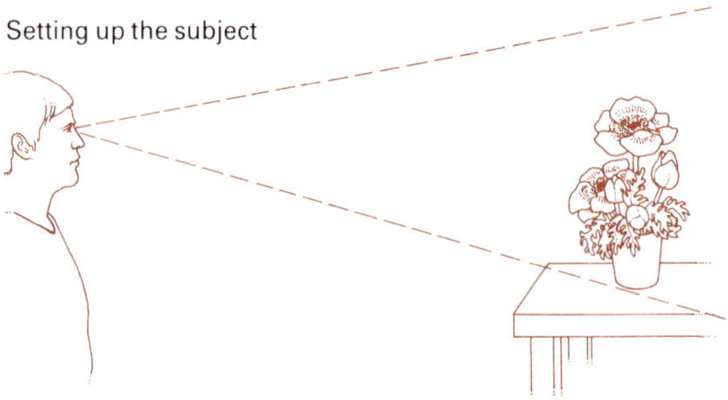

Choose a subject that you will enjoy drawing, such as a pot of flowers, and place it on a table about 1.5m from where you will stand to draw, far enough to see the plant as a whole, but near enough to see all the detail. The plant should be a little below the level of your eyes so that you can see how it grows up from the earth. Set up the drawing board vertically on the easel; if it is sloping it will distort the drawing (see p38). Take up a comfortable stance behind the board and mark the position on the floor to maintain a constant viewpoint.

see also pages 15, 34, 46–49, 114

Drawing the subject

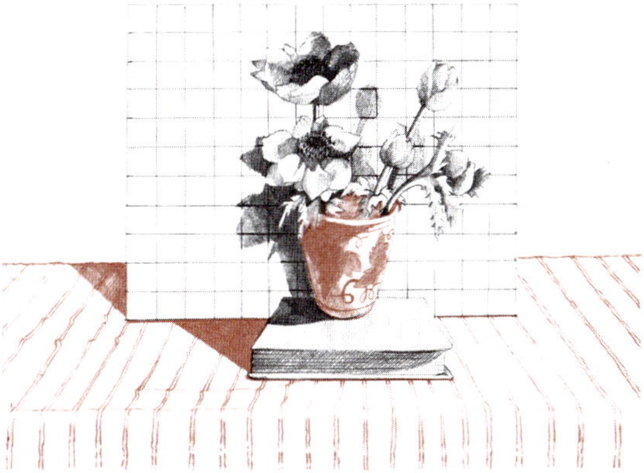

Glue or pin the grid to a board and place it vertically behind the plant, supported by books or propped up against a wall. The light should fall on the side of the plant to make the definition of the shapes easier to read. Observe the outlines carefully before you start drawing, and notice the contrast between the different lines. Simplify in your mind what you can see in front of you and think in terms of recording the silhouette; try to resist the temptation of conveying texture and tone at this stage.

Using a 2B pencil held loosely in the hand, not too near the point, start drawing a simple shape, such as the outline of the pot, noticing the space left on both sides of the line. Now move on to the more irregular shapes of the leaves, again choosing the simple shapes first. Plot in lightly their relation to the pot through the axes of the stems, tracing the direction of growth. Having established an overall outline begin to explore the more detailed shapes, relating each line to another within the confines of the square that contains it. This will enable you to describe easily receding lines by accurate observation of the angles they make on the grid.

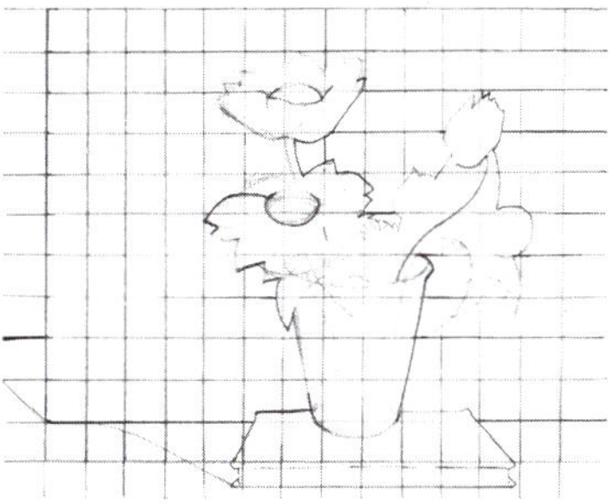

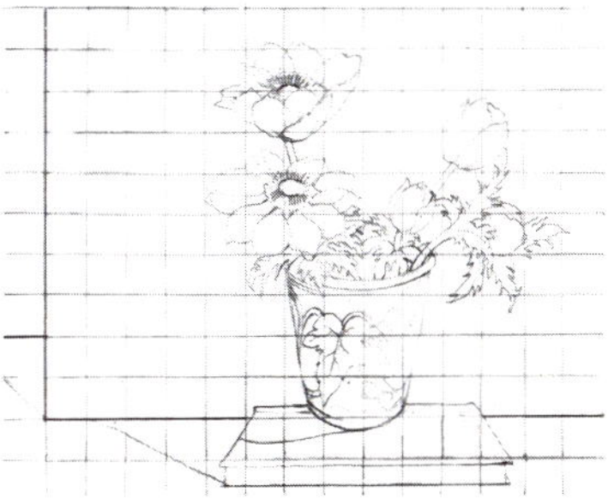

Natural grids

Having imposed a drawn-up grid on your subject you will begin to realize that everything can be seen in terms of its relation to its setting. The horizontal and vertical lines of structures that are found around the house, such as table edges and window frames as well as those outside, can be used in your drawing as a kind of grid that you will find less restricting than one that you rule up.

Having set up your subject against this 'natural grid' start your drawing by plotting in the horizontals and verticals lightly, using a loose extended arm movement to draw the straight lines. Try to avoid using a ruler as this will tend to give a mechanical effect to the drawing. Use the straight lines to help you see the outline of the subject and notice where all the lines intersect. If you feel confident about the shapes you are making, try experimenting with varying the weight and character of the line to introduce volume.

Variation of line

The character of your drawing will be dominated by the line you use. Your approach, the pace at which you draw and the pressure you use will be the determining factors in the kind of line that results.

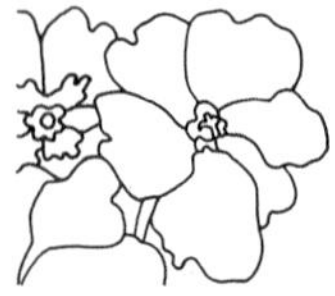

Simple, continuous outlines will produce a flat, decorative quality but can suggest volume.

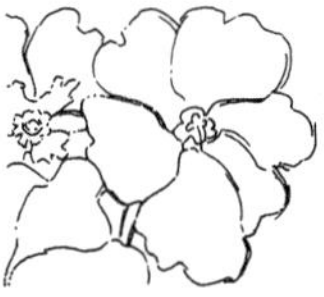

Broken outlines imply the fall of light on an object. Draw halted lines or rub out parts of the line.

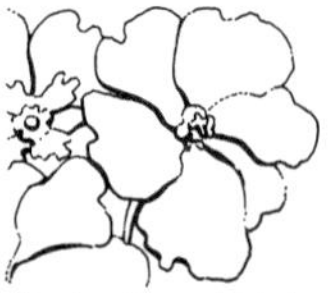

Varying the weight of the line by exerting more pressure or using a darker pencil looks lively.

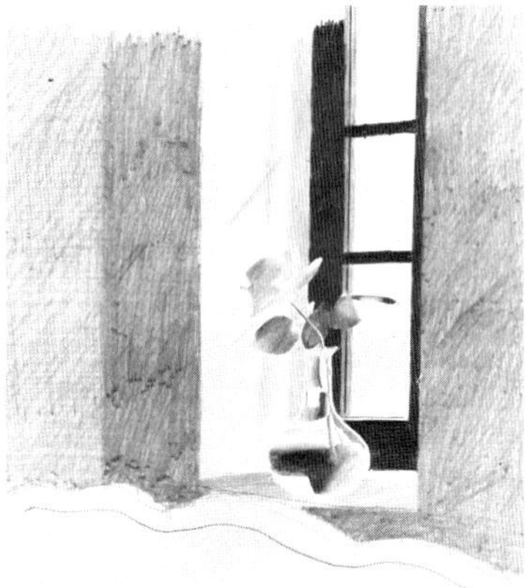

David Hockney
Le Nid du Duc
The vertical and horizontal lines of this composition are contrasted with the free though disciplined curves of the rose and the vase, dependent on the skilful use of light and dark tones. Shapes have been seen here, not in terms of linear outline, but as mass and contrast. Notice the treatment of the left side of the rose, drawn in silhouette against the white wall, and the similar treatment of the right side of the flask.

see also pages 23–33, 38–39, 59

Drawing the subject

Compose your picture by choosing an object whose shape will contrast with the straight lines of the background. Start by drawing in the natural grid of the background with particular attention to the accuracy of the verticals. Unless seen front-on the horizontals will be affected by perspective, as seen in the stripes on the cloth. Treat this sort of problem as pattern for now and use it as part of the grid. Draw in the main shapes of the plant, considering overall outline, helped by plotting in the main axes of the leaves. When the outline is right, convey a sense of volume by varying the weight of the line: give more emphasis to lines in shadow; erase areas to give highlights.

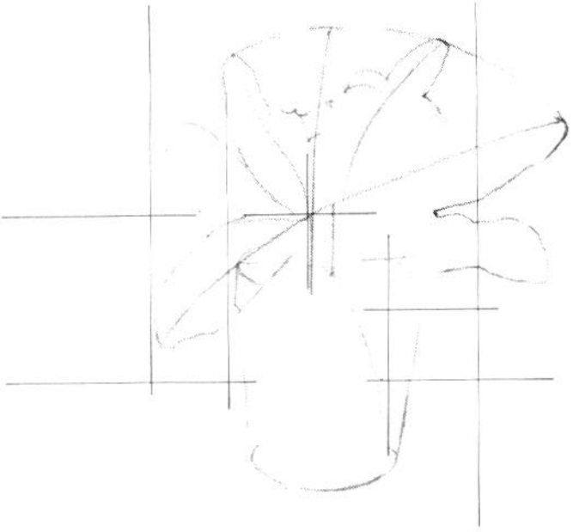

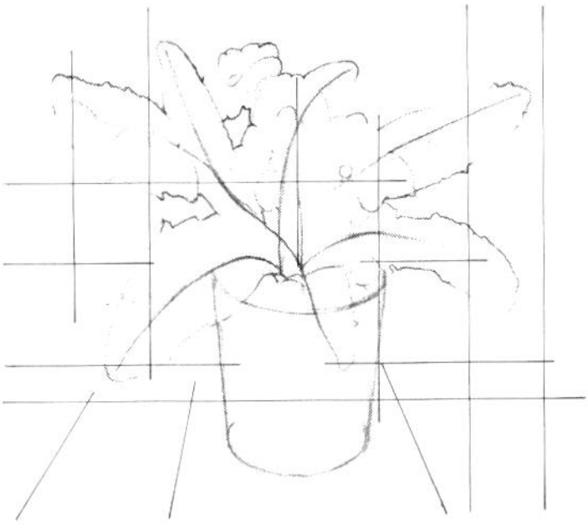

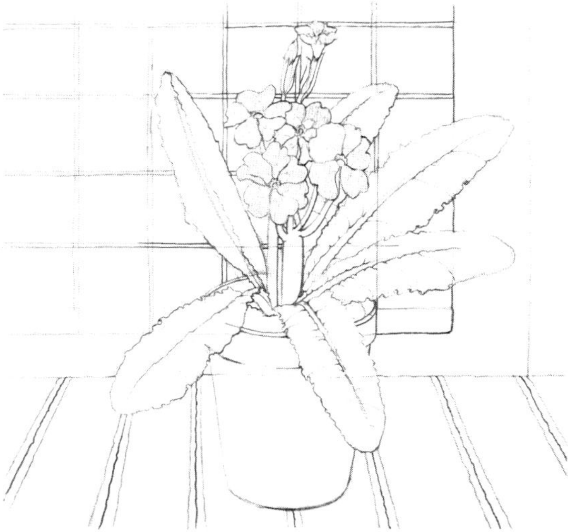

Planes and simple tones

To explore a three-dimensional form it is helpful to start off by drawing rectangular objects so that the eye understands the shape immediately and does not have to sort out the subtleties of the planes of organic objects. By setting such things as cardboard boxes and books (which you know have a top, side and front to describe) in a natural framework of horizontals and verticals you will be able to relate the edges more easily and this will leave you free to learn how to describe planes.

A single line can imply solidity and this is more obvious with angled shapes than with curved ones – you know that there is another plane on the other side of the line. The addition of tone confirms the change of angle and hence the change in the angle of light.

If you find that when you compose your arrangement you are distracted by the labelling on the books and boxes you have chosen, give them a coat of white paint to simplify their appearance and emphasize the planes.

Horizontal and vertical guides

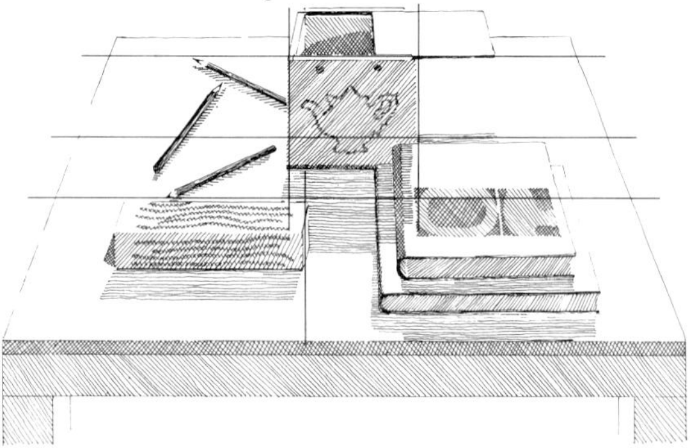

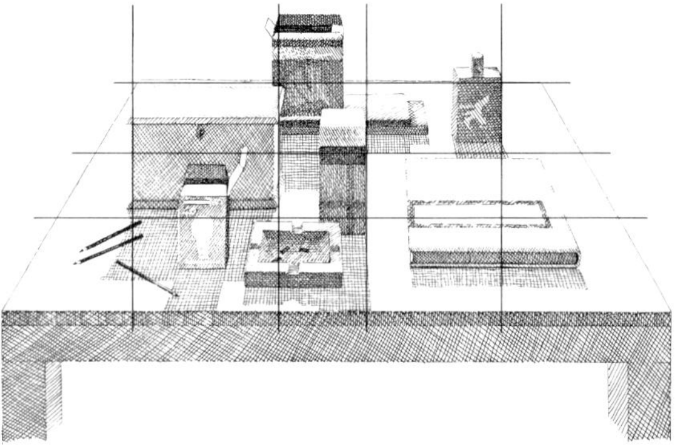

Arrange three or four objects on a table placed squarely in front of you, with the front planes facing you, a little below eye level. Consider the relationship of the horizontals and verticals of the objects in relation to one another and to the angles of the table, observing the way they overlap and the shadows they create. Now add more objects to your composition and change the light source.

see also pages 20–
21, 38–39, 59

Vertical guides

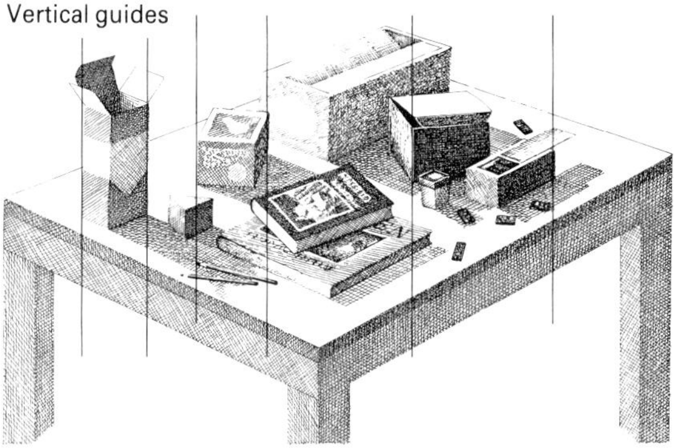

Vertical guidelines remain constant. Move the table at an angle, rearrange your composition and relate the objects to the verticals of the table legs. If the front faces of the objects are still aligned with the edge of the table you will now see two sides, or planes of the boxes as well as their tops. You will not be able to rely on any horizontal alignments and tone will come into play to describe form. Use two different intensities of cross-hatching to describe the surfaces and the shadows.

Hatching and cross-hatching

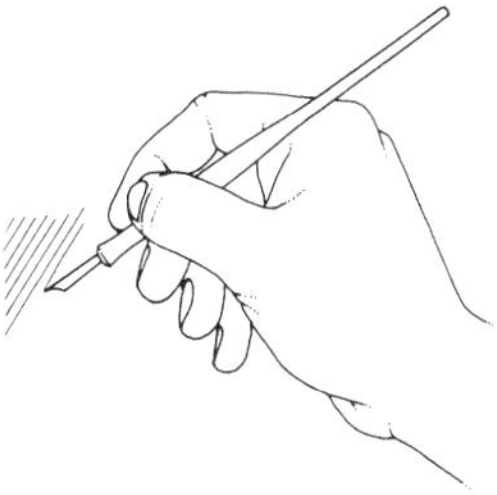

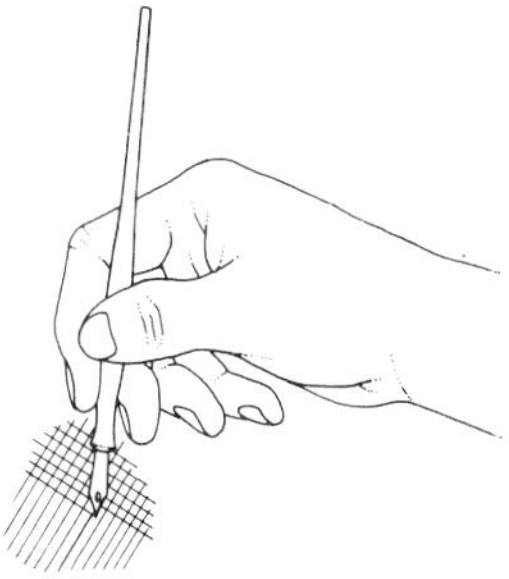

Hatching is used as a method of describing tone or shade. It is particularly effective if done with pen and ink, but can be done with most materials as long as you adapt your technique. Treat charcoal boldly to produce dramatic effects. Try even spacing, or, alternatively, vary the interval between the lines.

Cross-hatching can be built up by going over the hatching at different angles, increasing to a network of lines that will become darker and more intricate. Introduce a rhythm into your way of working, using crisp pen strokes. Patterns can be built up by changing direction in different areas.

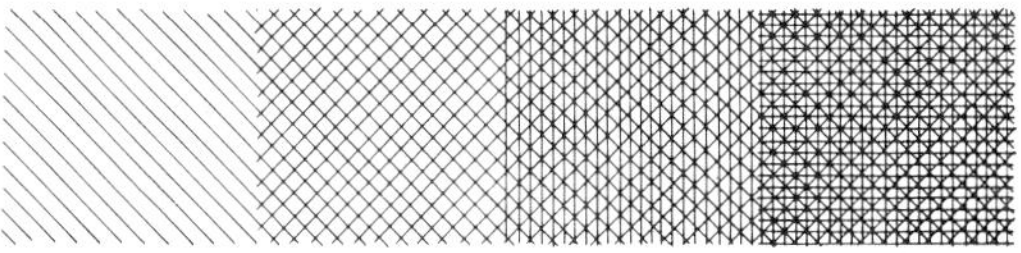

Sight size and scale

The field of vision that the eye takes in is in the form of a cone, known as the 'cone of vision', the apex of which is at the centre of the eye. It is easier to draw on what is called the scale of vision or 'sight size' since the mind is not concerned with interpreting scale and doing complicated geometrical enlargements or reductions. You will find that you tend to draw naturally at sight size.

Scale in drawing is concerned with the distance that the artist stands in relation to an object, which determines the size that it is seen. If you hold your hand in front of you at arm's length and gradually retract your arm, your hand will seem to grow larger and larger until it passes out of focus as a whole and only part of it can be seen. This concept is formally organized into the science of perspective.

Sight size

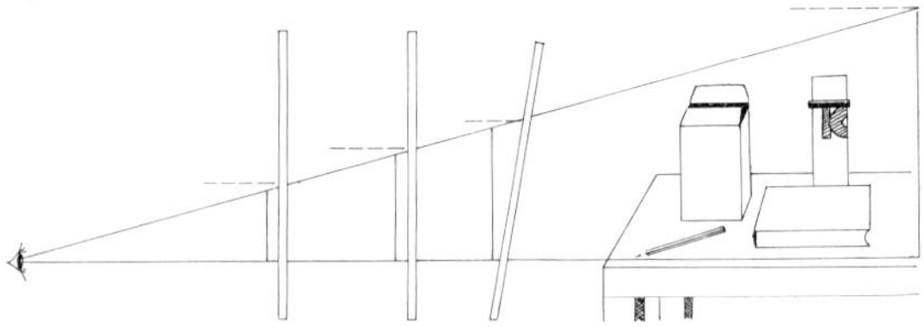

The size of your drawing will be determined by the distance that you and your drawing board are from what you are drawing. The nearer the board is, the larger the subject will appear; the further away you are the smaller it will appear. You will find by experience where the most comfortable distance to stand from the subject is (about 1.5m is generally suitable). Remember to keep your drawing surface vertical to avoid distortion. At sight size your drawing will appear on the drawing board at the size it would be seen if the board were a piece of glass and the image seen on that plane. To help your understanding of this idea you might want to try doing a drawing on Perspex (see p102). It will also help you to transfer lines that are seen at difficult angles.

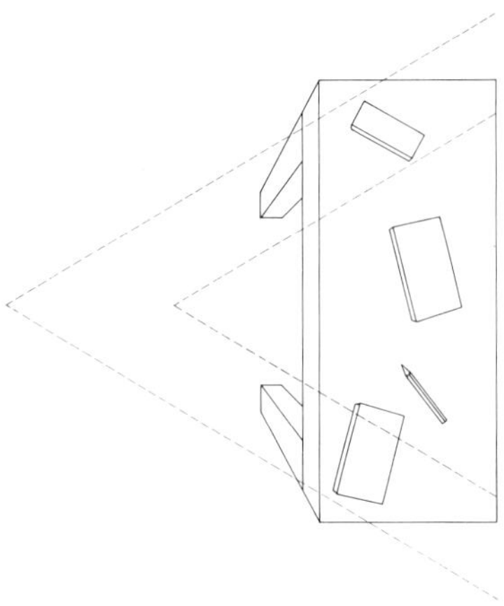

Your 'cone of vision' takes in everything within a 60-degree angle on a horizontal and vertical plane in front of it. The further back you stand from the subject the wider the area you see in focus will be. If you move your head to take in more than what is encompassed within your cone of vision you will be composing a picture from a multiple viewpoint and it will be distorted. Be aware of this when drawing landscapes and do not take in too wide a view.

see also pages 23, 82, 102–105

Scale

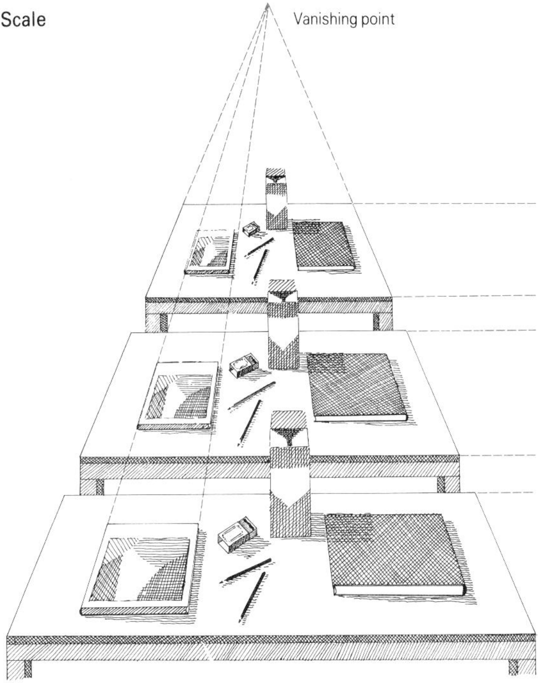

All parallel lines converge and objects diminish in size on the same scale as they recede from the eye. Notice here the diminution of the parallel sides of a table and the objects on it (which we 'know' to be square).

Drawing by direct transference

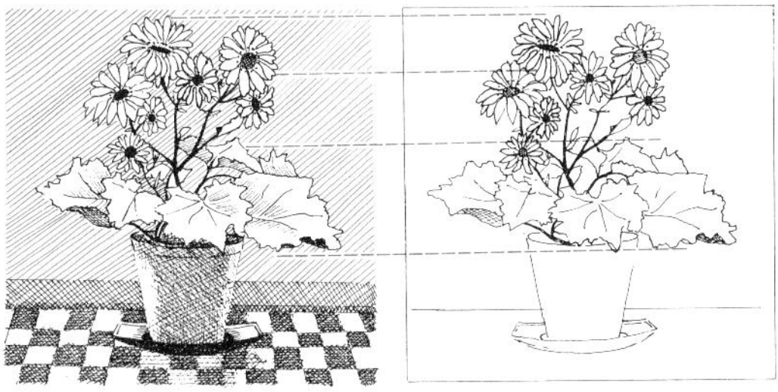

If you place the drawing board on the same plane as the object the drawing will be exactly the same size as the object and it will also be sight size. It will be easy to draw since your eye will not have to interpret scale and, since you are so near your subject, minimal time is lost between looking at the subject, memorizing it and transferring it onto the paper.

Measuring

If you train your eye to see accurately you will gradually become accustomed to judging proportion and scale and the relation of one thing to another in a composition. There are devices that will help you to check the lines that you draw and these can be useful, but try to rely first on your own observation and use these methods only as a means of double checking. It can be surprising to discover how the mind tends to read objects of a similar size as occupying the same dimensions irrespective of the distance between them. By measuring with a unit of comparison that is closer to your eye you will begin to find out about perspective and foreshortening.

Measuring with a pencil

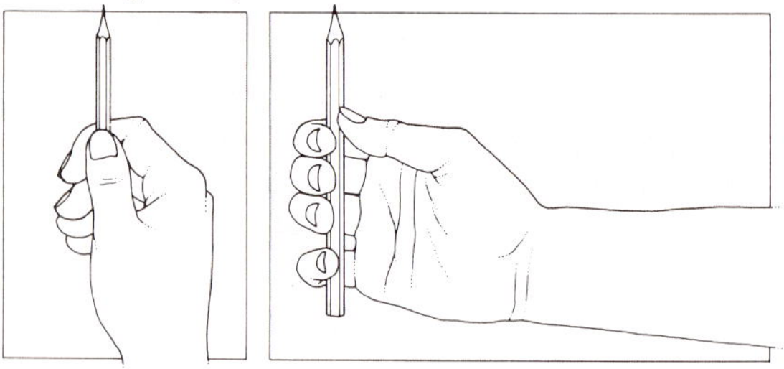

Hold the pencil upright in your hand, steadied by the thumb and gripped firmly by the fingers. When measuring verticals the thumb should be uppermost, for horizontals the hand is held level. The arm *must* be fully outstretched so that comparisons are constant. A ruler or piece of card marked with the units you want to compare can also be used.

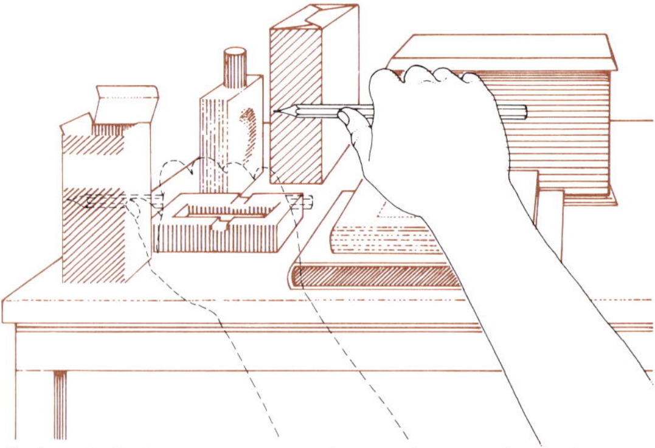

Find an edge that you want to measure in comparison to another line that appears to be a similar length. Line up one end of the pencil with an edge of the near object and mark the other edge with your thumb. Now move your hand, keeping your thumb still and compare the length marked by the pencil with the further object (holding it at arm's length). This method will work only within the range of your cone of vision since your arm acts as a pivot from your shoulder and describes the arc of a circle. Measurements made at the extremes of this limit would not relate to the flat surface of the drawing. Begin by measuring regular-sided objects; the contours of rounded objects are more elusive.

see also pages 34–35, 103

Measuring angles

Difficult angles can be measured easily by holding the edge of a piece of paper against one side of an angle and folding the paper to follow the line of the other side of the angle. The paper can then be laid on your drawing or held just above it and the angle checked since it has brought it into the same plane as the drawing.

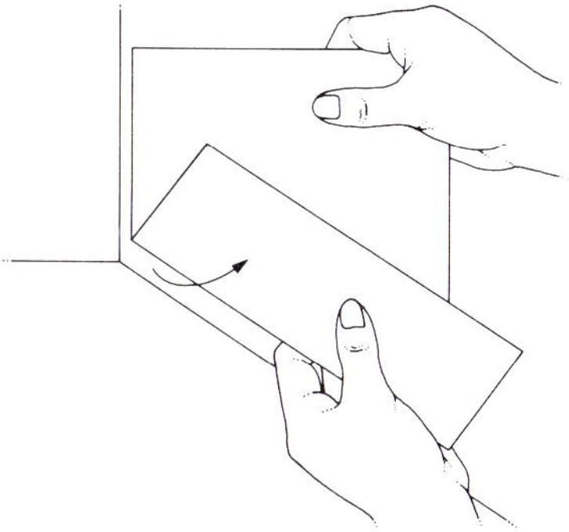

Using imaginary clock hands

Another way of judging angles, though relying more on judgement than on practical short-cuts, is by imagining the hands of a clock superimposed on the angle. This will reduce the scale and bring it into a closer plane.

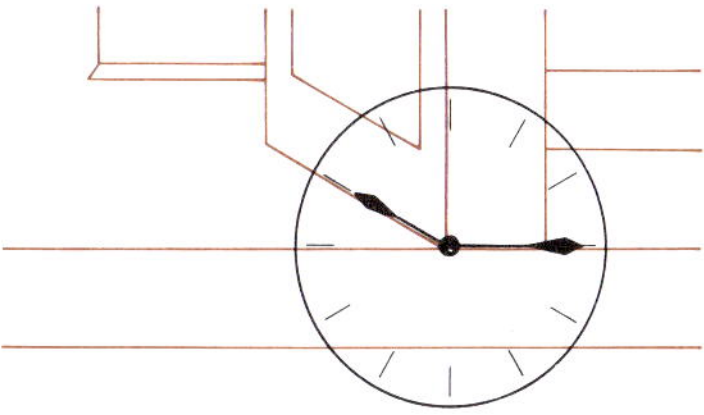

Measuring with a plumb line

A plumb line is a useful and accurate way of checking verticals and spotting what lies vertically beneath them. It is particularly useful in drawing the figure and in helping to determine the main axis of the body. A plumb line will correct any bias of vision that your eye may have in judging the position of the vertical (this can often be a surprising discovery). It will also relate parts of your drawing, from the back to the front plane. A plumb line is easy to make (follow the directions given below).

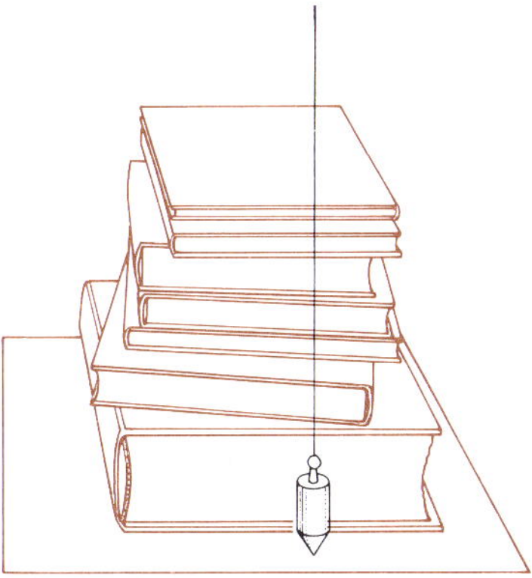

A plumb line can be made by tying a small lead weight (a fishing weight, a tube of paint or even a bunch of keys) to a piece of carpet twine, string or fishing line. The weight should be just heavy enough to keep the cord taut. Hold the plumb line out in front of you and regard it as a portable grid to check the edges of objects and line up things that appear to lie above or below each other.

Defining form

Tone is used to show direction of light and changes of plane on objects; it is a way of suggesting solidity and the illusion of the third dimension. In simple objects, such as cubes, a change of plane is always revealed by its angles and a simple change of tone which can easily be translated onto paper. In rounded objects the tone must be 'modelled' by following the curve of the surface as it turns from the light.

The use of tone

Cubic shapes can be described in linear terms; perspective and the relation of horizontals and verticals give enough clues to its form, although when the object is at eye level and part of the shape is not seen then tone is helpful. Cylindrical shapes can be understood when a cross-section is visible. As soon as it is not, it becomes incomprehensible to the eye and modelling must be used. The outline of a sphere, being the same from any angle, relies totally on modelling to define its form.

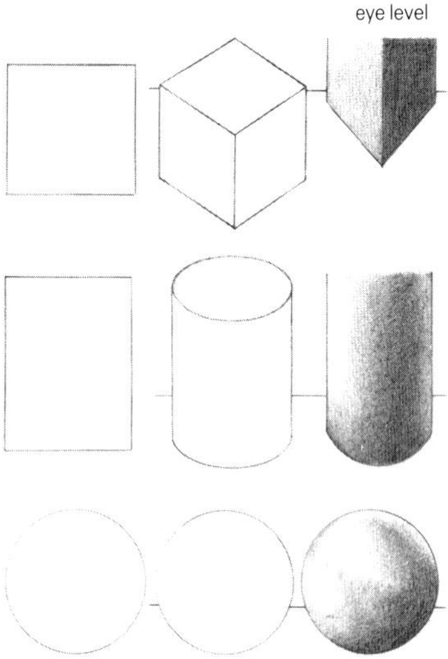

Light on a curved form

On a spherical object the light falls in a diminishing degree of brightness as it moves round the form from light to dark. At the centre and highest point is the highlight. Next to this is the broader main, or direct light, graduating down in tone as it moves from the highlight becoming darker until it begins to lighten up again by picking up indirect, or reflected light from nearby sources. It then casts a shadow, one cast by artificial light being sharper than a daylight shadow.

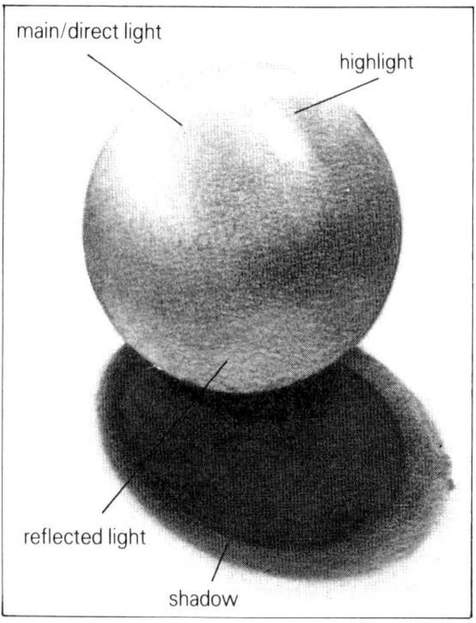

see also pages 14–15, 44–45, 48–49, 52–53

Making tones with pencil

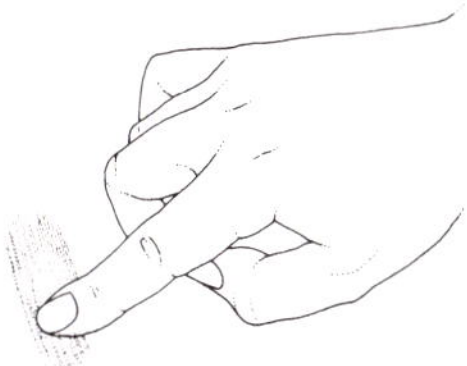

Lightly shade all the areas that you want to be toned with a 2H pencil. Increase the pressure of shading with the same pencil in the areas that you want to be darker. Lightly rub with the finger to soften the tonal gradation into the paper.

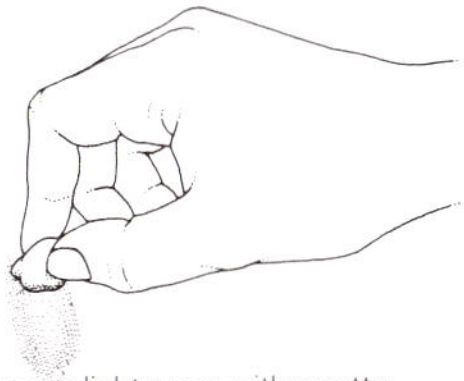

Remove light areas with a putty rubber, working slowly. The surface is now smooth and more responsive to increased toning with a B or 2B pencil. For a very dark area use a 4B. Dark tones can then be polished with an H pencil.

Simple forms

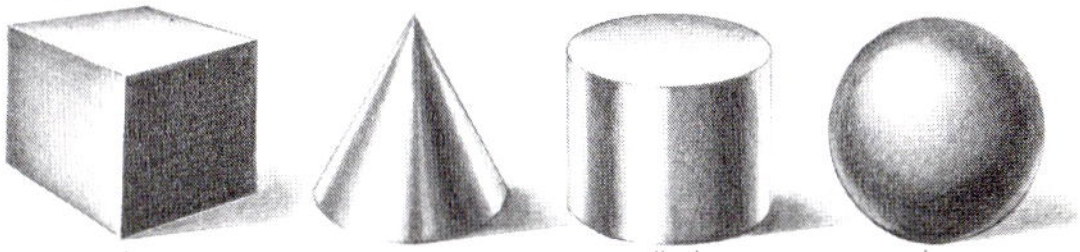

cube, cone, cylinder, sphere

These simple shapes are the main basic forms to be found in nature and can be used to simplify your understanding of any still life object, figure or flower. Proportions of any scale, from a flower to a building, can be worked out in simple three-dimensional terms. It was Cézanne who said, 'Treat nature in terms of the cylinder, the sphere, the cone . . . '

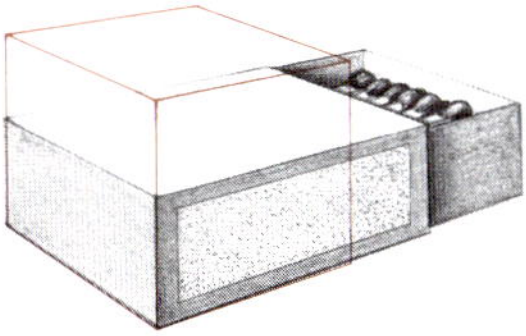

Cubes can be used to work out the basic shape of any regular sided form – from a matchbox to a building.

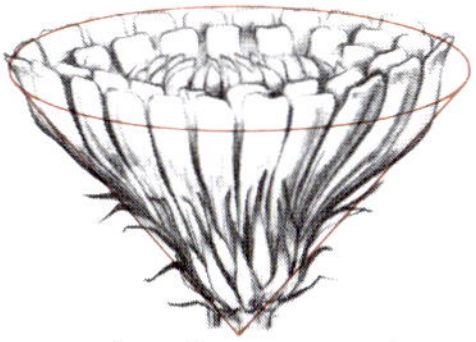

Cones are found in many organic forms; look at flower heads, carrots, or poplar trees.

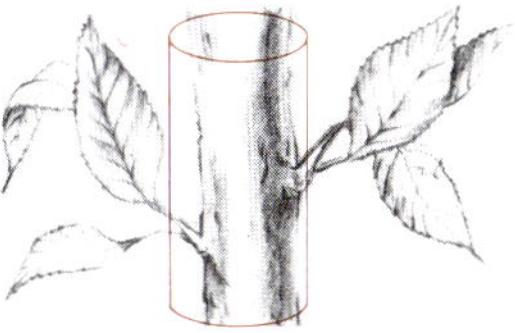

Cylinders will describe the structure of a flower stem, tree trunk, a leg, or an arm.

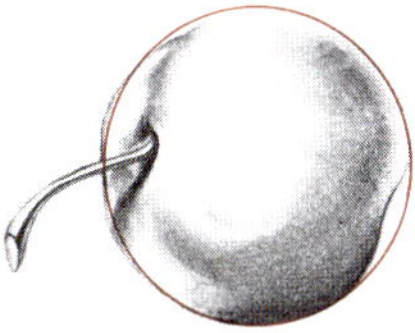

Spheres and their sections are seen in apples, tomatoes, cabbages, wheels, or umbrellas.

Drawing a still life

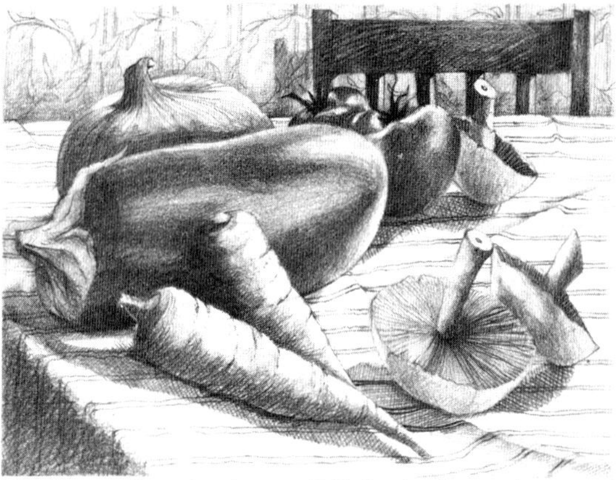

Whether you intend to draw a still life for the sheer enjoyment of the shapes, as a study for a larger composition, or simply as an exercise, you will find that this relatively simple subject opens up many interesting possibilities and poses many challenges. You may be tempted to draw an existing composition of 'found' objects or to set up your own arrangement. Explore the range of materials available to you; your choice will depend on suitability and on the character that you want your drawing to adopt, but more immediately on your mood.

Investigating the subject

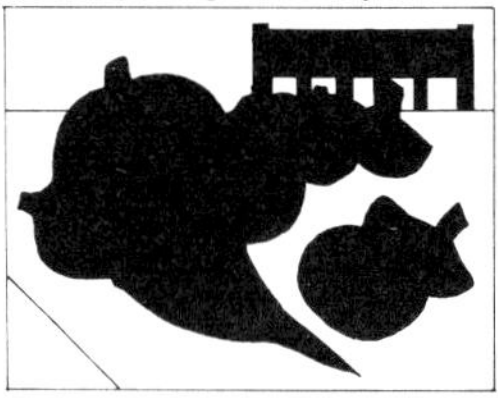

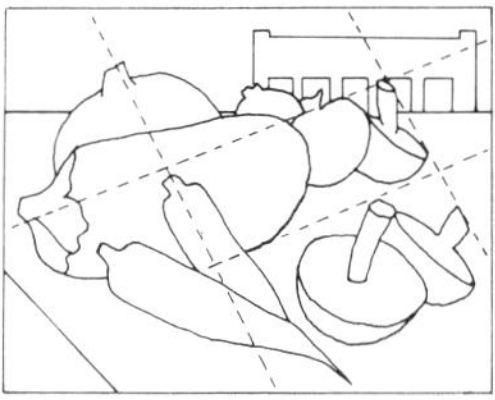

Consider the shape of the group you have arranged on the table. It may look pleasing, but the eye takes in everything and is not selective as your drawing will be. Do several quick sketches of the outline made by the shapes as a mass, shading in the solid areas. This will emphasize the positive and negative shapes created by the composition, their relation to the background, and their position on the paper. Alternatively, you might want to shade in the negative shape.

Now consider the individual shapes. Draw in the outline of each of the vegetables and place them in front of one another on the paper, at the same time building up a sense of direction that draws you into the composition. A diagonal force made either by the objects or by the space left between them will open up the picture plane and take the eye into the composition. Create a foreground, middle and background – it is possible, even on such a small scale as this.

see also pages 14–15, 32–43

Composing a still life

Vegetables and fruit make an ideal subject. Their shapes and textures are pleasing, enhanced by their colour which you might like to try to convey at this stage, or later, when you have first understood them in monochrome. A practical consideration when choosing fruit is their life expectancy: tomatoes and aubergines last well; carrots and mushrooms tend to wilt quite quickly so make individual studies of these to keep for future reference. The background is as important as the main subject; introducing a patterned wallpaper or tablecloth will break up flat surfaces. Make the composition easier to construct by including the vertical lines of, say, a chair back. Consider the direction of the light; daylight is more subtle, but remember that the direction will change as the day goes on; artificial light creates sharper shadows. Do you want the composition to be contained within the rectangle of your paper or to break out from it? Make preliminary sketches from different viewpoints.

Starting to draw the group

1 Having chosen your materials and found the best viewpoint start plotting in your verticals and horizontals and then the main geometric shapes. Draw in the whole shape of the vegetables to check that they really occupy the space you suggest. Emphasize roundness by adding contours.

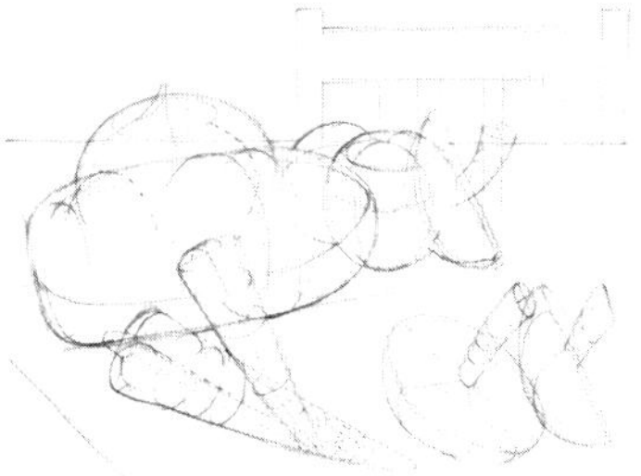

2 Begin to emphasize the stronger edges and add tone and the shapes created by cast shadows. Tentatively add in detail that gives clues to the character of the vegetable: the delicate gills of the mushroom, the gritty, whiskery lines of the carrot, the smoothness of the aubergine.

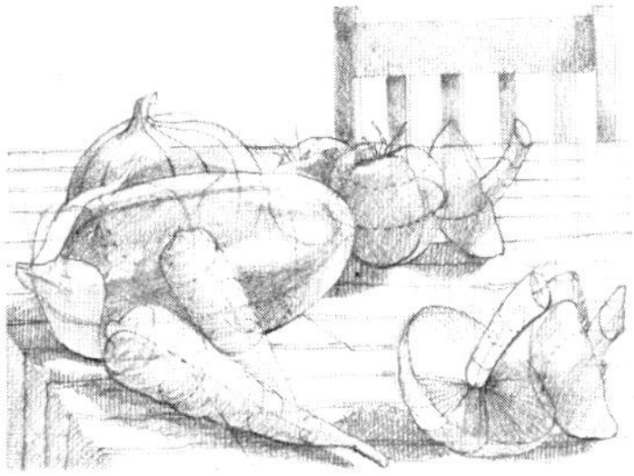

3 Now work up the texture and tones. Vary the quality of the line; if you cannot see an edge do not draw it in (notice where the top of the carrot touches the aubergine – the forms are understood). Do not lose any delicate detail. Lastly add the decorative pattern of the tablecloth.

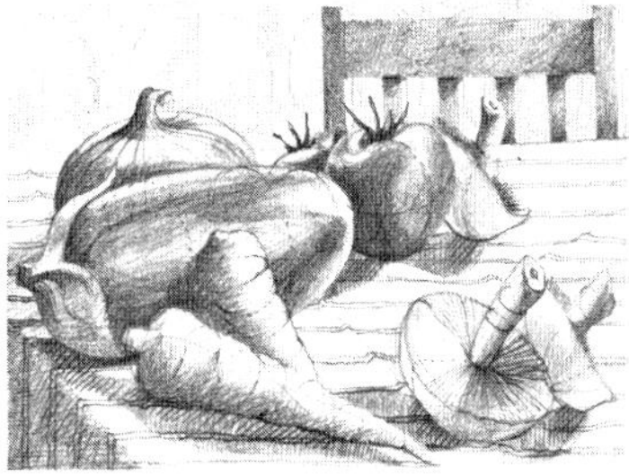

Flowers

A single flower or leaf, a bowl of arranged cut blooms, a bunch of wild flowers or a growing plant make absorbing and complex subjects. An ability to delineate outline and mass simply will form the basis of your drawing, but sensitivity in conveying fragility and a feeling of growth will give the subject its beauty.

Making sketchbook studies throughout the year will help you to understand the forms of various species and to see their different characteristics. Composing an arrangement for a finished drawing will set you a time limit. Buds become flowers, leaves will wilt and die. A composition might change enormously if you leave it for a day.

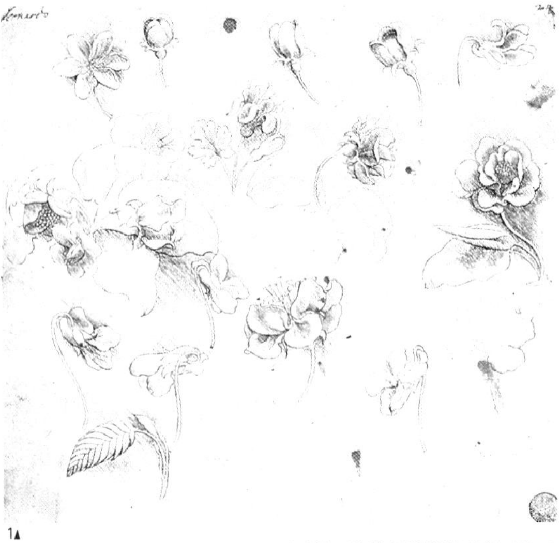

1▲

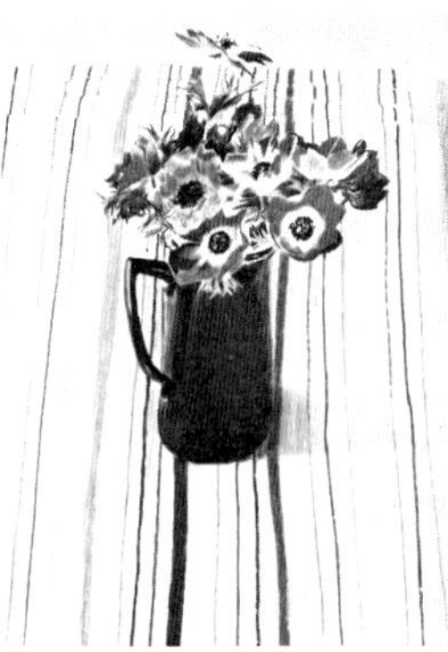

2▲

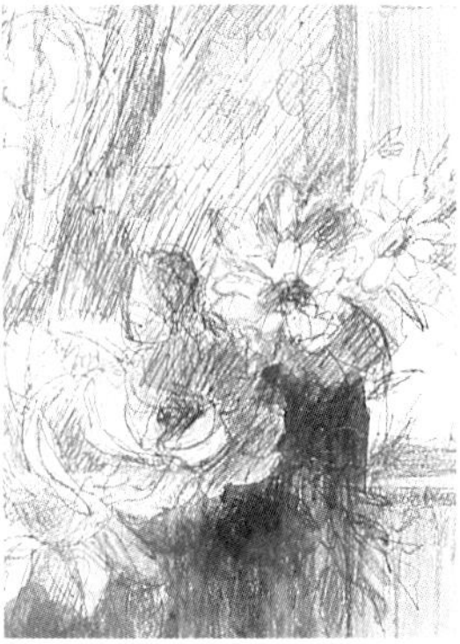

3▲

1 Leonardo da Vinci *Studies of Violets*; 2 Glyn Boyd Hart *Anemones (drawn in coloured crayons)*; 3 George Ainscow *Interior with Flowers (detail)*.

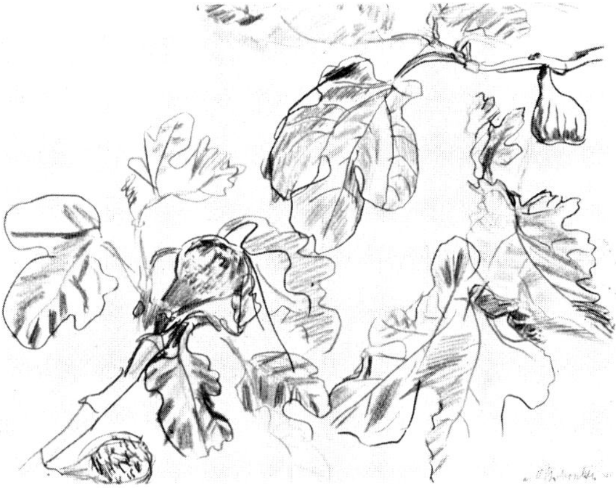

4▲

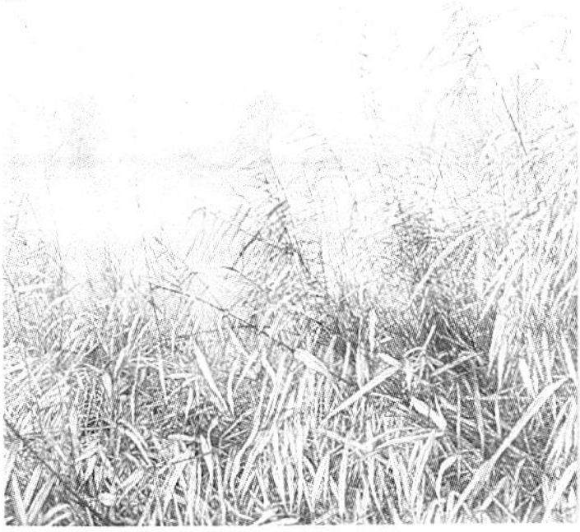

The detailed studies by Leonardo and the freer drawings by Oscar Kokoschka **4** both show how the beauty of flowers and leaves can transform even an investigative drawing into a satisfying composition. The pencil drawing by Jo Barry *The Field Beyond (detail)* **5** gives monumentality to a mundane subject that could be overlooked.

5▲

6▼

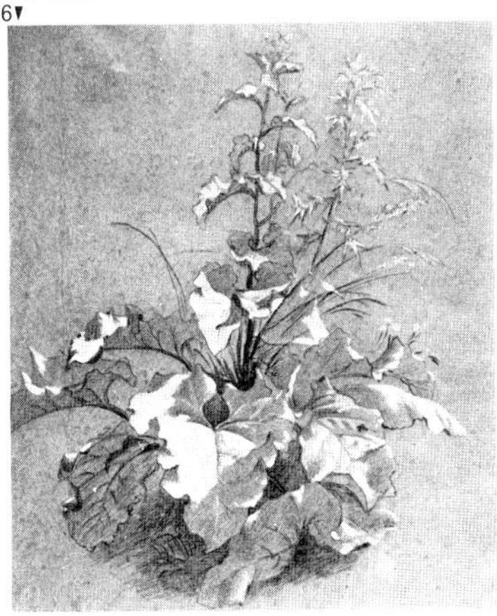

Drawing live wild flowers gives you a good understanding of the whole form of the plant and helps you to relate the various elements. In Charles Norris' drawing **6** note the broad treatment of the lower leaves and the more delicate handling of the new shoots at the top. The composition is ready-made except for its placing on the paper, unlike the two flower arrangements opposite that are much more formal.

The structure of flowers

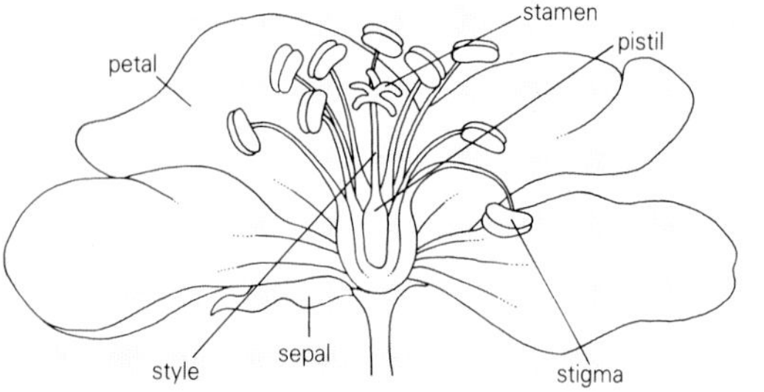

Flowers are, primarily, functional; their brightly coloured petals encourage pollination by attracting bees and other insects. This cross-section of a geranium shows the radial arrangement of the petals around the reproductive parts of the plant: the stamen (the male element), which releases pollen, and the female element, the pistil (a number of stigmas at the end of a style). The sepals are the outer covering of the original bud.

Drawing a flower

A simple understanding of botanical information will not only add to your interest in the subject but will help you to understand the structure of the plant. A careful drawing of one stem will give you the opportunity for detailed observation and to find the best way of gradually building up a drawing of what may appear to be a complex subject. Make things easier for yourself by drawing a single stem, such as this geranium, against a plain background so that the form is easy to see.

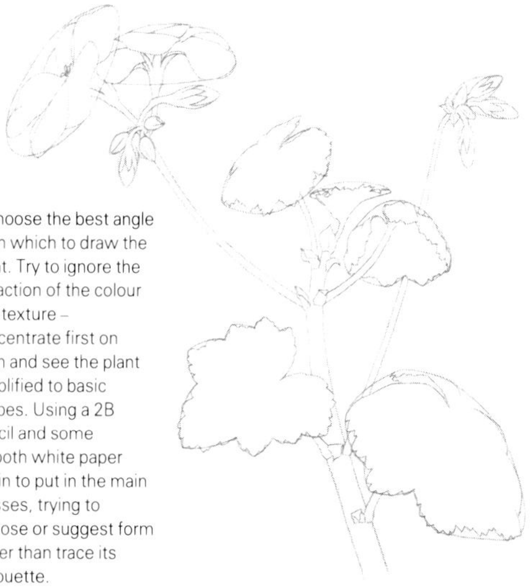

1 Choose the best angle from which to draw the plant. Try to ignore the attraction of the colour and texture – concentrate first on form and see the plant simplified to basic shapes. Using a 2B pencil and some smooth white paper begin to put in the main masses, trying to enclose or suggest form rather than trace its silhouette.

see also pages 42–43, 98

Starting to refine the details

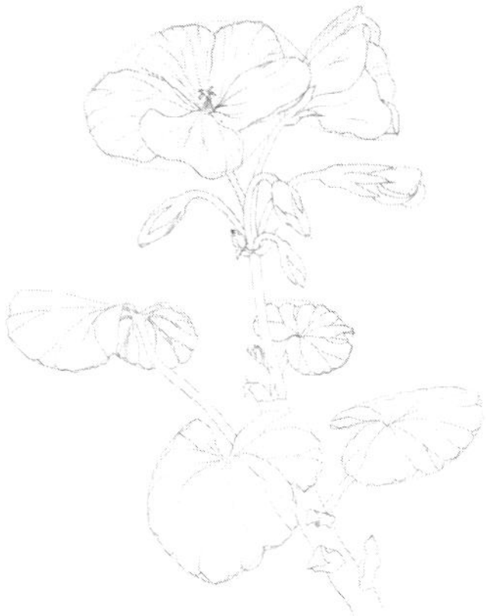

2 Strengthen the main structural lines and build up a rhythm along them. The play of light and shade on the upper- and undersides of the leaves gives a three-dimensional firmness and can be conveyed by varying the line. Careful depiction of the veins will give a convincing sense of growth and can reveal interesting patterns. Draw the plant from a selection of different viewpoints in order to discover its total form.

Working up to a finished drawing

Before you develop your drawing to a highly finished stage, sort out whether you really have all the information you need to understand the flower – could the stalk carry the weight of the leaves and flowers, are the curves natural? If information is missing, look closely at the plant and do small, detailed studies of parts that were not visible.

3 Give a sense of the space occupied by the plant by modelling the foreground more heavily and in more detail and sketching the further parts more lightly. Begin to suggest the texture of the leaves. Notice that there is a difference between the upper- and underside. Leaves are generally smoother on top and more woolly or hairy beneath. The join of the leaf stalk to the main stem should be well observed.

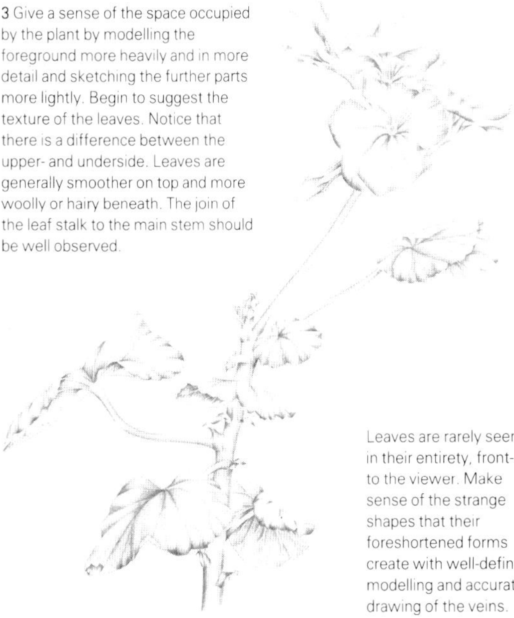

Leaves are rarely seen in their entirety, front-on to the viewer. Make sense of the strange shapes that their foreshortened forms create with well-defined modelling and accurate drawing of the veins.

Drawing the figure

The human figure has a particular fascination for artists. Possibly because the subject is human, it can be one of the most expressive of forms, capable of holding several layers of meaning. In exploring these possibilities, you should look beyond the optical facts and experiment with the rhythms of line and tone, light and shadow. On the following pages the essential skills needed for figure drawing are outlined – first a basic grasp of structure, including anatomy and how the figure moves, and then compositional questions such as viewpoint, pose and the setting in which the subject is placed.

1 ***Henri Matisse*** *Woman Kneeling; 2* ***Bernard Dunstan*** *Nude; 3* ***Henry Moore*** *Reclining Nude; 4* ***Henri de Toulouse-Lautrec*** *Woman Putting on a Stocking; 5* ***Le Corbusier*** *Women; 6* ***Angelo Visconti*** *Male Nude; 7* ***Jean Millet*** *Peasant.*

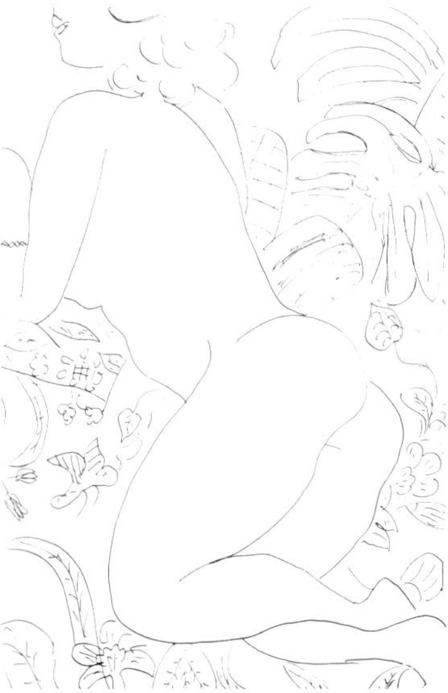

Three contrasting approaches to the nude figure: Matisse **1** produces a rhythmic design of simple line, while Dunstan **2** concentrates on the play of light. For Henry Moore **3** the weight of the subject is the most important element.

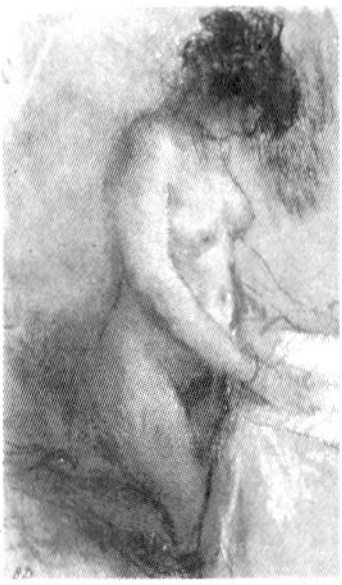

2

1▲

3▼

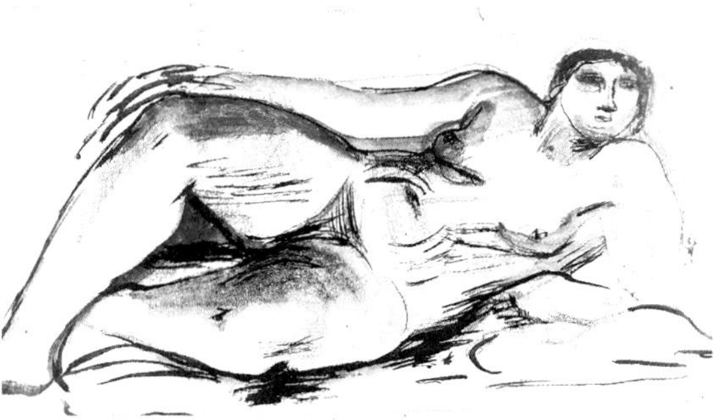

Direct observation versus free expression: Toulouse-Lautrec **4** drew what he saw, but the models were only a starting point for Le Corbusier **5**.

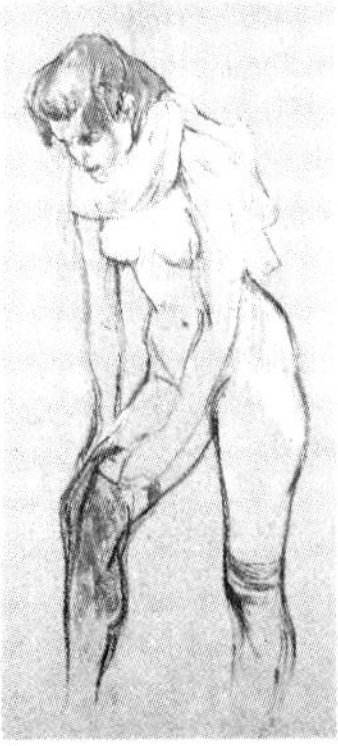

4▲

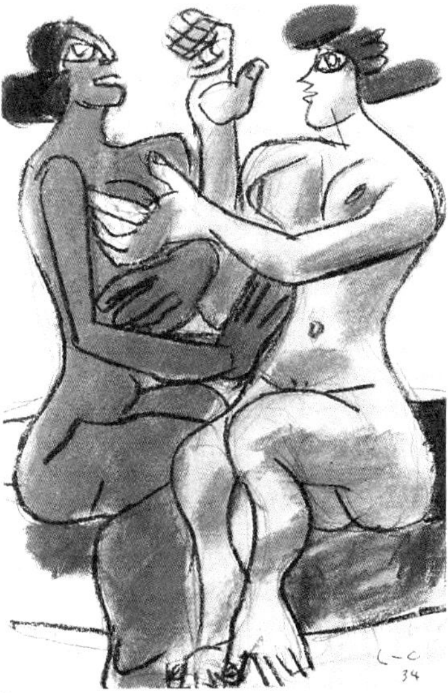

5▲

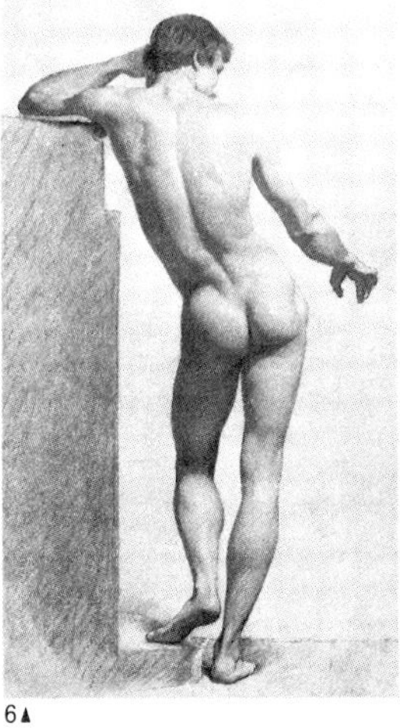

6▲

An academic life study **6** may be accurate and highly finished, but Millet's sketch of a peasant **7** shows that a freer approach can often come closer to reality, showing people as they actually appear, rather than in static and polished poses.

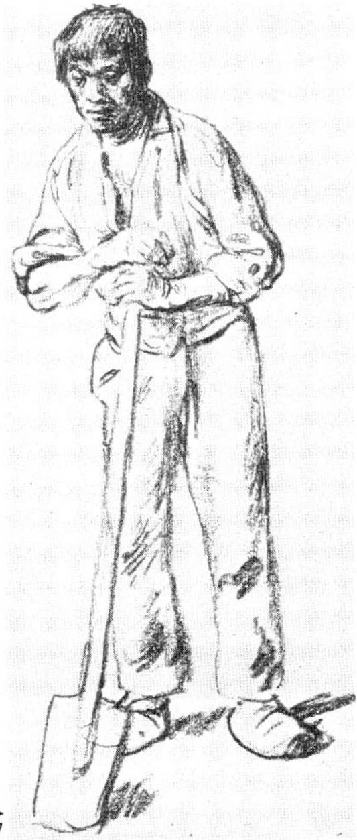

►7

Understanding the body

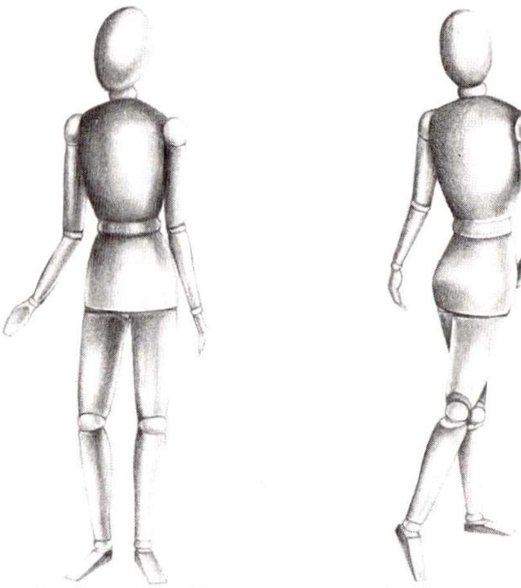

A figure drawing will seldom seem satisfying if it does not seem to represent the structure and movement of the body to some extent – translating into line and tone the workings of a three-dimensional, living organism. Rather than years of close study of human anatomy, however, what is really required is a grasp of the way the body's crucial joints move and a simple understanding of the geometrical forms to which the body can be reduced. Knowing how the body works will help you convey the way in which a figure sits and reclines – what it can and cannot do with its limbs. Even when you are drawing a figure that is fully clothed, this understanding will be of help.

Male and female shape

There are considerable differences in shape between men and women, and minor changes to the outline with which they are drawn can convey a great deal about their contrasting physical structure. Individuals vary a great deal and it is difficult to generalize. The following points, however, may help in characterizing a clothed figure as male or female. Men are generally larger, and their physical strength is particularly apparent in the upper part of the torso, where they are broader, with squarer shoulders. Women are frequently narrower at the waist, with the whole outline from waist to knee forming a single, full curve. Men may be more slender at the hips.

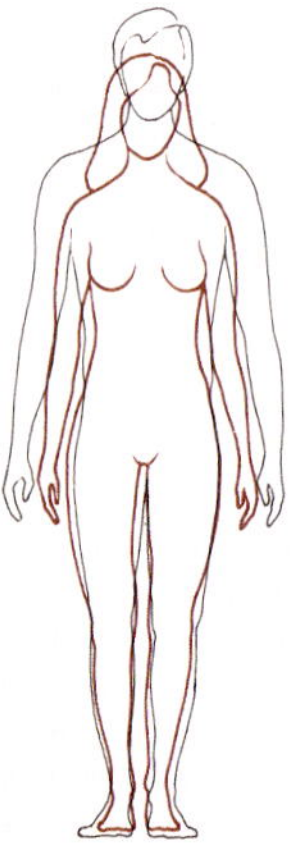

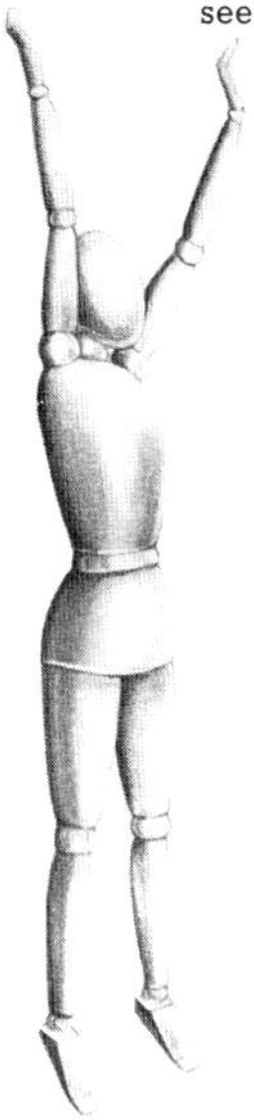

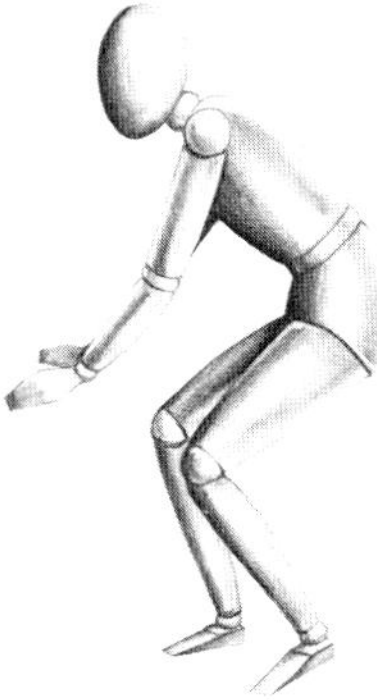

The lay figure is a useful device, both for visualizing the body as a construction of simplified forms and as a means to understanding how it moves. Note how the head tilts on the neck; how the rib-cage makes a firm, convex shield; how the hips and pelvis make a bell shape below the waist. Keep this in mind even when you are drawing the figure from the rear, with the shape of the bell flattened out by the buttocks. Consider the movement of the joints of the arm, at the shoulder, elbow and wrist. Do the same for the legs, which move not only forwards and backwards but also outwards from the hip. Note how the weight falls – on one leg or both. And note how the other parts, especially the arms and hands, are used to help maintain the balance.

The clothed figure

Even though they simplify outlines, reducing the varieties of texture and seeming to conceal difficult points of anatomy, clothes actually increase the problems of figure drawing. They disguise the articulation of the body, which has to be made apparent through the material. They also create distracting shapes of their own, with folds and drapes. To overcome this, you should try to use the folds to suggest the body beneath, as the artist has here by directing the folds away from the waist, which is clearly seen as the pivot of the body. Note, too, how the legs are given form by the rounded hem of the dress. Always think of the clothes as wrapping around the solid form of the body (which should be well understood), stretching over it, hanging from it or moving against it.

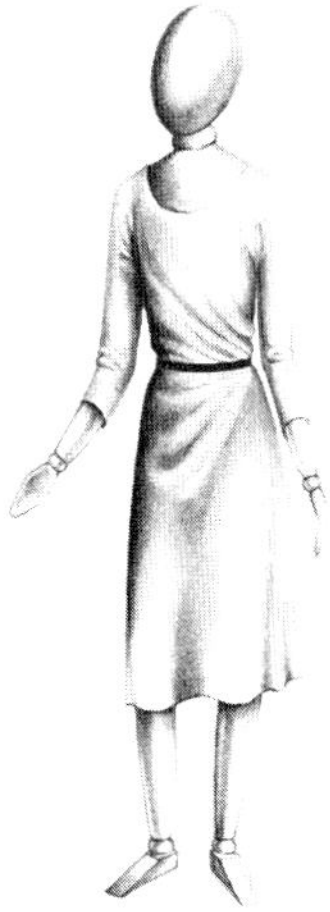

Anatomy and structure

The skull makes up about one eighth of the body's length, and decides the shape of the head. Note the very definite hollows and bumps of eye sockets, cheekbones and jaw.

The neck rises forward from the angled platform of the shoulders and collar-bones. The rib-cage is like a barrel, though the breastbone makes a strong vertical axis. All this is overlaid with complex bands of muscles, gathered in under the armpit.

The bones of the arms change character where they reach the elbow, to form the joints from which forearm, wrist and hand articulate. The upper arm is shorter than the forearm, and reversing this is a common drawing mistake.

The pelvis is like a chassis, supporting the weight of the spine and providing a base for the joints from which the thigh-bones rotate. Remember that it tilts as the weight of the body shifts from one leg to the other. And note that the point of the hip is usually found at the mid-point of the body's complete and extended height.

Thigh-bone and shin, together with their muscle forms, meet at the knee. Unlike the elbow, the joint is covered by bone and cartilage.

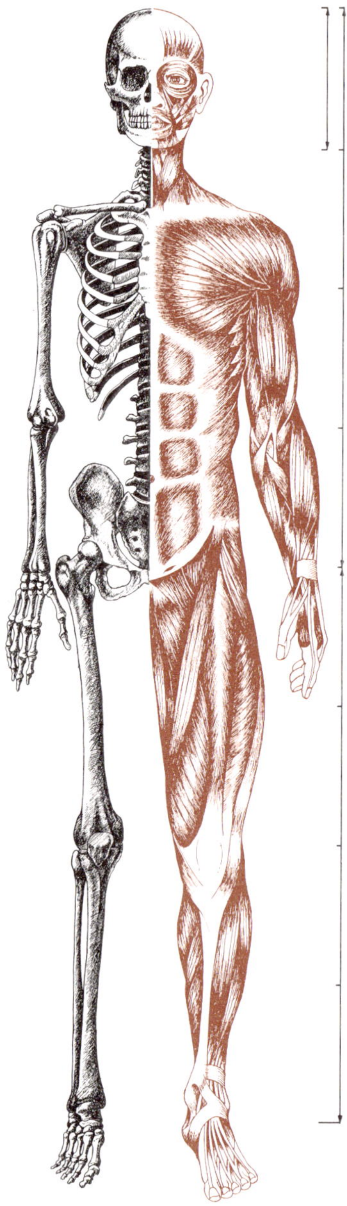

Knowledge of anatomy is not essential to figure drawing, but it certainly helps. A familiarity with the form of the skeleton will enable you to perceive the underlying structure of a body as you draw it. A knowledge of the elbow joint, for example, will give you a better idea of how the arm moves. On these pages the skeleton is shown from front, back and side, together with the muscles as they are built up and cover the bones beneath. Studying the skeleton should also help you to understand the proportions of the body and how the rigid bones are wrapped up, as it were, by the flexible tissue of the muscles, connected to the skeleton by a system of sinews and tendons. You will be able to represent the body's modelling with much greater conviction if you know where each muscle runs and what it is attached to – what each bulge and curve actually means.

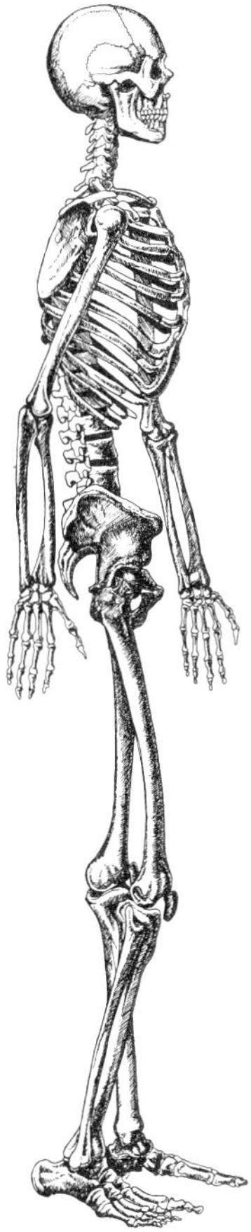

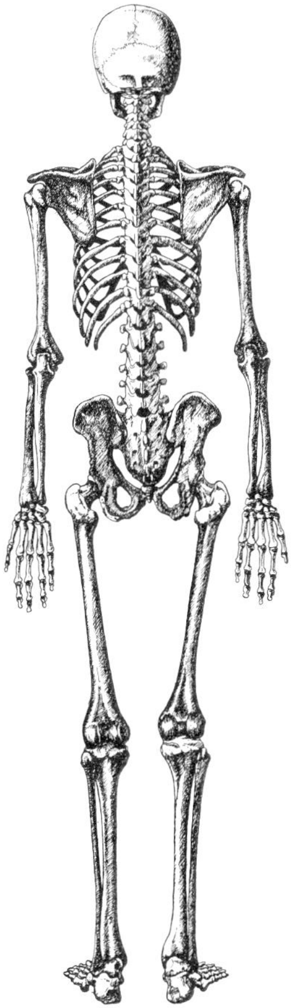

Hands

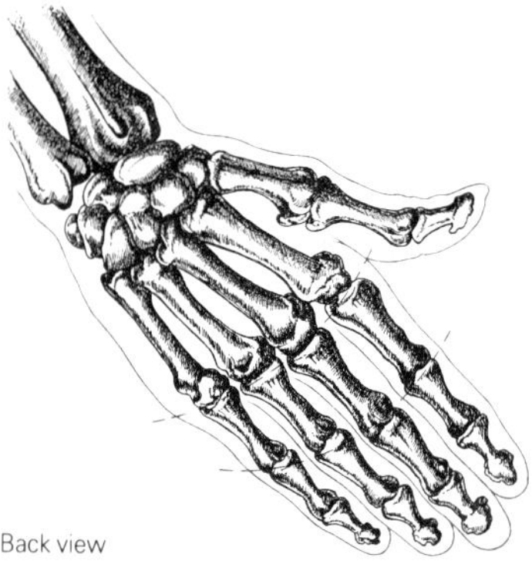

Back view

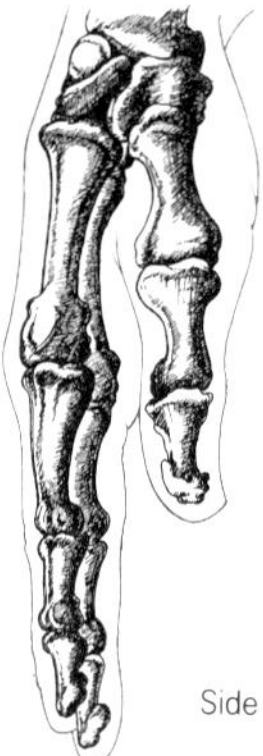

Side view

Hands are one of the most expressive parts of the body and by themselves can convey the mood of the entire figure. As a result, they are a crucial element in drawings of the whole figure and can also make superb and challenging studies on their own. Try to think of them as complete structures of bone and muscle and resist the temptation to draw them piece by piece, with the fingers added one by one to the base of the hand. Bear in mind that the finger-bones extend beyond the knuckles into the back of the hand, where they attach to controlling tendons. And note how the thumb is attached at a large joint which is positioned quite close to the wrist.

Movement of the hands

It is easy to misunderstand the way the hand moves and close observation is the only way to understand all its complex articulations. Note particularly how the hand bends at the wrist and rotates with the forearm. The fingers each have their own movements which need to be studied, especially the thumb.

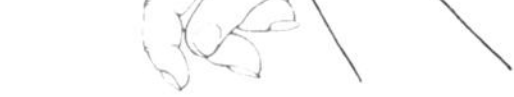

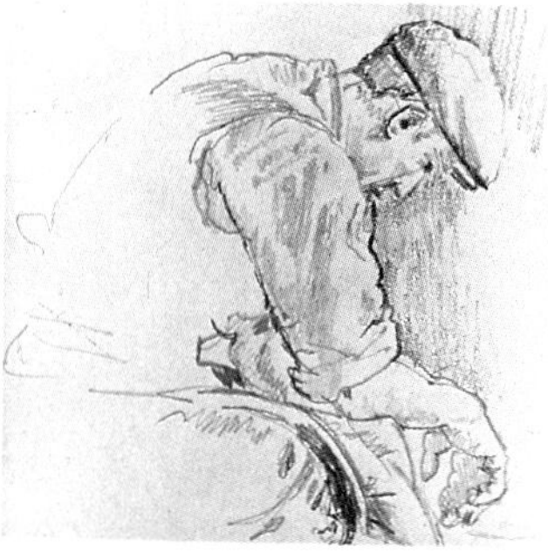

Walter Sickert
Despair (detail)
Sickert's drawing of a working man relies heavily on the limply hanging hand to suggest the subject's dejection. It is the most carefully executed element in the whole composition. But note how only the details needed to define the shape are included in the drawing.

see also pages 54–55, 69

Feet

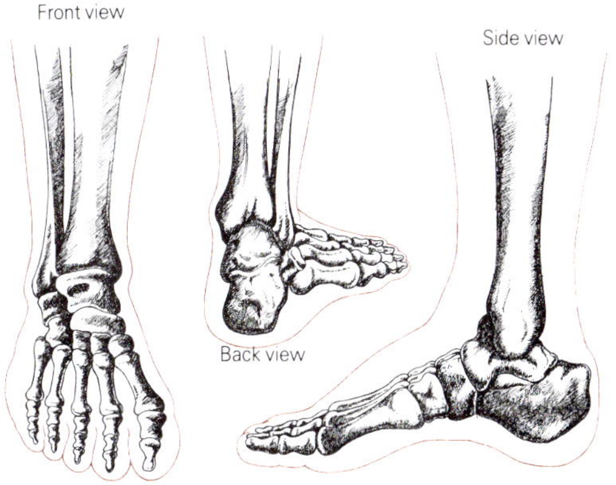

The feet are less critical than the hands. They are usually covered by shoes and rarely carry the same level of expressive potential. But if you are drawing a figure walking or in a turning pose you will need an understanding of the shape and the function of the joints of the feet. The ball of the foot takes the main weight of the body and is the fulcrum on which it revolves when walking. The ball is steadied by the toes and connected to the heel by a number of small bones which form a flexible arch. Remember that the feet always act in concert, balancing the body between them, and the movements of one are usually reflected in the other.

Movement of the feet

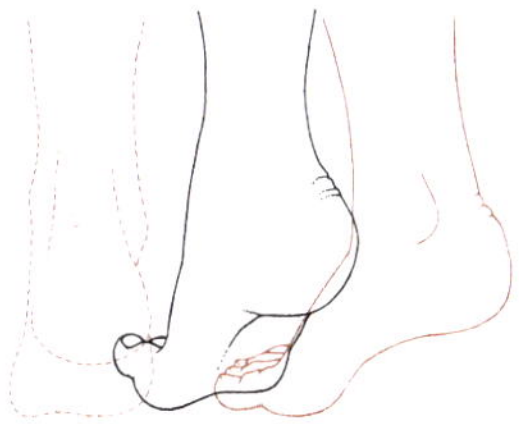

As the leg moves forward, weight is transferred from the heel, through the ball of the foot to the toes, which form a kind of platform. Note that the feet are normally set obliquely to the leg rather than pointing directly forward and that the ankle-bone is higher on the inside of the foot than the outside. Study the way the foot bends at the ankle.

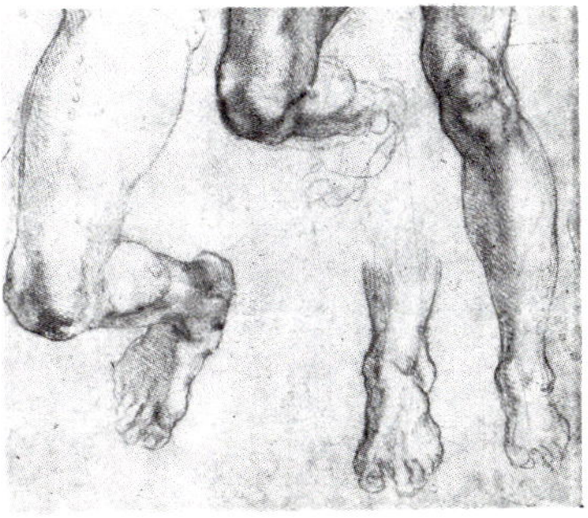

Michelangelo Buonarroti
Figure Studies (detail)
Perhaps the greatest master of figure drawing, Michelangelo certainly did not ignore the feet. These studies show a remarkable grasp of the way the foot bears the body's weight, with the bones spreading the toes to take the thrust from the leg.

see also pages 54–55, 69

Head

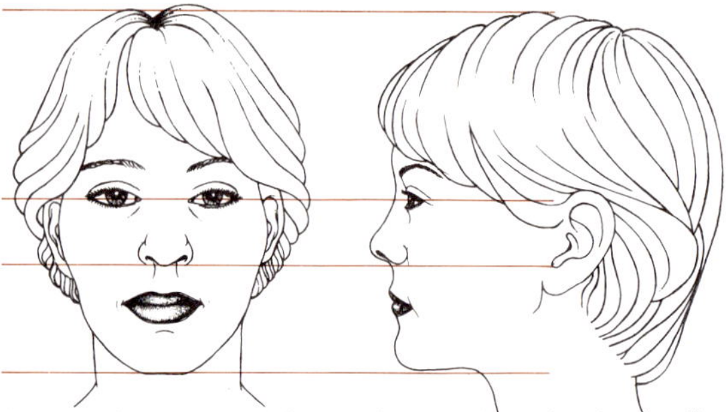

A drawing of a head is essentially a portrait, so even the smallest changes will affect the personality that emerges and certainly have a great influence over the degree of likeness. At first, however, ignore these considerations. Concentrate on the structure, building up the head from its main features – eyes, nose, mouth, ears and hair. Study their relative positions and scale, leaving the details of expression or personality until later. An important point to remember is that the eyes are at the mid-point of the head and that the base of the nose is about one-quarter of the distance from the chin.

Finding a pose

Simple full-face and profile drawings have a very formal look – rather like passport photographs. Varying the pose involves greater difficulty with, for example, foreshortening, but a much greater range of expression can be introduced. A glance directed downwards suggests thought, for example, so try varying the viewpoint.

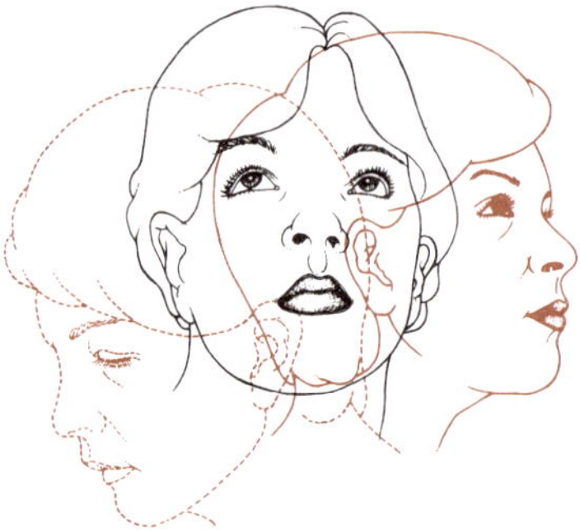

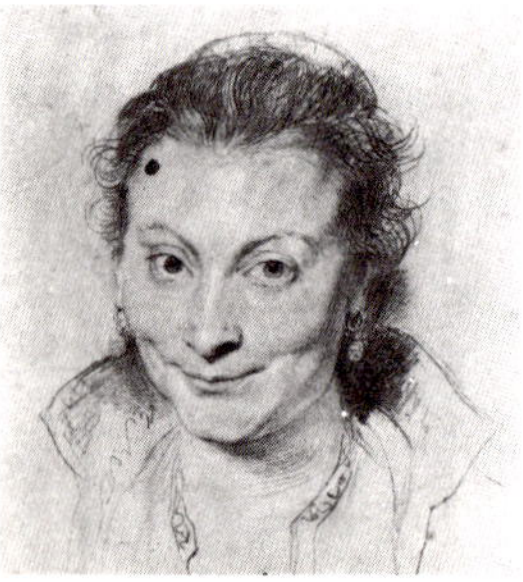

Peter Paul Rubens
Portrait of Isabella Brandt
Rubens' study for a full portrait starts with a firm understanding of the subject's bone structure. The modelling of the high forehead with arched eyebrows, prominent cheek-bones and pointed chin have all been clearly set down in black chalk before the artist went on to add interest and liveliness with red and white chalks. The result is a truly remarkable portrait – a simple likeness charged with the most vivid characterization.

see also pages 34, 36–37, 60–63

Styles of figure drawing

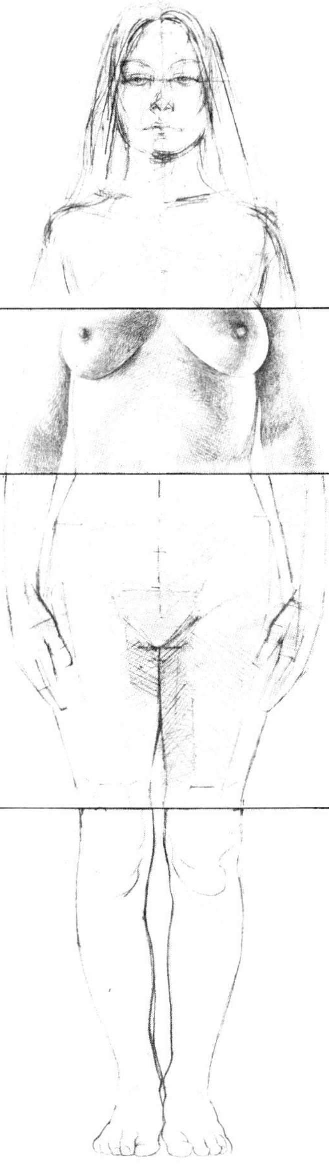

Broken outline

Broken lines do not define the form but suggest it in short stabs and darts. This free style gives a sense of movement and flickering light and shade. It is an effective form of artistic shorthand, but beware of the stylization that can result from loose treatment.

Tonal hatching

Hatching and cross-hatching (see p37) make it possible to achieve detailed modelling of the form.

Simplified planes

Reducing the body to a geometrical study can be a useful and instructive exercise. Such drawings help you analyse the structure of the body as a construction of surface planes, making you more aware of how the light falls on and defines the solid volumes before you.

Line drawing

The use of line alone creates the most simple type of image, with no attempt to show the modelling of the figure. It is often not as easy an approach as it seems, for the outline has to define the form with firmness if it is to convey the shape of the body and a sense of implied volume convincingly.

Life drawing

The nude body is one of the most challenging of artistic subjects, so life drawing is an extremely instructive exercise. It teaches a thorough understanding of the proportions and movements of the body and also develops skill at interpreting and representing solid forms. It was once a central part of every artist's training, and a few great artists produced studies of extreme technical beauty and expressive power – even in the unpromising circumstances of the academic life studio. Life drawing still has its place, although there is now a greater emphasis on the creative and imaginative role of the artist in interpreting the nude figure.

The best way to take up life drawing is to join a class. Otherwise, you can use a friend or a member of your family as a model, or perhaps hire a professional model with other artists sharing the cost. In front of the posed model, look and think before your start. Draw lightly at first, perhaps swiftly sketching out the complete figure. Take in the proportions of the whole form rather than concentrating on details, working from the general to the specific. Avoid too much correction or concentration on fussy details. A simple drawing will almost always be most effective, so try to make every line count.

Setting up the model

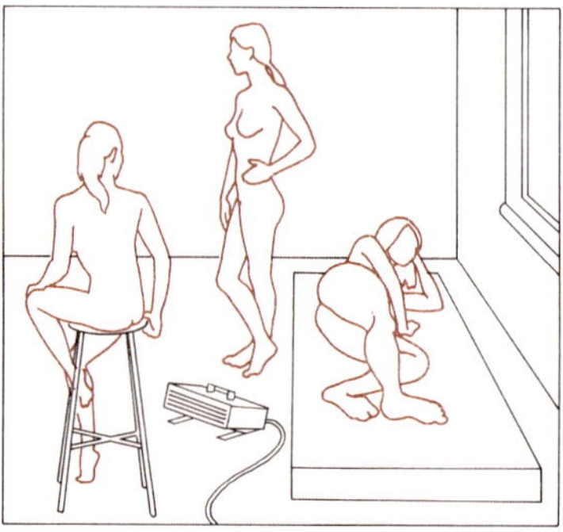

For life drawing, you will need a large, well-lit room, out of direct sunlight and with about two metres space around the divan or chair on which the model will pose. Wall lights will cast more interesting shadows than overhead strip lights. Provide a small fire to keep the model warm – this may even be necessary in summer.

Starting to draw: selecting the pose

Choose a standing pose to begin with. It will be easier to see the structure of the body and how the weight is carried. Make sure the model is comfortable or it will be difficult to hold the pose for long. Walk around the model before you draw and experiment with the pose. Try to see the figure as a whole, from head to feet as you consider the best angle.

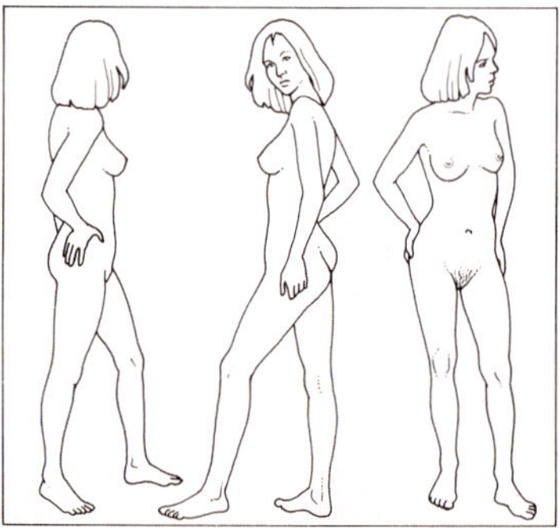

see also pages 12–13, 18–19, 40–41, 52–59

Step-by-step

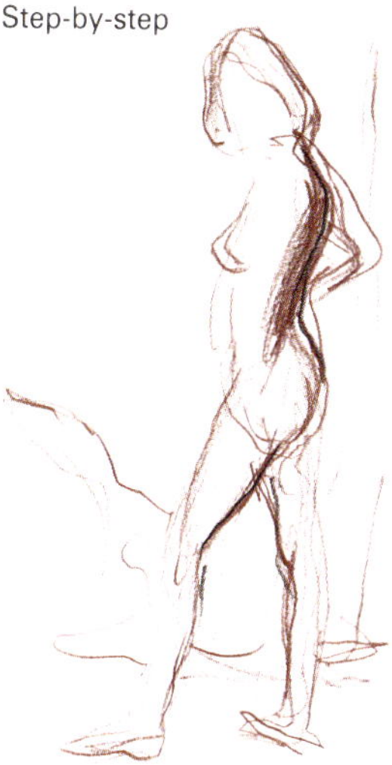

1 Look for the essential elements in the pose – here, the swing of the back and the hips – and try to put these down with simple strokes.

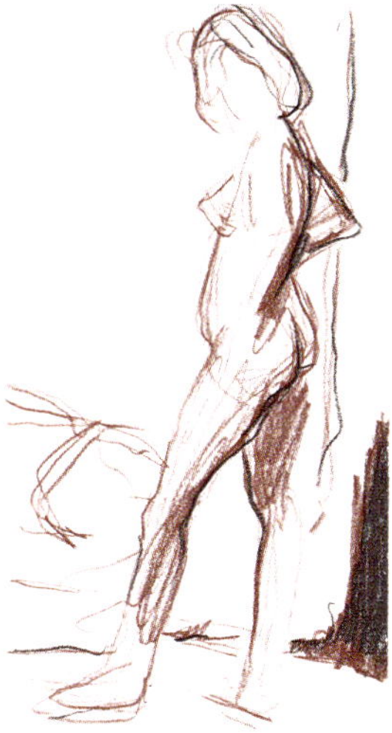

2 Begin to introduce some definition to the shapes of the body, identifying the main areas of tone in both the figure and in the setting.

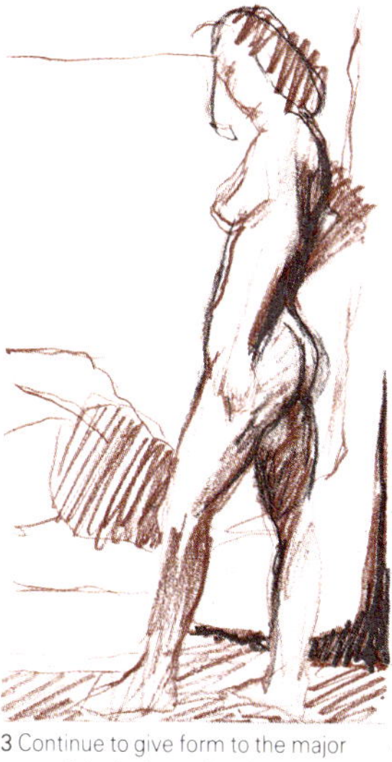

3 Continue to give form to the major parts of the body, such as breasts, buttocks, knees and hands. But leave the face for the time being.

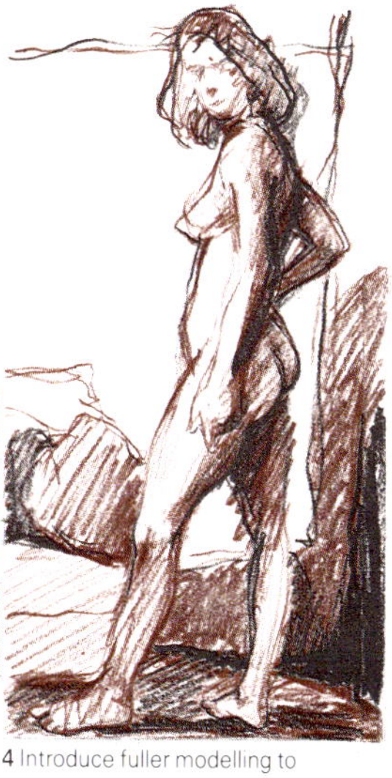

4 Introduce fuller modelling to balance the pose and assert the correct stresses. Suggest the face and block in the middle tones.

Quick sketches

As an exercise, try drawing from the life with great rapidity. Ignore the results to start with, for you will be learning something quite different than you would by completing a more laborious study. Drawing at speed forces you to identify the important facts and to appreciate the overall unity of the pose. You will also acquire a much better feel for the energy and movement of the figure.

Start with 30-second sketches, purely as an exercise, timing yourself rigorously. Then move on to one minute. You should be able to produce quite developed and expressive studies like those below. Move on to two minutes. By now, having become used to working at great speed, this will seem like an acceptable time to set down what you see. Finally, allow yourself five minutes for each sketch. The examples below right, by the same artist, show that it is possible to produce complete figures in this short time, with a strong suggestion of the figure's modelling as well as its linear shape.

30-second sketches

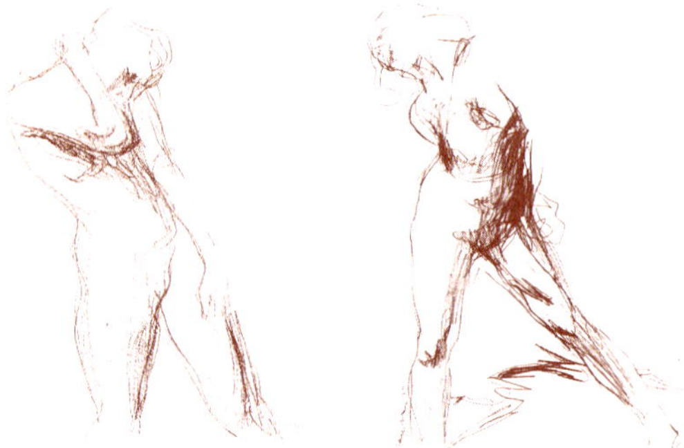

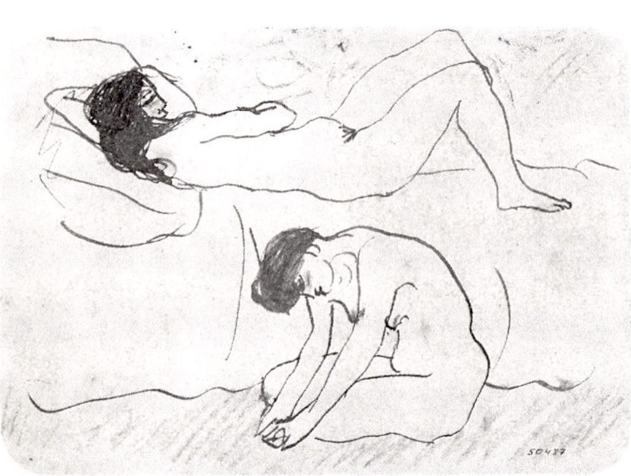

Pablo Picasso *Two Nudes*
With the simplest outline of ink and minimal crayon colour, the young Picasso's drawing reveals complete economy and sureness of touch.

see also pages 14–15, 40–41, 52–59

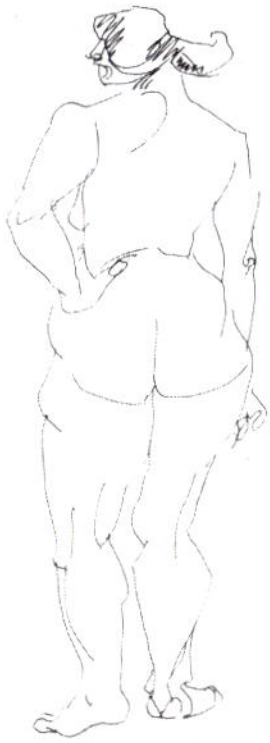

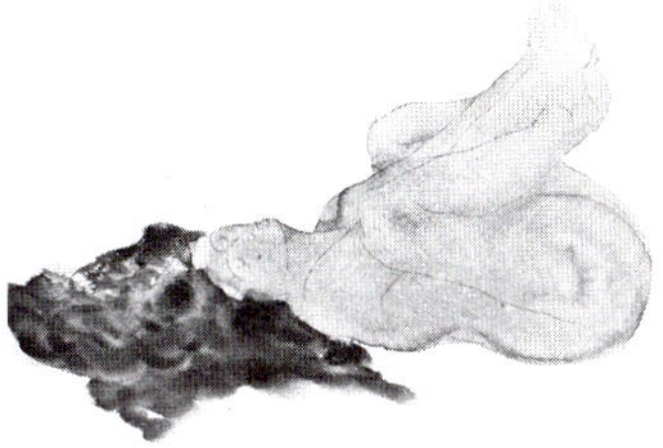

Henri Gaudier-Brzeska *Standing Female Nude*
Without using shading, Gaudier-Brzeska gives solidity and weight to an informal study.

Auguste Rodin *Nude on her Back*
A complex pose captured in line and wash.

Five-minute sketches

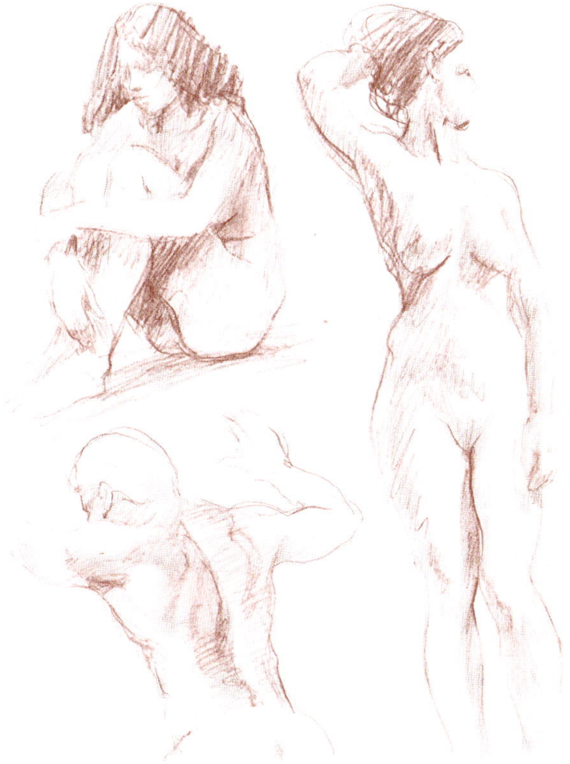

Foreshortening

A problem to be overcome in figure drawing is the effect of perspective – foreshortening. This radically alters the body's appearance, and the first task is to draw what you see rather than what you know is there. The solution, however, is not the meticulous delineation of an outline in perfect perspective but the suggestion of the space that the figure occupies. Firm modelling of the forms in the foreground will help. Set off these areas with blank spaces – the imagination will fill in what you have merely suggested. You should also study the drawings of other artists and even photographs to see how the parts of the body change shape with foreshortening.

Reclining figures

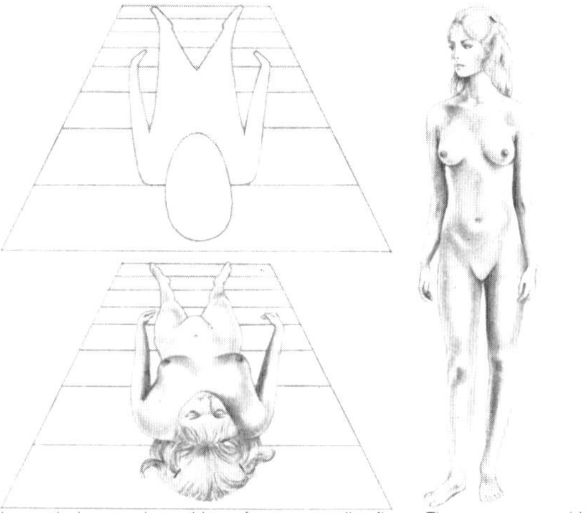

In practical terms, the problem of foreshortening is to adjust the relative sizes of the parts of the body in relation to the effect of perspective. Train your eyes to see the body's foreshortened shape as a simplified outline, forgetting what you know about the actual size of its parts. If you find this difficult, devise a scale by marking off the main points of the standing figure. Then construct a grid (see p106) or mark off those same points on the surface your model is lying on. Having found the overall shape, you must observe the figure before you as a set of solid forms receding from the foreground. In the illustration the modelling of the head and breasts is crucial to the illusion of foreshortening.

Oblique foreshortening

Foreshortening usually occurs at an oblique angle. The same method of measuring as above can be used, although it will be more difficult. More modelling has to be introduced in distant parts of the figure.

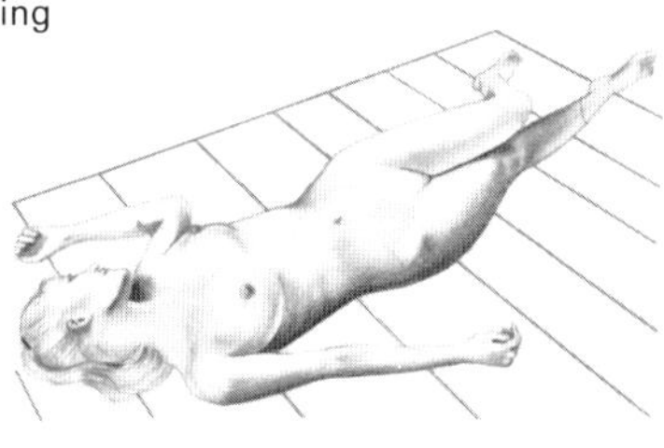

see also pages 102–105

Seated figures

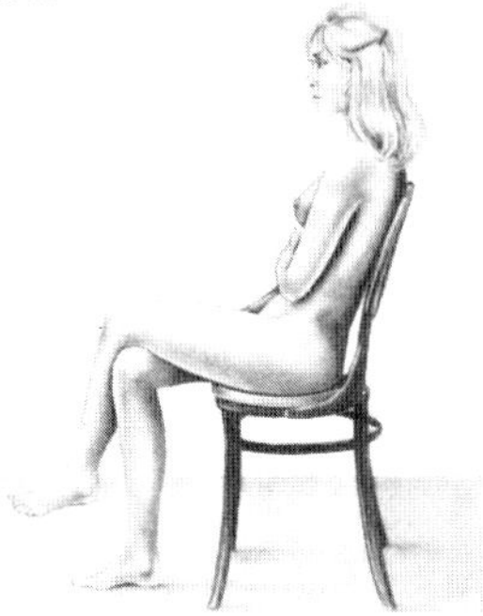

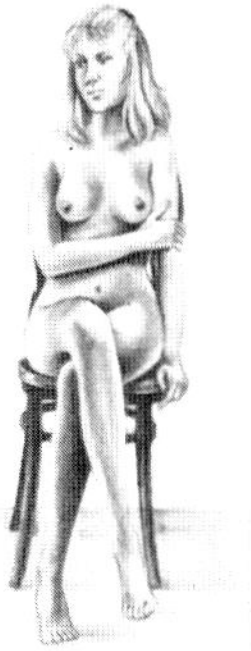

When drawing a seated figure, use the proportions of the chair as a guide. Within this frame, make the points where parts of the body begin or end as clear as possible and let the foreshortening look after itself. The legs can prove difficult, however, particularly when crossed. Use shading to contrast the upper leg with the shadowed leg below. Shading on the arm, breasts and chin adds to the effect of modelling. The chair also helps to establish the proportions of the clothed figure, with the shadows emphasizing the sense of space.

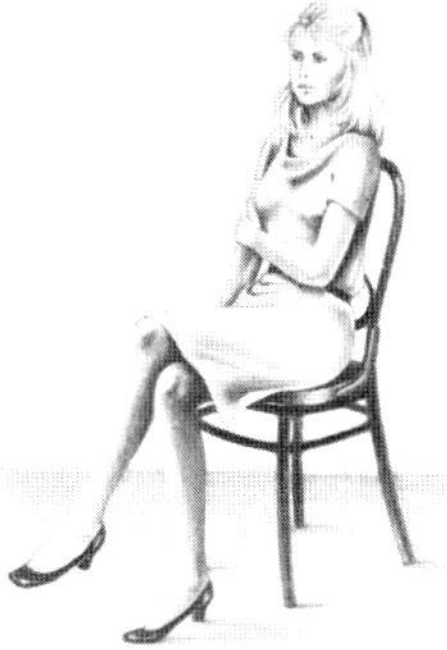

Deliberate distortion

Wyndham Lewis
Crouching Nude
Lewis, an artist with a bold and energetic style, here demonstrates that even the most complex poses can be convincingly handled. Some deliberate distortion has been introduced – the head, for example, should be larger. Other parts of the body including the raised knee, however, have been perfectly rendered in their foreshortened shape with a few vigorous but accurate pencil strokes.

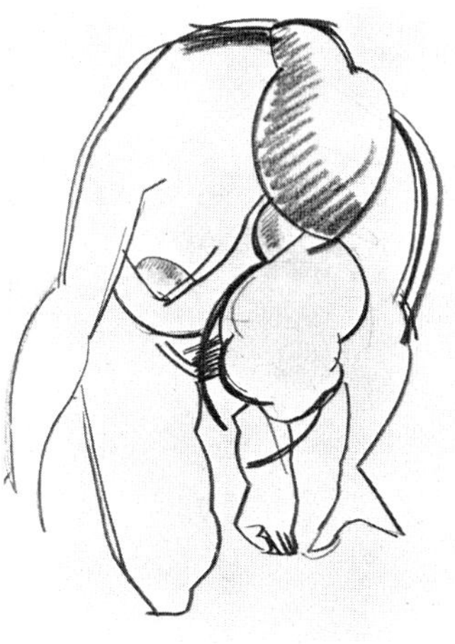

Composition

Making use of the studies you have made, you can now plan a composition – deciding not just what you are going to include in the drawing but also how best to organize the various elements. The setting of the figure in space and the direction of light are crucial. In addition, the shapes and shadows should be balanced to lead the eye around the composition and give the drawing an expressive impact. Although this quality will be developed as you actually work, it is more likely to emerge if you have a clear conception of what you are trying to achieve at the outset. Try to form an image of the complete composition in your mind before you start and resist the urge to fill in details that attract you until the drawing is nearing completion. Remember that composition comes before style.

Scale and distance

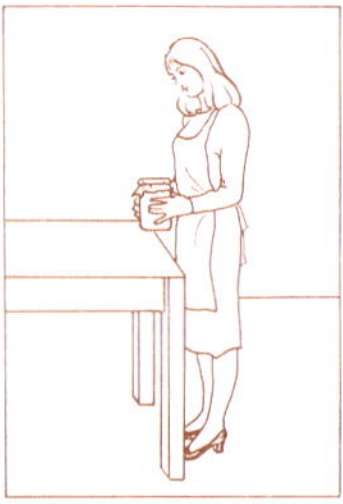

If your drawing is to include an illusion of space, start by defining the main spatial planes at the front, middle and back – the table front, the figure and the wall behind which closes in the background.

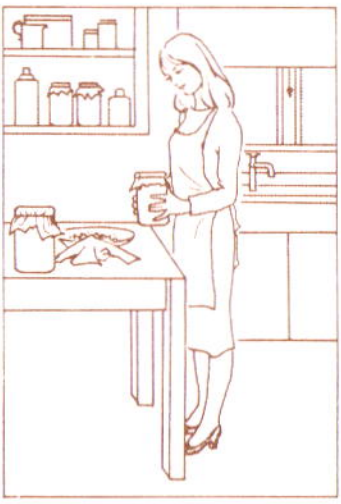

By adding elements to the composition you can elaborate the surface design of the drawing. This may reduce the spatial clarity – perhaps to the detriment of compositional unity.

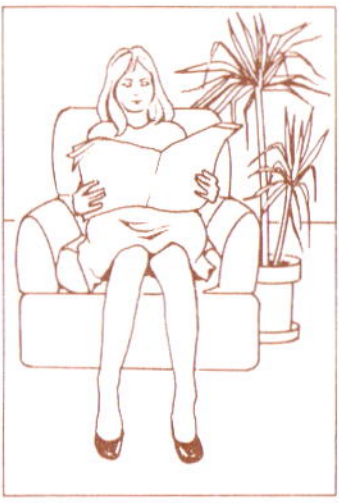

The figure itself may occupy more than one plane. Here, the knees, magazine and head need to be placed in space. Other objects, such as the chair, can help to establish these different planes.

Shape and proportion

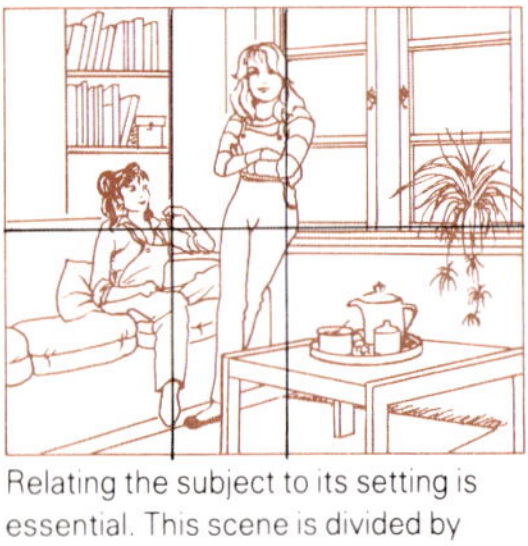

Relating the subject to its setting is essential. This scene is divided by several main verticals. These help define the shapes of the figures and also their relative positions in the room. Establish them as the main structure of the composition before starting the figures.

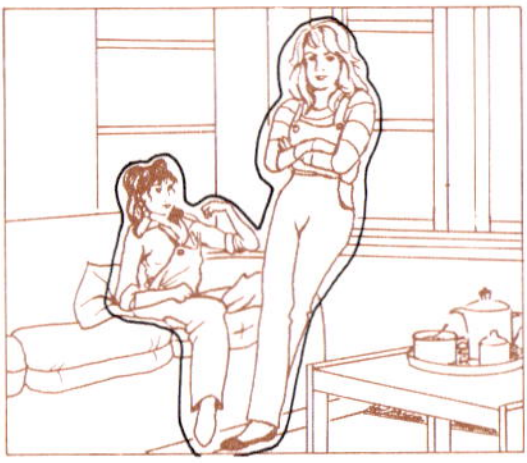

Try to identify the main shapes created by the figure in outline, relating them to the negative shapes around them. Both must be pleasing for the drawing to work satisfactorily. These broad shapes are likely to make up the main compositional elements in the scene.

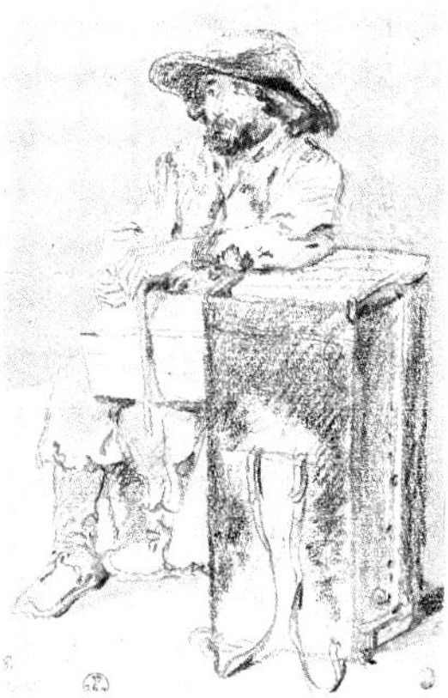

Antoine Watteau *Old Savoyard*
Sketched quickly from the life, Watteau's drawing is composed in real space, with the old man's backpack in the foreground and a shadowed wall behind. The minimal detail is concentrated largely on the subject's face, achieving the great pathos of this fine study.

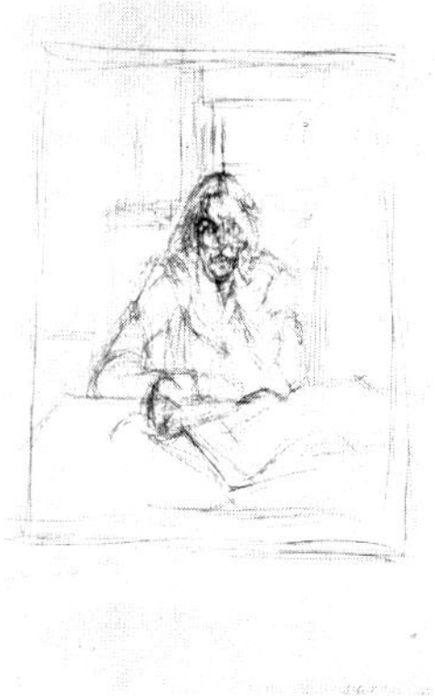

Alberto Giacometti *Annette Reading*
In this rapidly executed and strangely expressive sketch, Giacometti uses a rigidly geometric structure to establish a firm composition, focusing on the dramatic face. The desk and figure form a triangle with the head at the apex. Just enough background is included to set the figure in space.

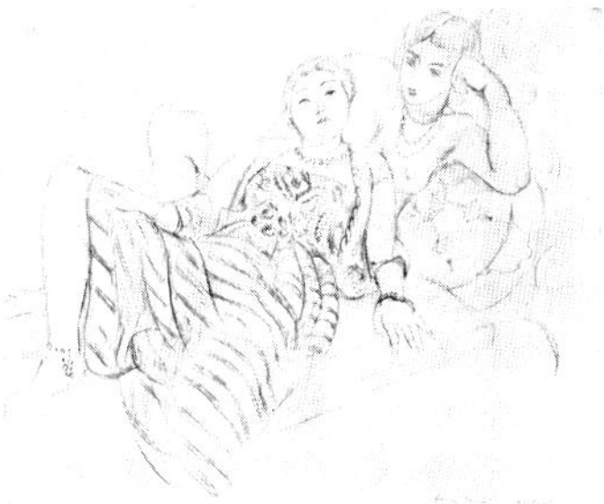

Henri Matisse
Two Odalisques
Matisse is concerned entirely with the surface of the drawing and shows little interest in defining a real space, concentrating on the sensuous rhythms of the lines as they curl around the forms. The intricate linear patterns of the composition are given some stability by a simple diagonal structure. Style and composition match perfectly the sensuous mood of the subject.

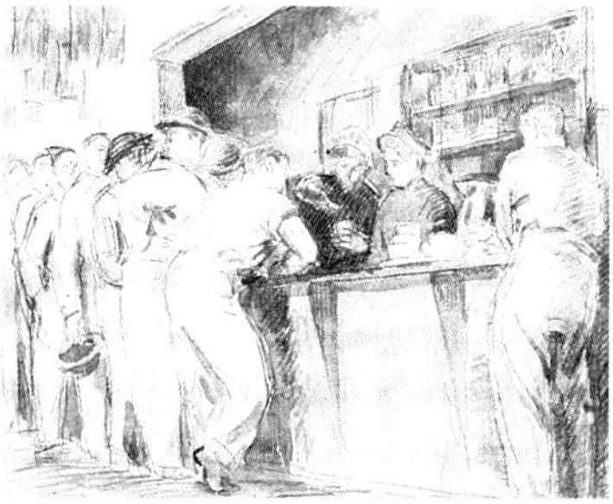

Henry Lamb
Men Drinking
Here, Lamb uses a low viewpoint and strong perspective to create depth and unity in this drawing of a group of figures.

Movement

see also pages 16, 56–58, 62–63

Drawing moving figures is as dependent on understanding how the body is constructed as it is on observation. The general movement of the joints must be understood, together with the broader twists and bends of the torso. It is particularly important, for example, to grasp the way the shoulders rotate in relation to the hips. Beyond this, you must study the characteristic ways the body leans and turns in movement. Adopt a free, experimental style – quick strokes will express movement more effectively than a static, finished drawing, however accomplished. Be prepared to repeat edge lines for an effect of blurring.

Drawing a moving figure

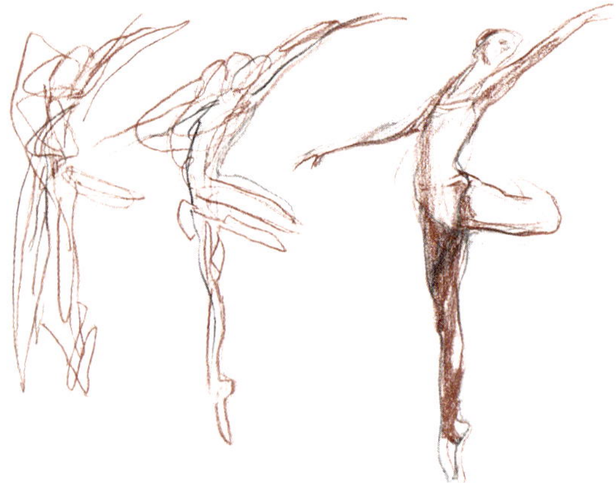

As an exercise, try a series of quick sketches while watching a moving figure such as a dancer. First, try to identify the general shape of the body with a series of quick strokes. Then produce a more refined version, leaving out the lines which seem least accurate. From this basis, you should be able to produce a more complete, but still free drawing.

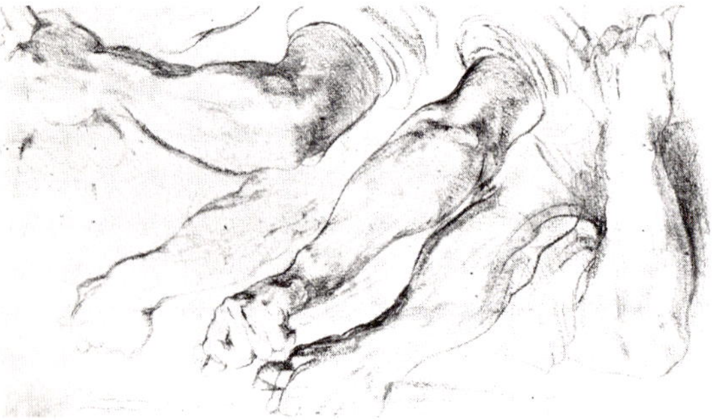

Peter Paul Rubens *Studies*
In order to express the movement of a flexing arm, Rubens was prepared to exaggerate the musculature, strengthening the contour with white.

see also pages 66–67, 87–88

Groups

Groups and crowds of figures involve considerable problems, for a group is both a single, broad mass and also a collection of individuals that may need fairly accurate drawing. Begin with a visual analysis of the whole. Is it a compact mass or spread out? What is the difference in scale between the nearest and furthest figures? Which figures come in front and which are partly hidden? When you have loosely mapped out these major elements, choose the figure that seems to be the focus of the composition and establish its scale and relation with the surroundings. Then build up the other figures, always referring back to the key figure and the broad structure you have set up.

Analysing the group

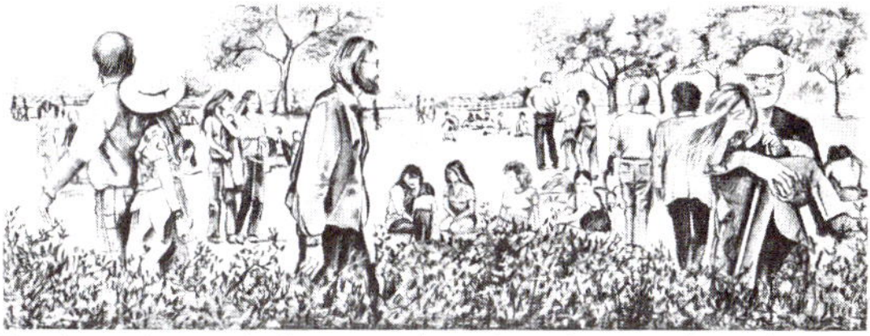

Even in complex crowds, figures can almost always be seen as interacting groups. In this scene, very few figures are totally isolated, and most are engaging companions in conversation or responding to the actions of others. Identify the connections and make them the focus of the drawing.

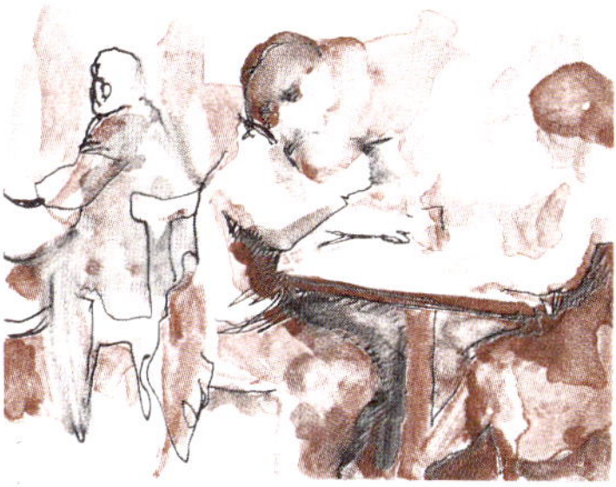

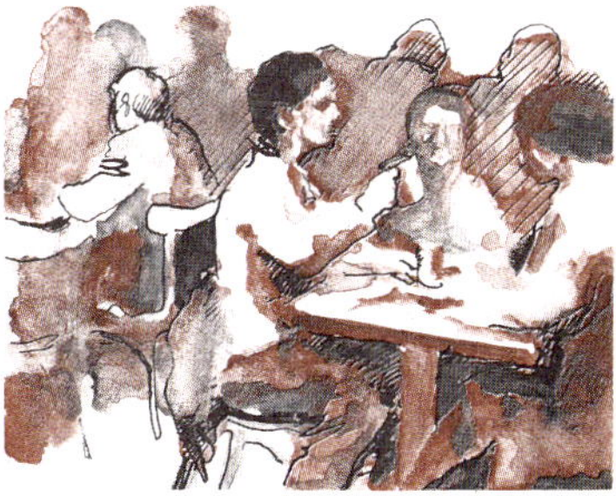

Faced with a busy scene, try to decide in general terms what you intend to show – in this case the central figure is the man seated in the foreground and the composition should be built up around him. First, the main shapes and shadows have been put in with various dilutions of wash, then defined with ink line. Having established the broad shapes of the composition, the depth is added with darker washes and hatching. If you are unsure of any of the gestures, ask a friend to repeat them as you work up the drawing. Do not overelaborate – it will be clearer and more effective through suggestion of the forms.

Drawing children

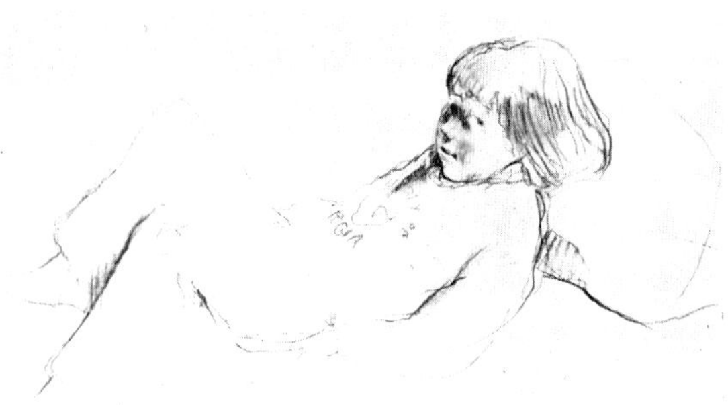

Marc Winer *Catriona*

There are special factors to be considered when drawing children. Their bodies are still being formed and they are so active that study of their structure may seem irrelevant. Indeed, many of the individual and lifelike characteristics in the drawing will come from the choice of a pose that shows some particular behaviour. The shape of the head and the body changes markedly as the child grows, however, and an understanding of this process can be very useful, putting you in a better position to catch the fleeting features of one particular pose. You should match your drawing style to the nature of the subject – a light, swift stroke will be truer than a hard, pedantic line.

Children at play

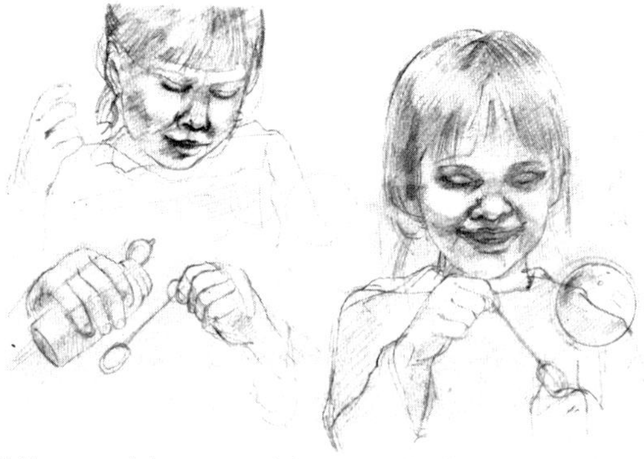

Children are at their most natural when engaged in a favourite activity. Their obvious enjoyment and absorption can make fascinating study. Concentrate on the essentials – the head, hands and the main gestures. Study the shape of the head. How like a globe is it? Where and how does it differ from this simplified geometrical shape? Think less about achieving a likeness than defining the main shapes of the body and the characteristic movements of the activity. Notice how the head tilts and the hands move. Above all, try to capture the enthusiasm and spontaneity of the child in its own world, so distant from that of adults.

Child portraits are quite difficult. There are fewer individual points such as lines and blemishes to fix the likeness. Note the chubby volume of the cheeks and other facial features. You may also find that children are easily bored and will not hold a pose for long. Try drawing them with something to read (below), or watching television.

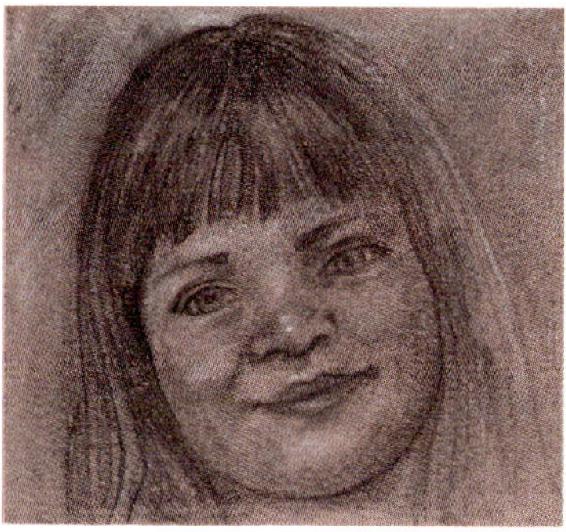

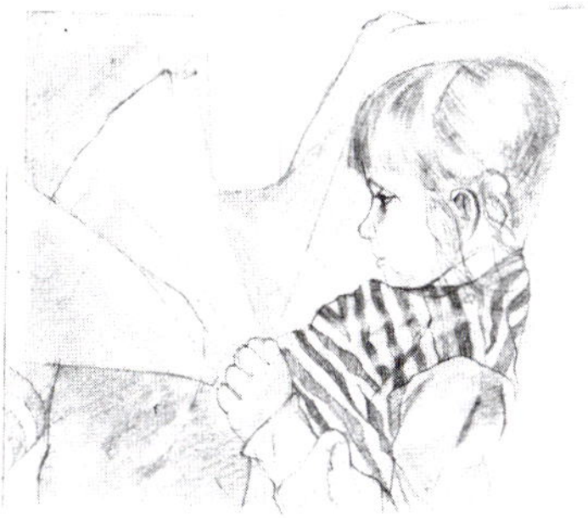

Selecting a medium will probably be influenced by the fact that you may have to draw with speed to capture an expression. Conté crayon (above) is a good 'instant' medium. When used with tinted paper (which establishes a middle tone) it is effective for portrait studies. Pencil sketches (left) allow for linear variety.

Changing proportions

The growing child will alter in other ways than becoming taller (below). The general proportions of the body change, with the head becoming smaller in relation to the body. During adolescence, which begins more rapidly with girls, the body becomes more muscular and loses fat, with the sexes becoming noticeably different.

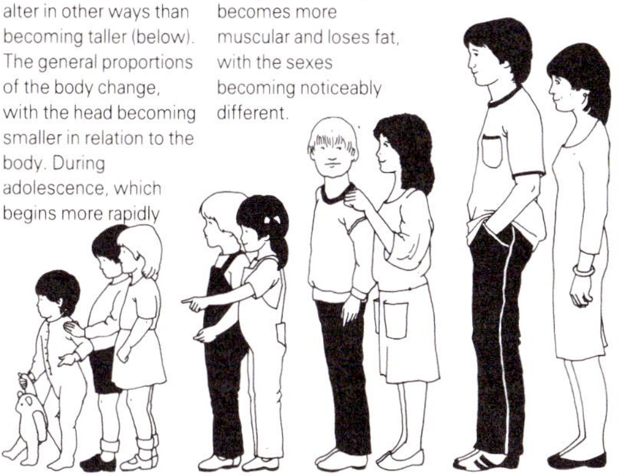

Portraits

A portrait is more than a study. It attempts to do justice to the personality of the sitter. Look at the subject and ask yourself: what is it that makes this person individual? Choose a comfortable pose and give the model a point to focus on. Allow the model to move around while you are working, however, as long as you can fix the position of the element you are working on at any given time. Avoid fussy surroundings – the main area of interest should be the personality of your sitter.

Drawing a portrait

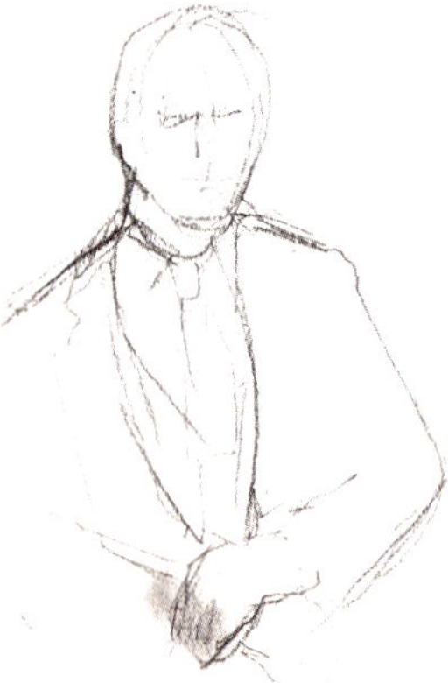

1

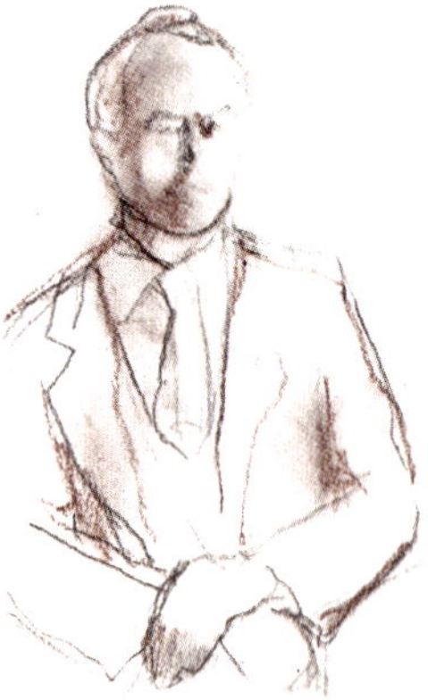

2

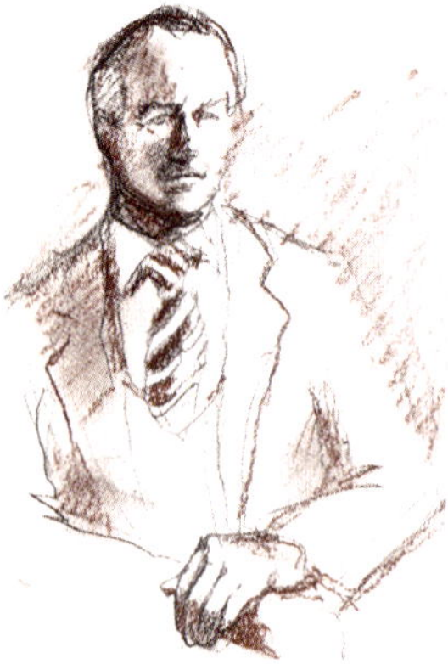

3

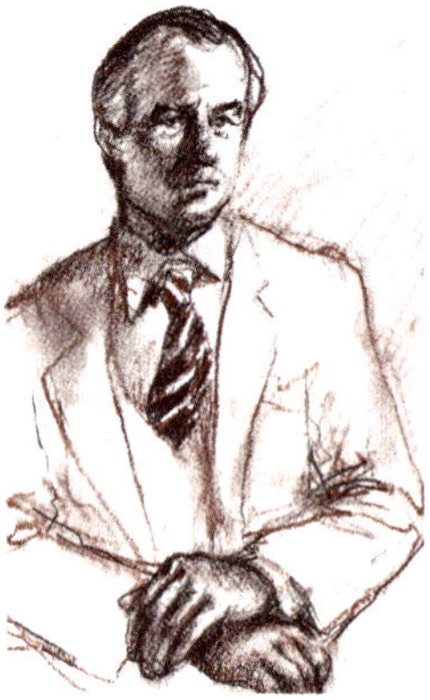

4

1 Lightly sketch in the general position of the figure, ideally with the head placed off-centre. 2 See how the head sits on the body and outline its shape, positioning the eye sockets, hairline and nose as accurately as you can. 3 Develop the modelling of the form by introducing the main areas of shadow. Refine the likeness, working on different features simultaneously so they relate to each other. 4 Pick out reflected light with a rubber and deepen the shadows.

see also pages 18–19, 58, 66

Portrait drawings can be produced in many different styles, with widely differing intentions. Some artists deliberately intend to flatter, with attractive and fashionable images. Others try to achieve an intense study of personality. Still others have used the portrait convention as a starting point, pursuing their own pictorial aims.

1 ***Pablo Picasso*** *Ambrose Vollard;* 2 ***Wyndham Lewis*** *Virginia Woolf;* 3 ***Jean Auguste Ingres*** *Josephine Lacroix;* 4 ***Henri de Toulouse-Lautrec*** *Profile.*

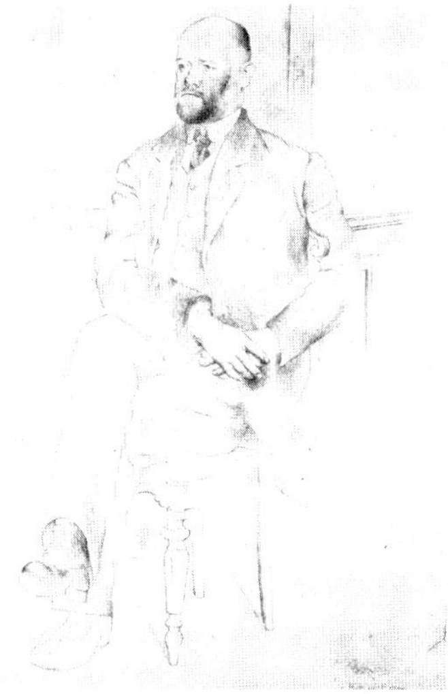

1▲

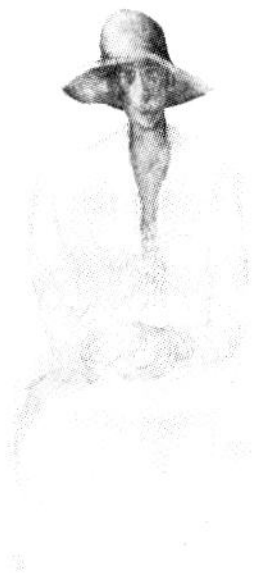

2▲

Picasso's entirely conventional drawing of Vollard **1** in fact penetrates deep into the psychology of the sitter. Lewis's *Virginia Woolf* **2** shows greater concern with the expressive study of form.

3▼

Ingres' portrait drawings **3** show superb technique, creating a refined atmosphere with precise and controlled line. For Toulouse-Lautrec **4**, a freer approach achieved movement and vivacity.

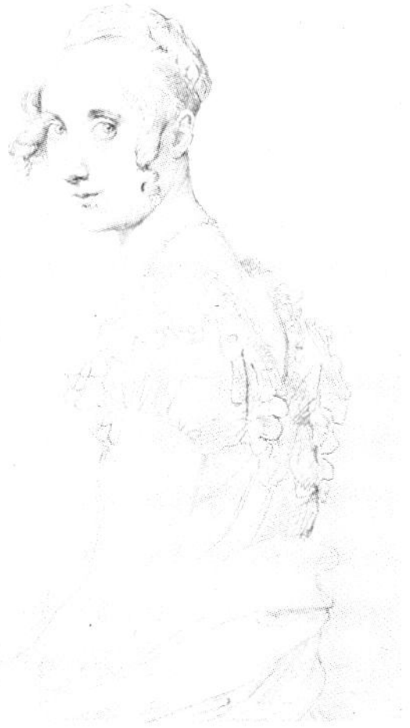

4▼

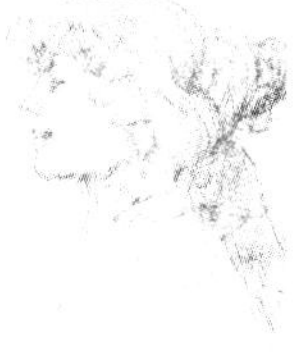

Animals

Drawing animals presents a problem rather like that of drawing young children since they cannot be asked to pose for you, so you will have to rely on preliminary sketches and a good background knowledge of the underlying structure of the animal. Start by drawing your own pet, which is more likely to keep still for you. If you find that you develop an interest in this subject go on to study the wonderful animals and birds on farms, in zoos and in the wild, exploring different ways of conveying movement, character, and the texture and markings of fur and feathers.

1 John Swan *Leopard;* 2 Theo van Hoytema *Pelicans;* 3 Henri Gaudier-Brzeska *Wolf;* 4 Nitten *Bird on a Branch;* 5 Thomas Gainsborough *Goats.*

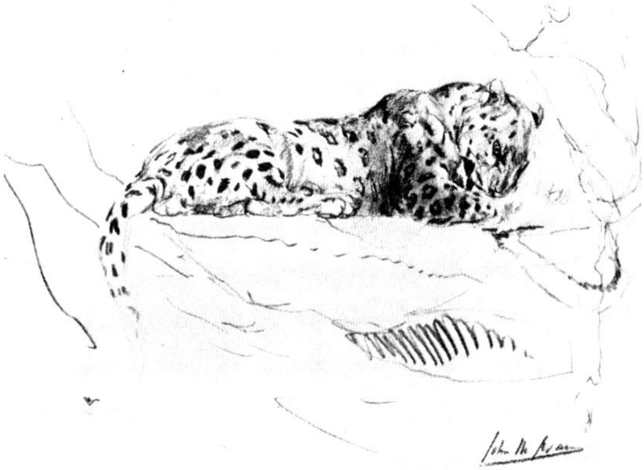

1▲

2▼

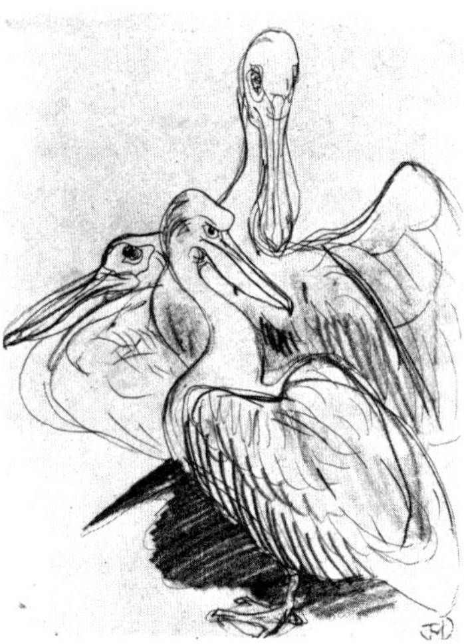

These drawings show the differing approaches of several artists. The dominant markings of the leopard **1** follow its strong, underlying form; the spots flatten out at the edges. There is strong characterization in the pelicans **2** exaggerated by the rhythm of the outline of the group and the cast shadow. A simple ink line has caught the leanness of the wolf **3**, while the rough texture of the paper and the sketchy chalk marks suggest the shaggy fur and something of the character of the two goats **5**.

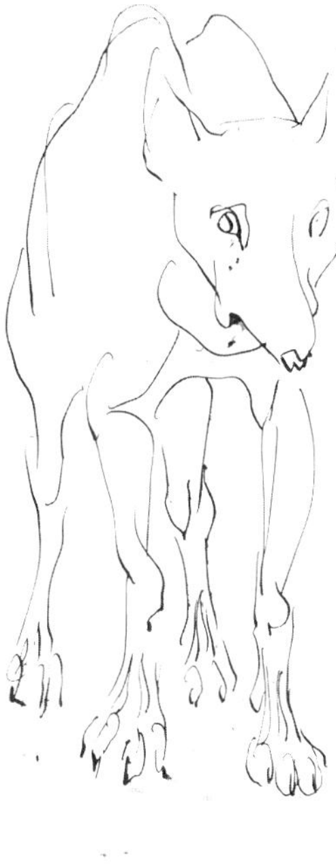

This drawing by a Japanese artist conveys texture and volume with simple brush strokes.

4▼

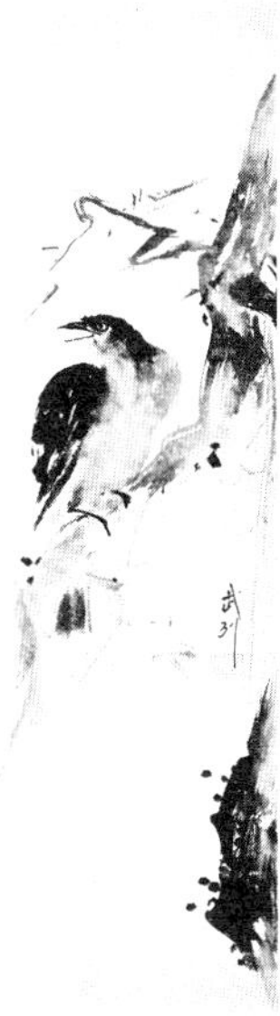

3▲

5▼

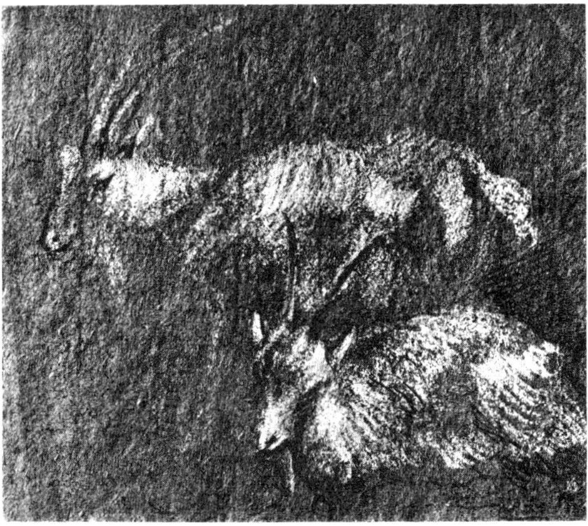

Studying the structure

The best way of finding out what information you need to make a lifelike drawing of an animal is to do several quick pencil sketches. It may be difficult to determine the basic structure that lies beneath the fur or feathers, or what position the legs are in when the animal is moving. So make detailed studies in museums and zoos. You will find that knowledge will help you work more quickly when drawing from life.

Stuffed animals give you the opportunity for study at close range, giving you long periods of time to make detailed drawings. Start by making several two- or three-minute sketches of the whole shape of the animal, trying at the same time to grasp their movement. Then go on to make detailed drawings of more complex parts, together with markings and texture.

Zoo animals tend to repeat their pattern of movement so work on several drawings at the same time. When an animal goes back to the appropriate position, add to the drawing. The difference, however, between an animal in captivity and one in the wild may be considerable.

Photographs will give you a good insight into movement. The micro-second stills of the American, Edweard Muybridge, revealed in the nineteenth century for the first time how animals really move. Photographs like these will show you the position of the legs and where the weight is carried. They can, however, be misleading and can give a very artificial appearance.

Anatomical study will reveal the basic structure and give you a knowledge of how the animal moves.

Four-legged animals

The spine is the main support. Its design (as the rest of the skeleton) is adapted to the behaviour of the animal. A peaceful grazing animal, such as a cow, is sturdily built, its bones are heavy; a fast animal or a hunter, such as a gazelle or wild cat, has a much lighter structure.

The horse Note that the bulk of the weight is carried by the heavy shoulder bones. The pelvic joints in the rear legs cannot be fully understood from a living animal.

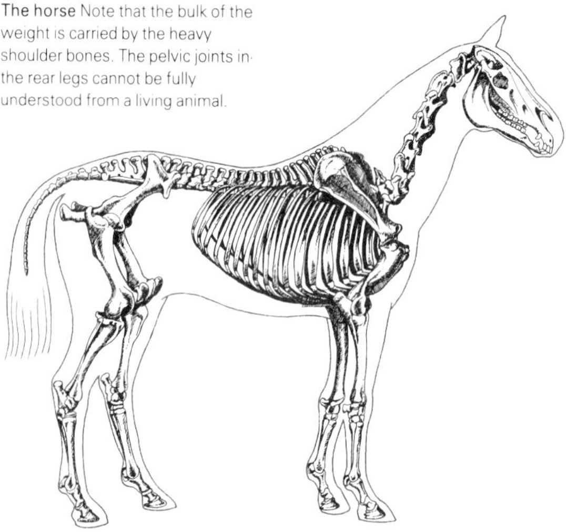

see also pages 54–55

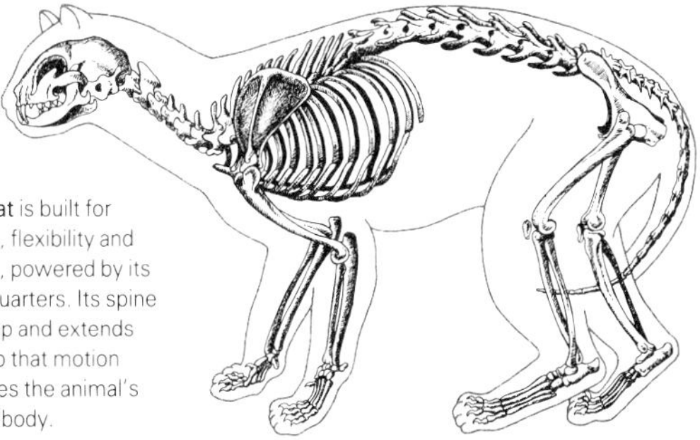

The cat is built for spring, flexibility and speed, powered by its hind quarters. Its spine coils up and extends out, so that motion involves the animal's entire body.

Birds

A study of a bird's skeleton will help you to understand its mechanics in flight. Notice where the wing joins the shoulder – this is difficult to see even when the bird is resting. For details of feather markings study from stuffed and, if possible, dead birds. Once understood, getting a feel of the rhythm made by the markings will be more characteristic than minute reproduction of detail.

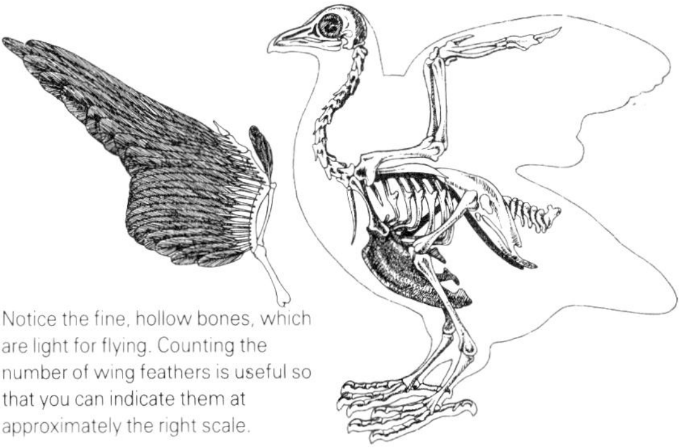

Notice the fine, hollow bones, which are light for flying. Counting the number of wing feathers is useful so that you can indicate them at approximately the right scale.

Fish

Beautiful drawings can be made showing the pattern and colour of the species bought from a fishmonger or seen in an aquarium. But if you want to convey movement it is useful to know the position of the fins and tail which propel the fish and the underlying structure. This will remind you that as the body shape changes with every twist, further distorted by the refraction of the water, there is still a bony skeleton beneath.

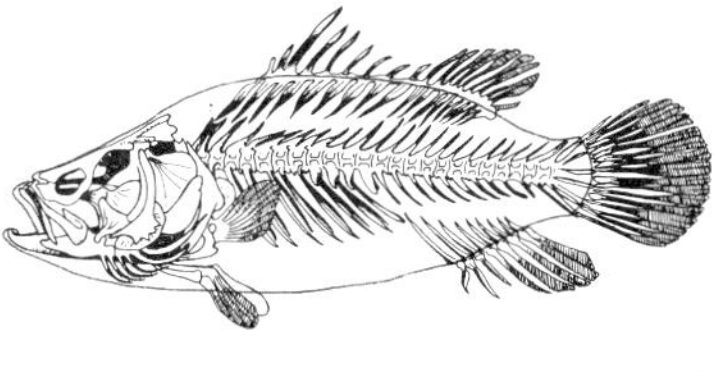

The fish's skeleton has a large head with the rest of the body carried on a long spine. The length and shape of the tail and the number of fins vary widely between the species.

Sketches and composition

Sketches enable you to explore behaviour and characteristics – an expression, an attitude or an action – and to discover suitable drawing media. A simple line drawing can convey movement, a conté or a pastel may already give a sense of the texture you want to draw. Use the medium to help you in your drawing, and let the paper represent tone and colour.

Making a drawing that sets an animal in its own environment, whether it is a cat sunning itself in the garden or cows in a field will tell the viewer more about the animal.

Quick sketches

Draw the animal in as many different poses as you can, catching it asleep or eating are good times, making a number of small studies on a page of your sketchbook. If the animal moves, abandon the drawing and go back to it when it resumes the same position. Use pencil or conté and make the outline suggest the texture.

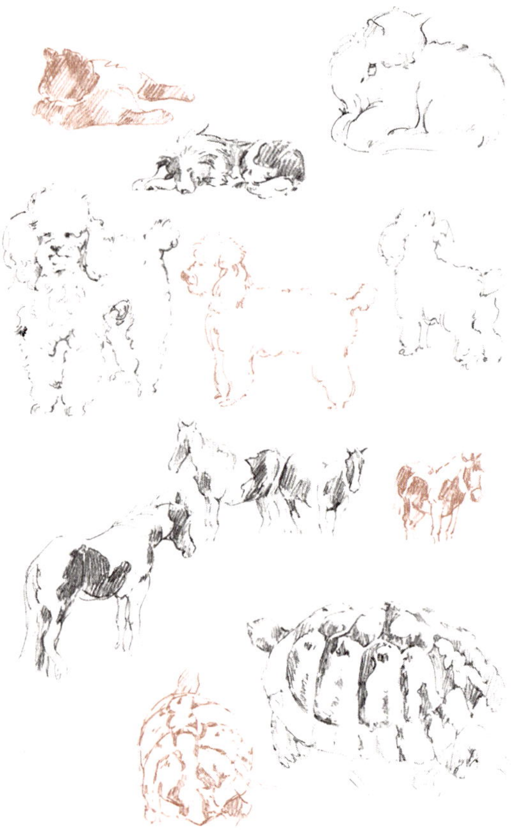

see also pages 14–15, 20–21, 69, 100

Composing a picture

Introduce other elements into your drawing that will say something more about the animal. The relation of a cat to its owner can make a good composition. Although the cat is not central to the composition it is the focus of it. The girl in this drawing is looking straight ahead but her attention is directed towards her cat and the drawing is very much of the two of them.

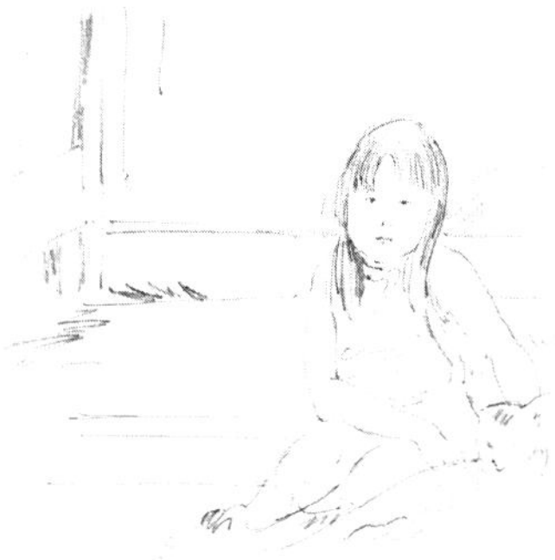

Emphasizing mood in the composition

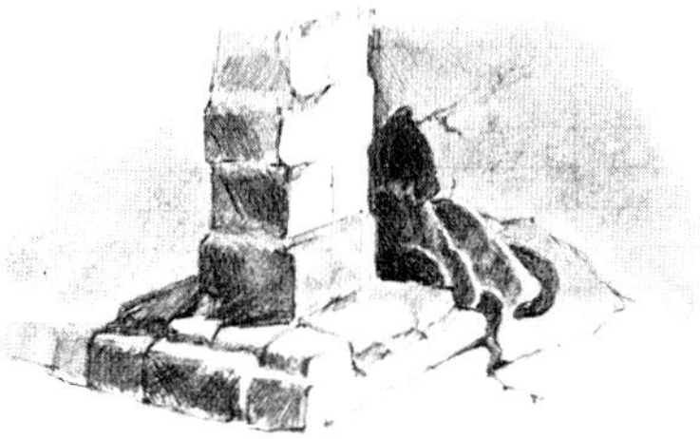

Character can be enhanced by the mood of the drawing. This sleepy cat was drawn in soft pencil in tonal masses, suggesting the form of the cat without outlining it. The contrast between the black cat and the highly lit stone pillar is central to the composition, framed by the shadows.

Drawing fur

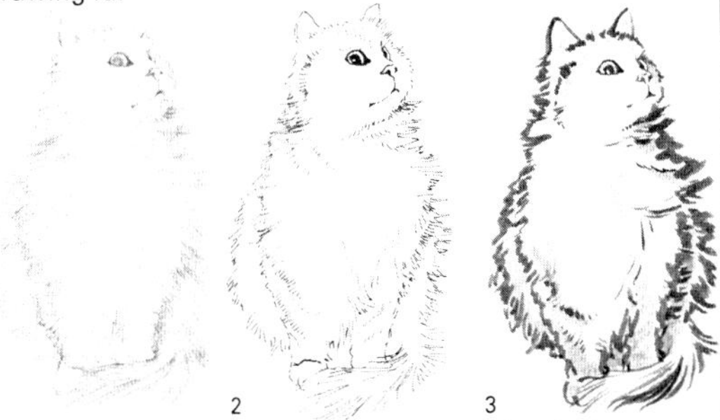

1 2 3

Fur grows in the direction that follows the structure of the animal, so an ability to draw it effectively will give a better sense of form. This does not have to depend on reproducing each hair but on building up the marks with a rhythm in certain areas that implies their continuation around the form. Pencil **1**, pen and ink **2**, and brush and ink **3** can be used in this way. Tone can be built up by varying the density and pressure of the marks.

Landscape drawing

Drawing landscape provides a complex challenge – you will be dealing with still life, flowers, people, animals, sky, trees, sea and buildings. And each landscape not only has its own characteristics, as diverse as lush green forests and dry waste lands, but it also changes every minute, with the season, with the time of day and the weather, each producing a different effect on the viewer. So the problem is one of being able to select, of drawing from the landscape the quality that interests you most, to intensify that feeling and to put it down on paper.

1 ***John Constable*** *Fir Trees at Hampstead*; 2 ***Alexander Cozens*** *Blot Landscape*; 3 ***Vincent van Gogh*** *The Countryside on the Banks of the Rhône*; 4 ***Rembrandt van Rijn*** *River with a Sailing Boat*; 5 ***Ker-Xavier Roussel*** *Le Grand Parasol (detail)*; 6 ***J.M.W. Turner*** *Rome from the Garden of the Villa Lanti (detail)*; **Alexander Cozens** *Classical Landscape*.

1▼

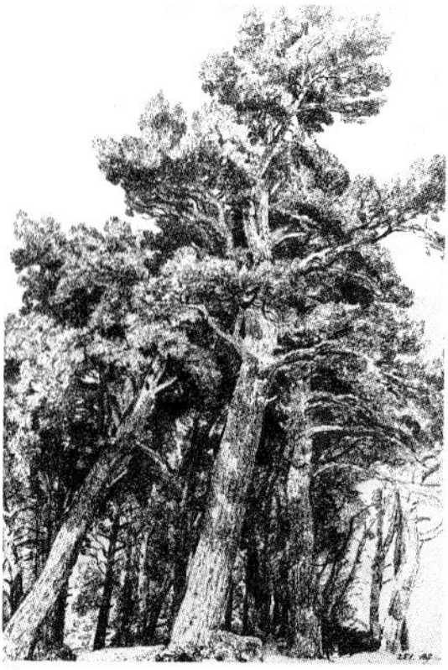

Constable's detailed pencil study 1 gives a sense of the light and air that surrounds the trees and defines the space in which both they and the artist stand. Cozens created an imaginary landscape 2 by means of ink blots which has produced a powerful abstract image. Van Gogh 3 achieved an expressive textural effect with marks made by a reed pen.

2▼

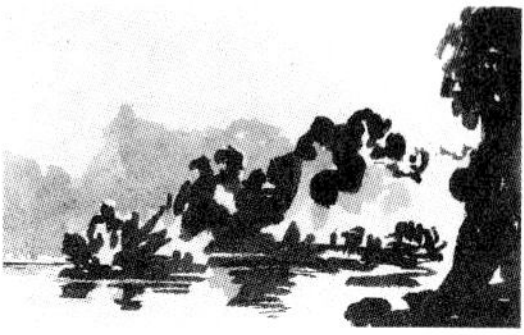

3▼

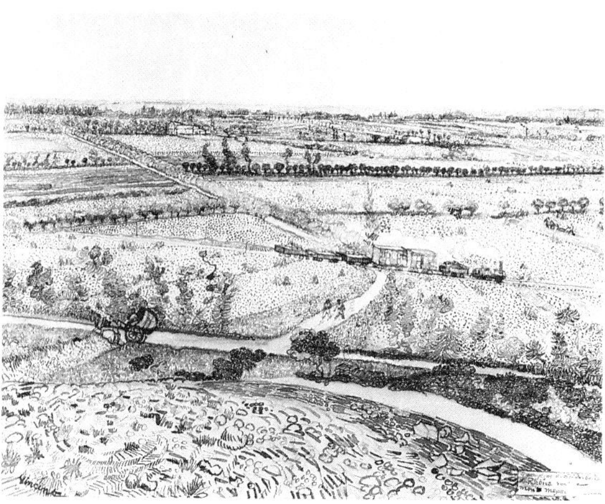

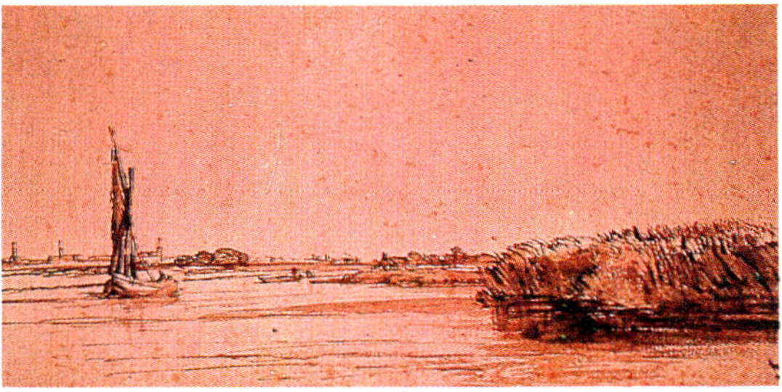

4▲

6▼

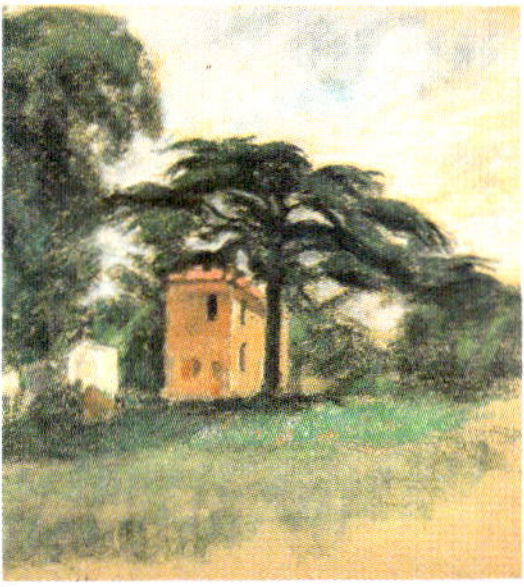

5▲

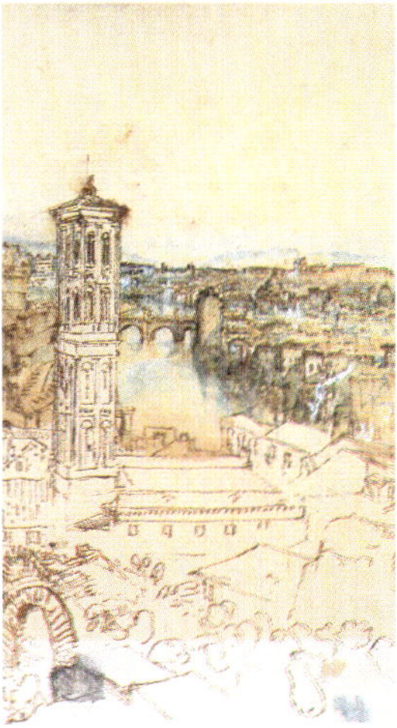

The wide, low horizon of Rembrandt's pen and ink landscape **4** is given scale by the boat. Roussel's pastel composition **5** has a more enclosed effect. Turner **6** suggests distance by the gradation of colour washes and the diffusion of detail. Cozens **7** carefully defines the planes by tone.

7▼

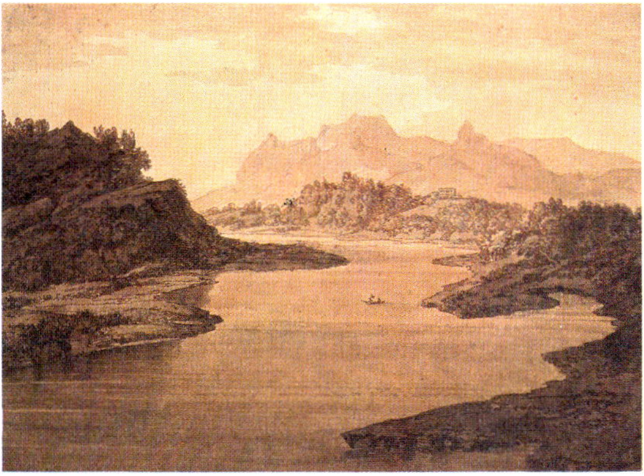

Working outside

First you must decide what sort of landscape you want to draw. It is helpful to jot down a list of all the places you have seen that you think will make interesting pictures. You will tend to find that it is not necessarily the most spectacular views that make the best drawings and that it is largely up to you to interpret what you see into an interesting composition. Selection is your first task; a landscape changes continually as you walk through it or shift your gaze so you will have to decide what it is about a particular landscape that interests you.

Selecting the subject

It is helpful to isolate a part of the landscape by looking through a viewfinder (which can easily be made by cutting a window out of a piece of cardboard). Restricting your view of the landscape will stop your eye from taking in too much and will clarify the composition. Pick on some strong lines, such as a tree in the foreground or the horizon.

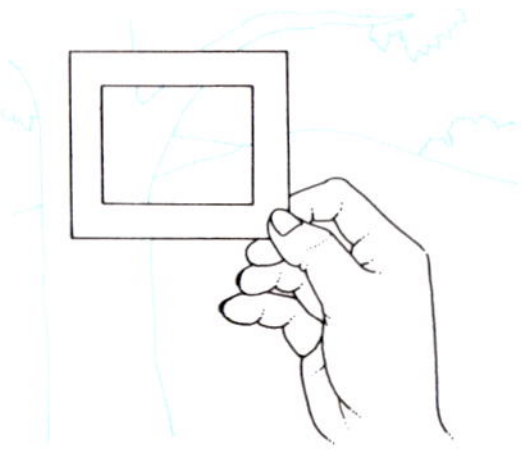

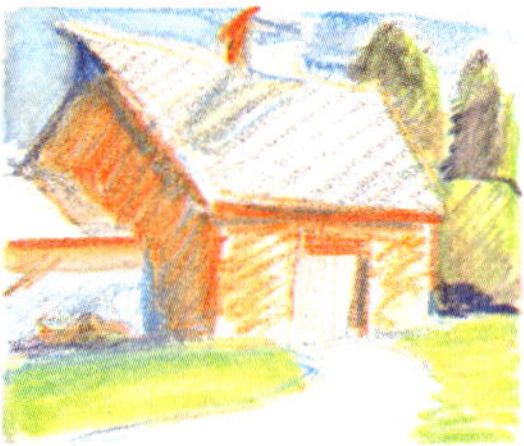

Take time selecting your subject and walk around looking from different viewpoints, varying the amount of distance that you take into the subject. Start by choosing a subject with fairly shallow space, such as a garden that is bounded by a fence, or close in on the main point of interest, such as the barn shown here. Restrict the number of elements in your first composition.

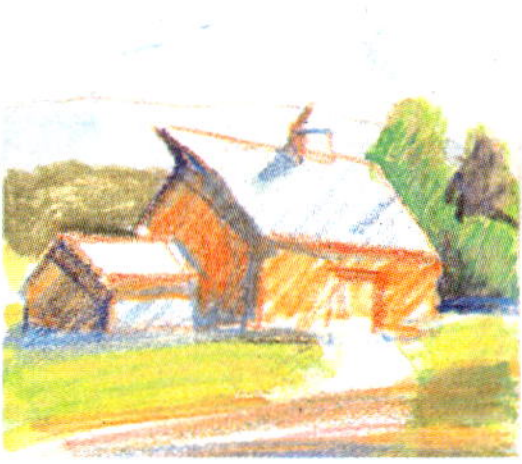

Moving away from the focal interest of the composition, notice how the extra depth of field pushes the barn into a deeper middle distance – it is still the centre of your drawing, but there is more space around it, and this must be organized. Indicate bands of different tones to lead the eye into the composition. Here a cast shadow emphasizes the foreground, with the sky as the background.

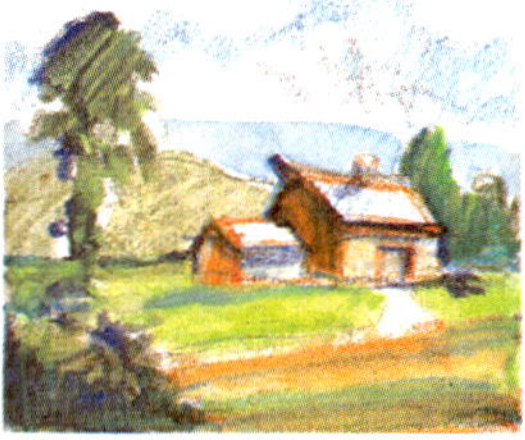

When you move to a far view, the object is no longer dominant enough to anchor the composition. Instead, set up a horizon, or clear middle division: on this the barn will now sit. Behind and in front of the line place other objects – the tree on the left sets up a diagonal with the barn and this invisible line is echoed in the foreground shadows. A bush defines the very front plane.

see also pages 16–
17, 24–25, 38, 87

Setting up

For an idea of the sort of equipment you are likely to need turn to page 24. A main consideration when drawing outside is the elements, so make sure that you are dressed for the weather – a sun hat for bright days and warm clothes for cold days (you will probably be standing or sitting still for several hours at a time). The lightest breeze will lift your paper from the board so it is important to pin or stick it down securely. Take enough materials to last you through the day, particularly plenty of paper. A pad of newsprint or other cheap paper should be used for a series of preliminary sketches, which will help you to loosen up before developing a finished drawing. Charcoal is a good medium to use to begin with as tonal areas can be blocked in quickly, but since colour is one of the most exciting things about the landscape you may also want to take a variety of colour media.

Establishing distance

An awareness of the difference in visual impact made by a change of viewpoint is the first step to understanding the problems of setting a landscape convincingly in space. There are some simple devices that will help you. Objects or landmarks become smaller and higher up on the picture plane as they recede. And with distance also become less distinct, with changed colours. Making a simplified tonal arrangement of foreground, middle- and background will help you isolate the separate planes before you put in any detail so that objects that appear to be tonally similar remain in their own plane.

Work either from a dark foreground to a light background or from a light foreground to a dark background (below), thus creating layers of space rising up the paper. Define the edge of each plane with pencil or charcoal and shade in the tones, or, as here, brush on freely three graded dilutions of sepia ink for the fore-, middle- and background.

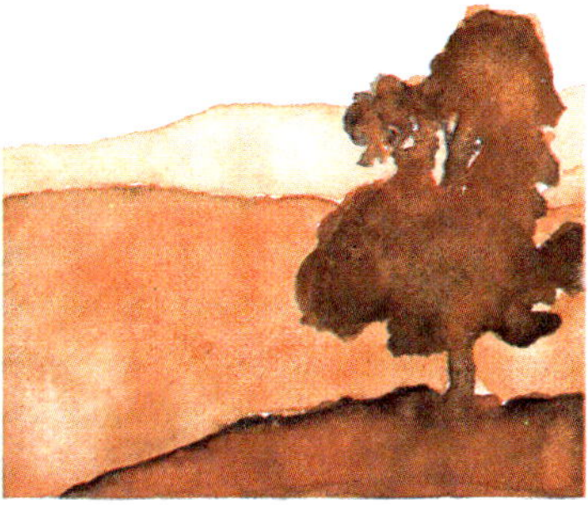

The purpose of this exercise is to simplify the planes, to put each element firmly into its own space, so do not add any detail at this stage. Concentrate on the power of the silhouettes and be aware of the suggestion of space that can be made by a firm overlapping of shapes on one another in the basic structure.

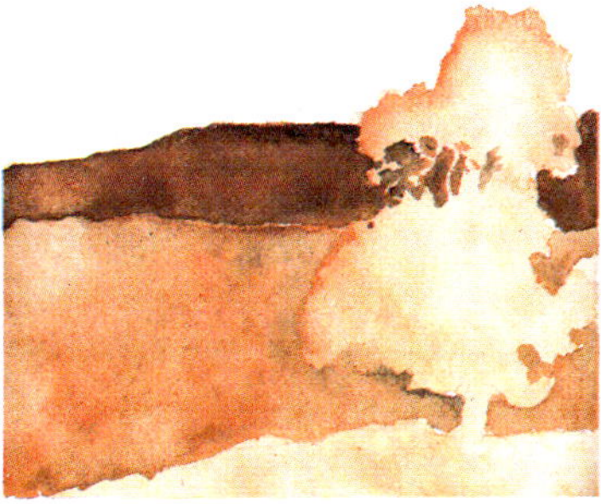

Composing the picture

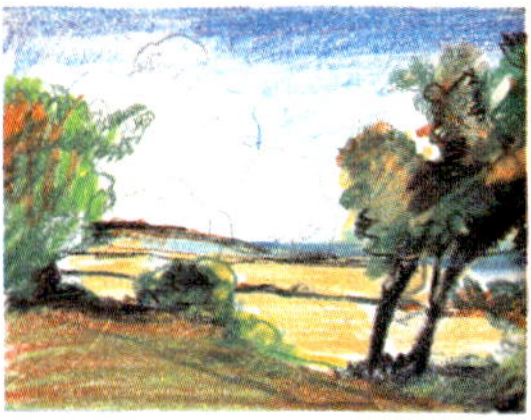

1

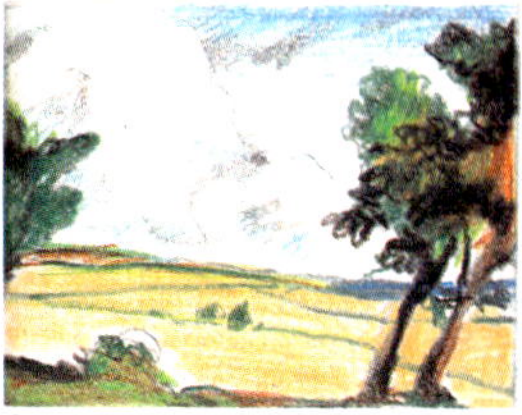

2

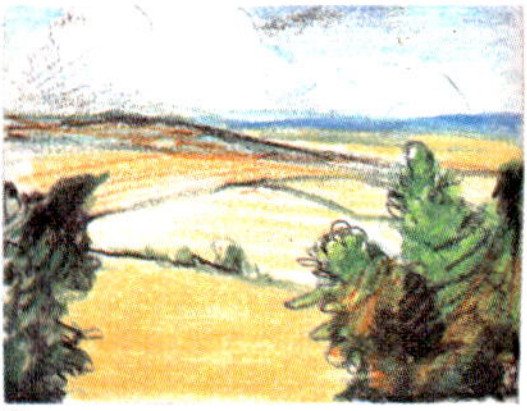

3

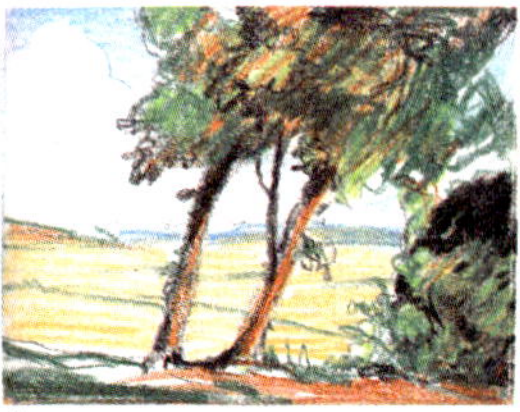

4

Having chosen a landscape, make quick sketches to see how the composition looks on paper and also to practise your technique. You will soon see the difference in the emotional effect of a drawing that a slight change of viewpoint can produce. As in these quick crayon sketches start with the horizon, then lightly draw in the shapes of the foreground, and especially those which stand out against the sky: these are the most important ones. Will you use them to frame or to be the centrepiece of the composition? As you experiment, try to depend less on outline and compose in tone and colour masses.

Developing the drawing

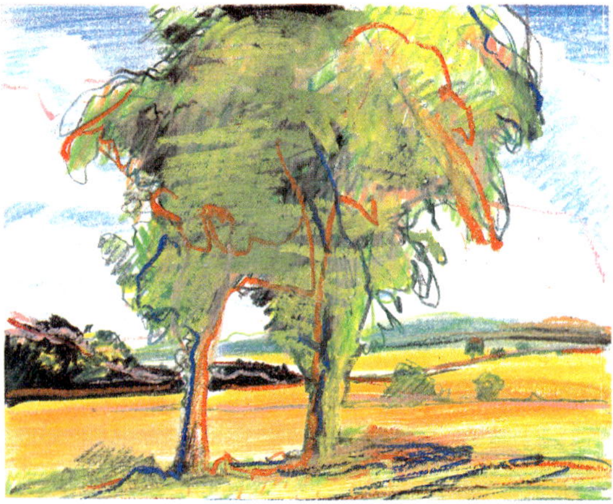

This drawing develops sketch **4**, above. As you refine the composition its character will inevitably change – parts will be accentuated, rearranged or lost. Note here the alternation of lights and darks on the field behind and the importance of negative shapes.

see also pages 16–17, 88

Different developments

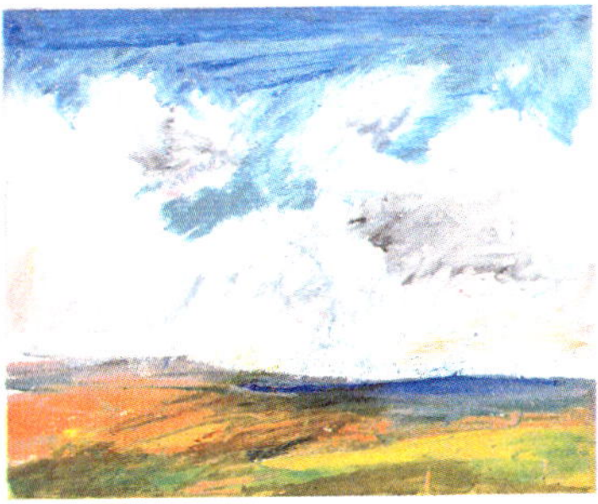

The sky naturally tends to take up a greater area of the drawing the further and wider the view chosen. It is given shape and form by clouds so concentrate on these and leave the paper bare between them. Oil pastel is a good medium in which to get a sense of their movement with a rapid technique.

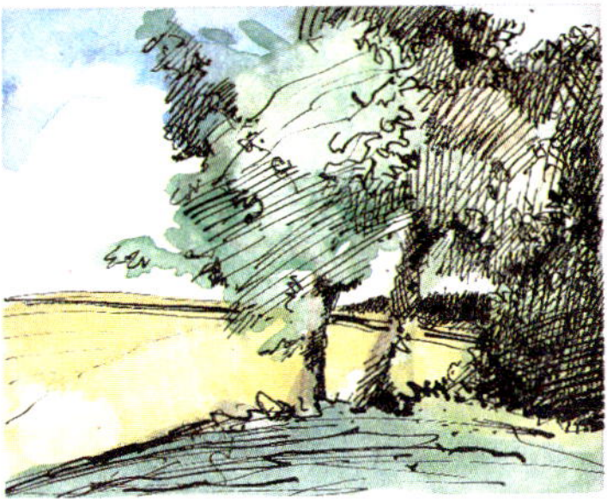

This is a sketch in pen and ink and wash, but, like the cloud drawing above, it is a study in tone and texture. It was begun as a sketch in wash; then, when the wash had dried, the pen was used to firm up the horizon and to strengthen the darks. The design is in wash – the pen only strengthens.

Composing with light and shadows

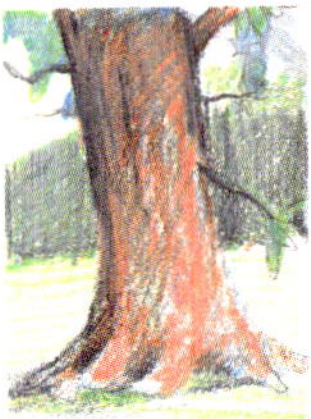

In even light the shape of the tree is clear, the colours are true, the space is uncomplicated. The drawing is simply organized and the light has flattened out the planes. The effect is undramatic, quiet, and perhaps subtle, even wistful.

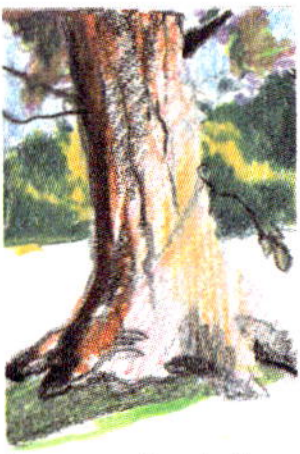

A strong, directed, harsh light breaks up the form of the tree into dramatic shadows and colours. It stands out in stark relief against a background which is in high contrast of lights and darks. The diagonal cast shadows dictate the composition.

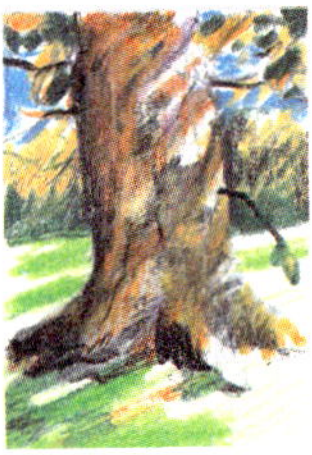

Dappled light, typical of afternoon, is thrown by the leaves of this and other trees and creates a mellow or even nostalgic mood. The light fragments the form into abstract shapes of light and shade, and the drawing can easily lose coherence.

Colour media

The crayon drawings on the previous pages show how useful colour can be in drawing landscape, helping you not just to outline objects but suggest the space, light and air that surround them. Pastels, and ink or watercolour wash are also good media. They naturally demand a free, impressionistic approach, although when starting to use these media it is advisable to sketch a preliminary outline in pencil. Soon you will get used to composing in shapes or masses of colour, building at first on your experience of creating planes with contrasting tones (see p83) and virtually no linear control. Line can thus achieve expressive texture.

Pastels

For an introduction to pastels, and suitable papers to use with them, see page 18. When working outside with pastels, carry them in a box and bring tissue paper and cardboard and tape to protect the finished drawing. Soft pastels can be used either by building up a series of cross-hatchings (below) or, for a more painterly technique, by blending. Oil pastels can be built up in thicker layers.

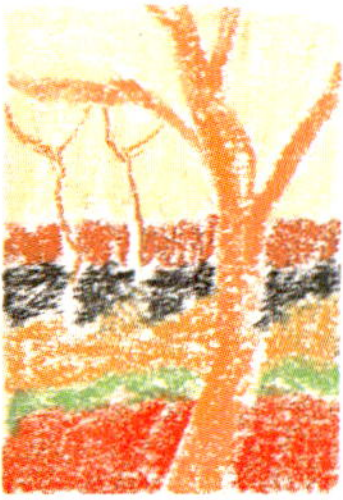

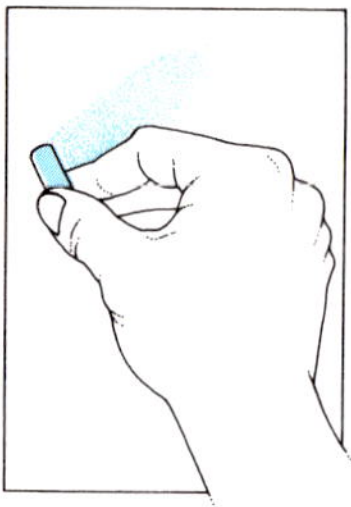

Soft pastels As a first stage in your drawing, block the composition out over a pencil outline in broad strokes with the pastel-stick turned on its side. This will give you the basic colour design of the whole composition over which details can then be built up.

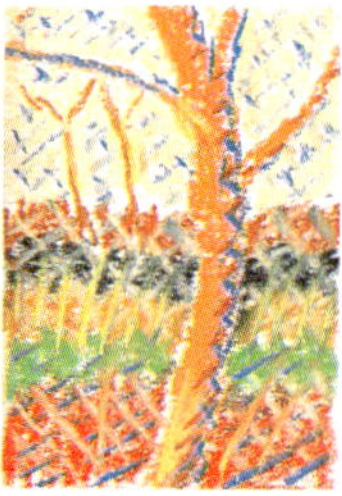

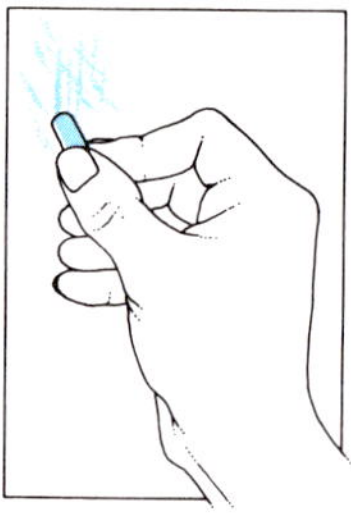

As a second stage, use the point of the pastel to make cross-hatchings, and so refine the impression. For the maximum effect, put warm colours over cool ones, or vice versa, as here in the foreground strip – cold blue sets off and contrasts with warm red.

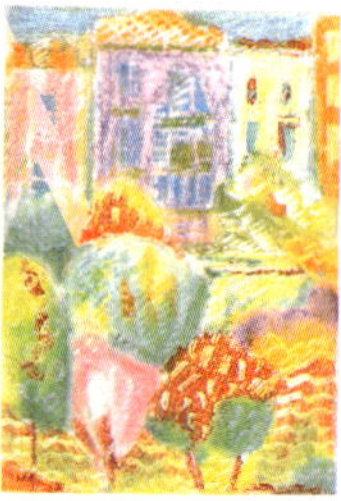

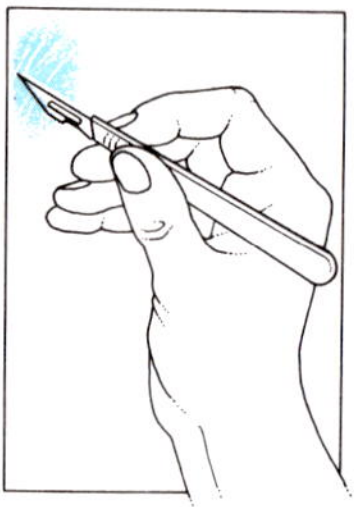

Oil pastels First sketch in the composition lightly, as shown above. Then overlay other colours, blending them in, or, with a sharp blade, scrape at the pastels in linear strokes, thus revealing the paper or the colour beneath depending on the pressure applied.

see also pages 18–
19, 21, 23, 25, 130

Watercolour

Watercolour is available in **1** tubes or **2** pans (more suitable). Start with a range of 12 colours: viridian, chrome yellow, Naples yellow, yellow ochre, raw umber, burnt sienna, alizarin crimson, cadmium red, cerulean, cobalt blue, ultramarine and violet. **3** A watercolour box provides a palette. **4** Have two pointed sables and a flat one or **5** a natural sponge.

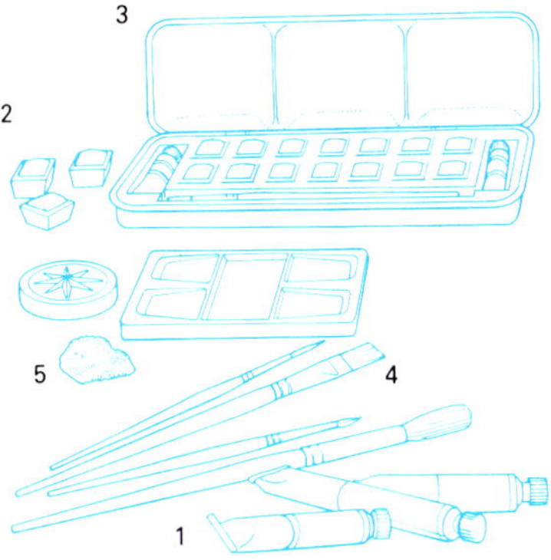

Mixing a wash

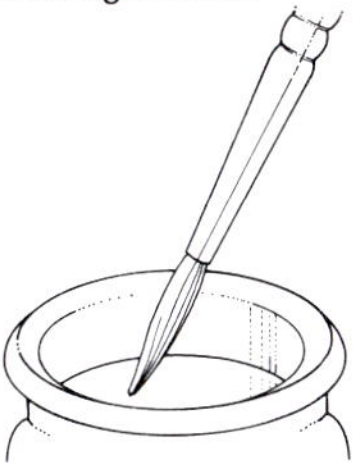

Dip a sable brush into clean water, shake out then dab on the colour and transfer it to the palette.

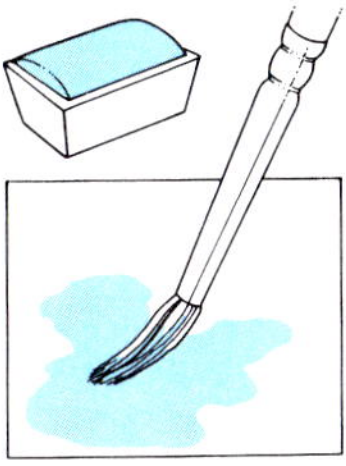

Test the colour on a spare piece of the same paper as you are using – the surface affects the colour.

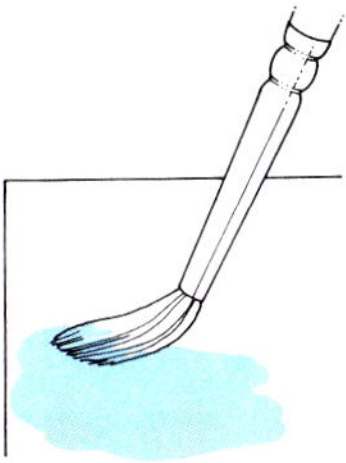

Mix up enough of one colour for a wash. Clean the brush in fresh water between different colours.

Laying a wash

To lay a flat wash and to understand how to control the flow of the colour see page 132. First consider the surface you want to draw on and whether the paper should be stretched (p130). The key to successful watercolour wash drawings is the ability to work with speed and confidence. Remember to work from light to dark – the process is irreversible since the washes are transparent. However, the colours do lighten as they dry.

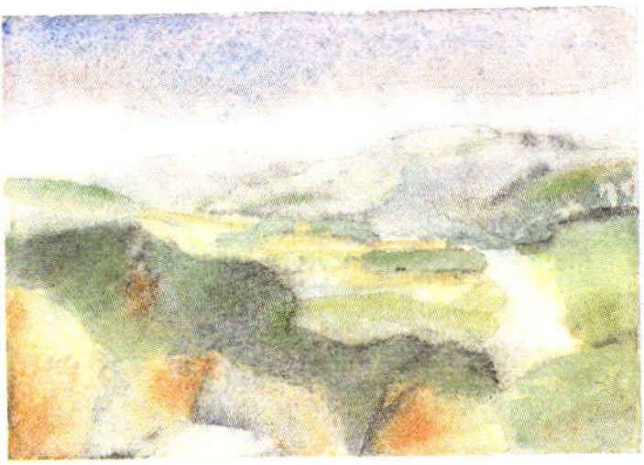

Wet on wet method to create blurred edges. Pencil in the main shapes then soak the paper with water with either a wide brush or a sponge. Work the colour into the wet surface, starting with the lightest colours. If the paper starts to dry re-wet it with a brush.

see also pages 20–21, 29, 87

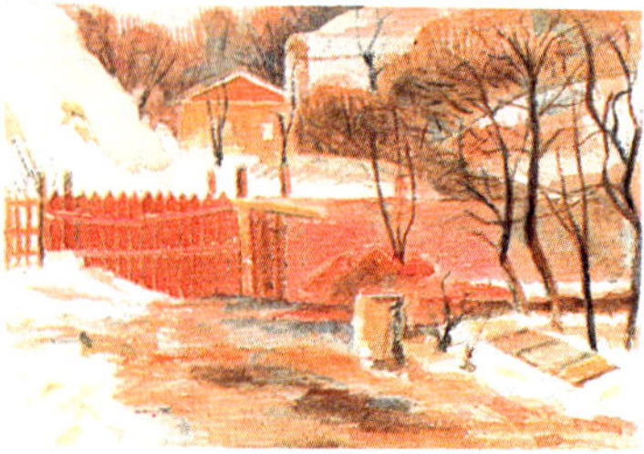

Dry wash technique retains crisp edges. Rough in the outlines in pencil on the stretched, dry paper then brush in your washes starting from light to dark and allowing each to dry before applying the next. Work on two or three drawings at a time if you like to work quickly.

Combining pen and ink with wash

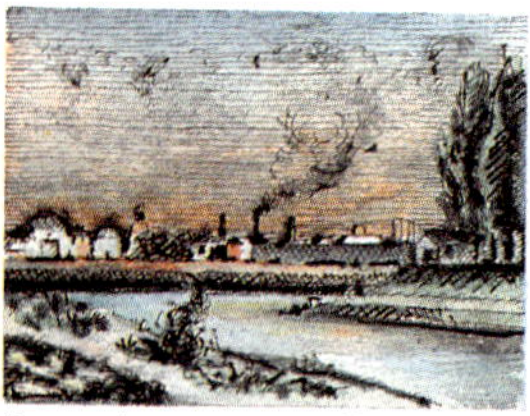

Pen work over a composition of dry colour washes gives a crisp line, which contrasts to good effect with the more atmospheric washes.

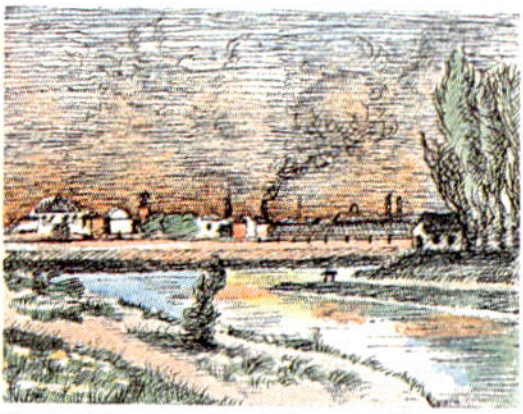

For a different effect, dampen the surface of the colour wash slightly, then add pen work. Alternatively, lay a wash on pen, using non-waterproof ink.

Creating texture with watercolour

For the sky, or for a distant wood, try applying a number of washes with a sponge. Dissolve the colours into pools on the palette, then dip in the sponge and apply lightly to the paper. You can achieve bold shapes and the tiny bubbles introduce a new textural variety.

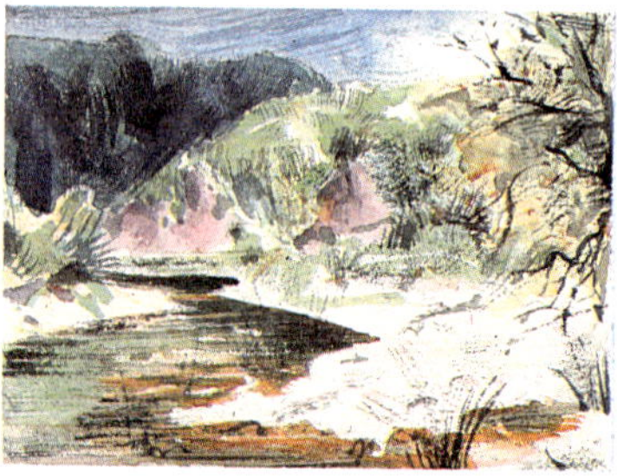

A splayed brush is useful in creating a kind of shimmer, especially in foliage. Pinch the hairs of a brush loaded with fairly dry pigment, so that they splay out, and draw the forms freely. Make use of the parallel lines this technique tends to produce revealing the underlying wash.

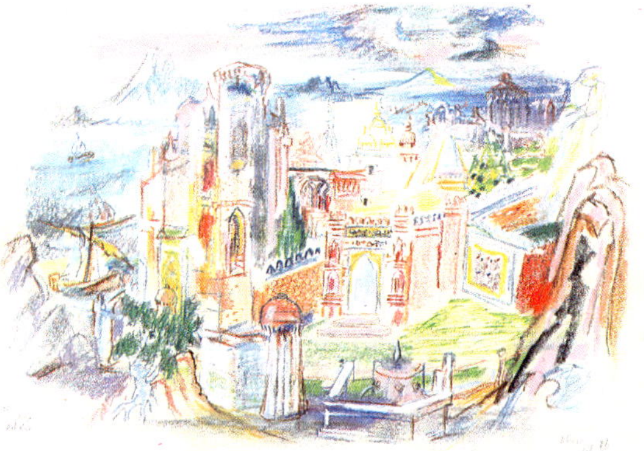

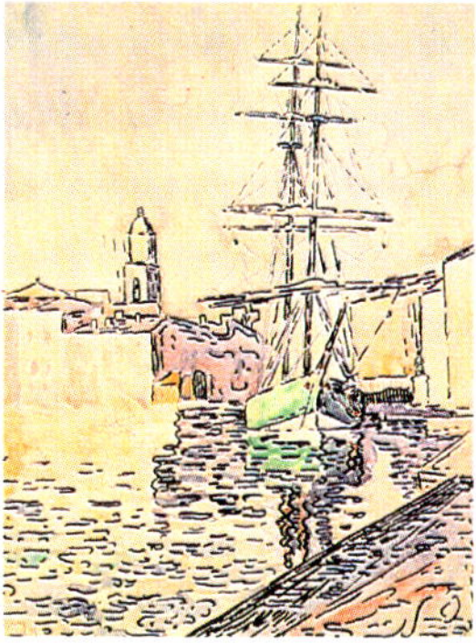

Oscar Kokoschka used pastels for this magical castle scene (top). Samuel Palmer's more stylized treatment of the imaginary *Early Morning* (above) was done in brush and pen with ink.

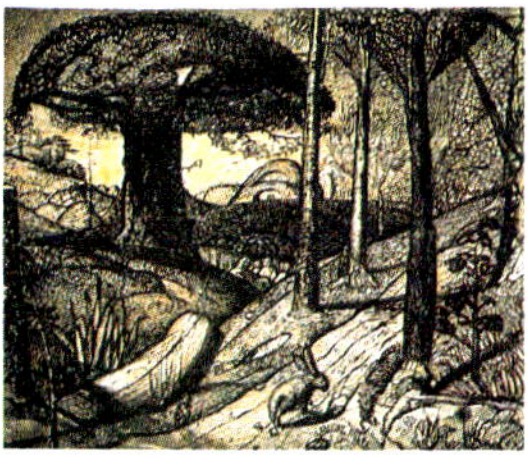

Paul Signac used thin layers of wash as background colour in *Green boat, Port of St Tropez* (above). The vibrant black ink line of the drawing defines outlines and the agitated shapes of the reflections. In John Constable's *Study of Cloud Effect*, detail (right), the underlying quick pencil line is almost covered over by rapid wash brushstrokes which capture a fleeting impression of the scudding clouds.

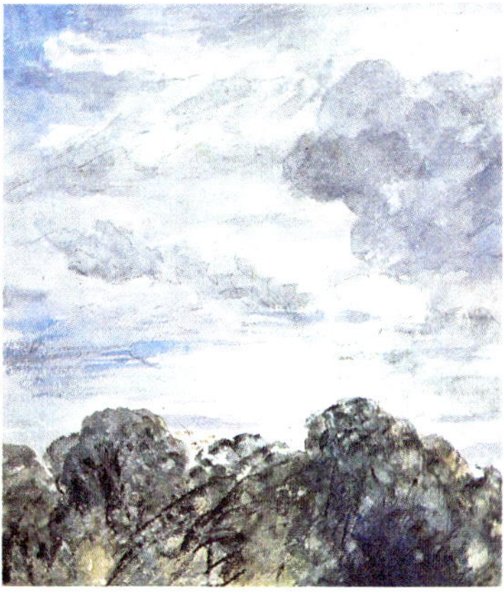

Sky and water

The sky determines the mood of the landscape and changes its colours, so it is important to make detailed studies of it. Think of clouds as mass and treat them not just as flat outlines but as three-dimensional forms, with their own areas of light and shade, that cast shadows on the landscape. Do rapid sketches to capture fleeting effects and use these studies to build up a knowledge of characteristic conditions.

Clouds

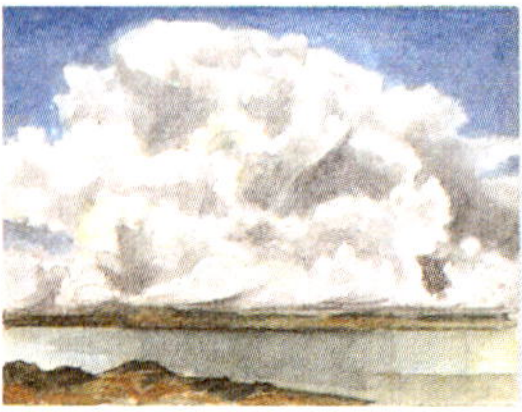
1

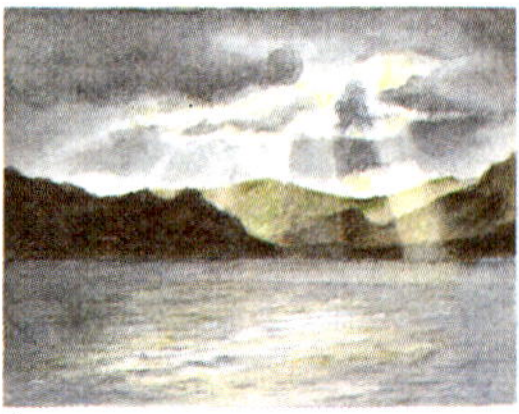
2

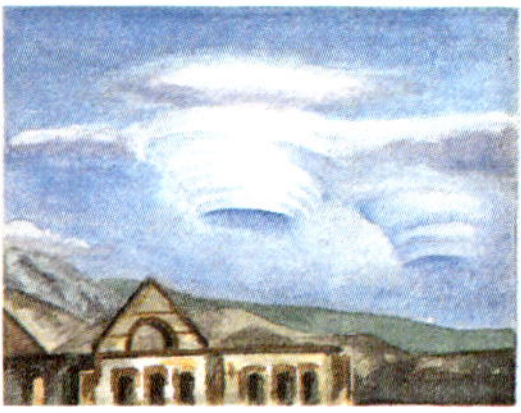
3

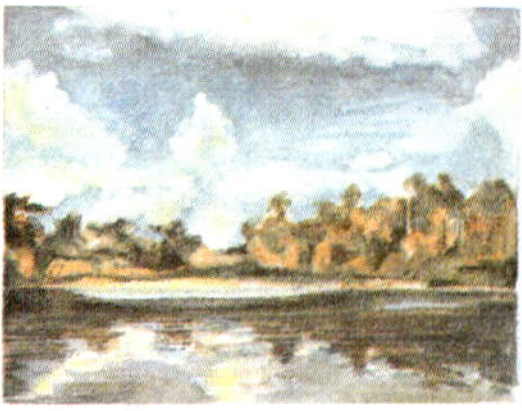
4

Every part of the world has its distinctive cloud formations, just as each has its distinctive landscapes. These watercolour studies show four different relationships of clouds and sky to water and land. **1** The cumulus cloud massed in sculptural shapes stands over a low horizon in contrast to the flat land. **2** Shafts of light burst through the cloud, leading the eye down to the water. **3** An unusual formation of clouds makes the architecture below seem more solid. **4** The surface of the river mirrors the shapes of the clouds.

Colour and time of day

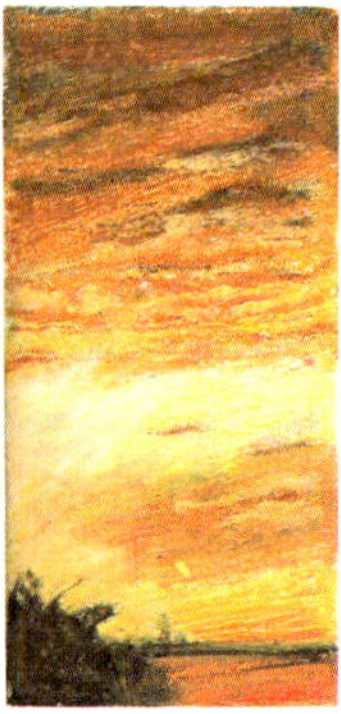

Notice the change in shape and colour that happens to clouds throughout the day. These oil pastel sketches contrast the clouds lit by the midday sun from above with those at sunset, when they are lit from below. A bright blue midday sky has subtle colour variations that should be observed. It might be a pinky blue near the horizon, becoming more purple higher up.

see also pages 18–19, 86–88, 94–95, 102–105

Water

You should make studies in different ways of drawing water, too, since it is almost as changeable as the clouds and needs practice to be drawn with conviction. The surface of water varies not only with the weather but also with its surroundings, and reflections can play an important role in the colour and the composition of a drawing. Water is always in movement, and this must show in the patterns of its surface, whether matt or reflecting.

Ripples and reflection

As water recedes you will see less of the dark, transparent surface and more of the reflection of the sky, caused by the changing level at which the angles created by the waves or ripples are seen. If you simplify these shapes into rounded patterns to suggest liquid form the water surface will recede convincingly back to the horizon.

Water movement

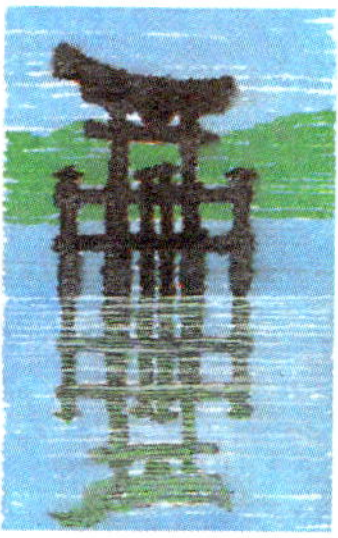

1

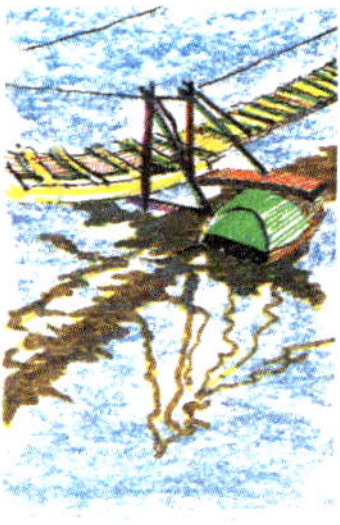

2

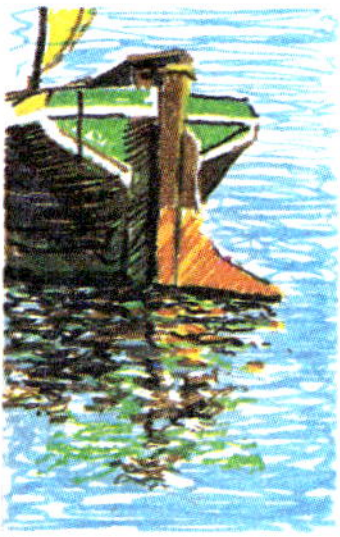

3

1 Slight movement can be indicated by a horizontal division in the reflection. **2** The image is broken into distorted, rounded shapes by rippled water. **3** In rough water the image is fragmented and only colours are seen.

Problem areas

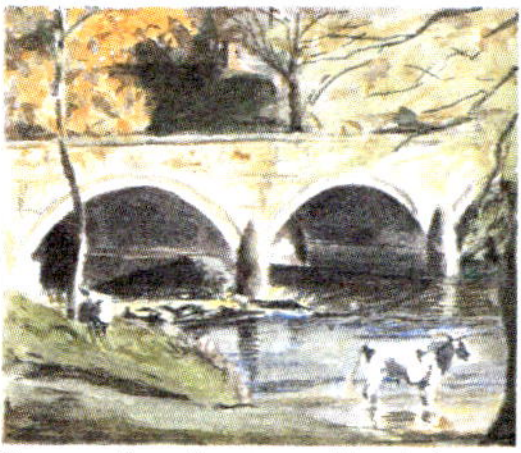

The meeting of water and land often causes difficulty. Reflections are one means of leading the eye across the break. When there are none, try including elements that lead out into the water.

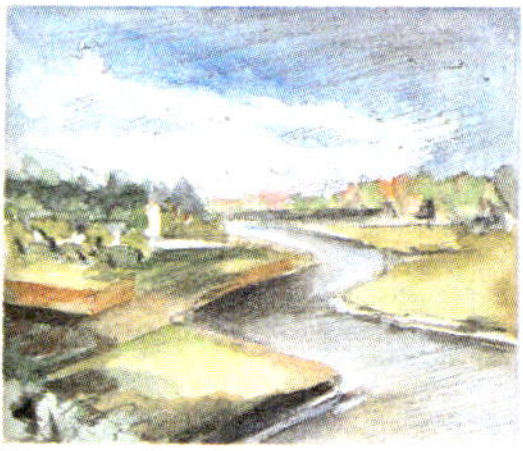

The recession of a river back into the landscape is often particularly difficult. To avoid letting the river mount up the sheet, work out the plane along which it runs, and then indicate curves within these limits.

Trees

Trees make a fascinating study in themselves. Draw them at different times of year and see the change from the skeletal winter outline to the abundant green masses of summer foliage.

An understanding of the basic structure, approached with a study of botanical details in the same way that you might study the anatomy of the human figure, will help you to understand their growth and so enable you to draw with ease the characteristic quality of a particular species in relation to the landscape.

Understanding the structure

Before you start to draw a tree first look at its overall shape. Notice the proportions of the trunk, and then half close your eyes to see patterns made by the foliage, noting in particular the shapes left between the leaves. These glimpses of sky behind add interest and increase the feeling of the tree as a massive free-standing form in the landscape.

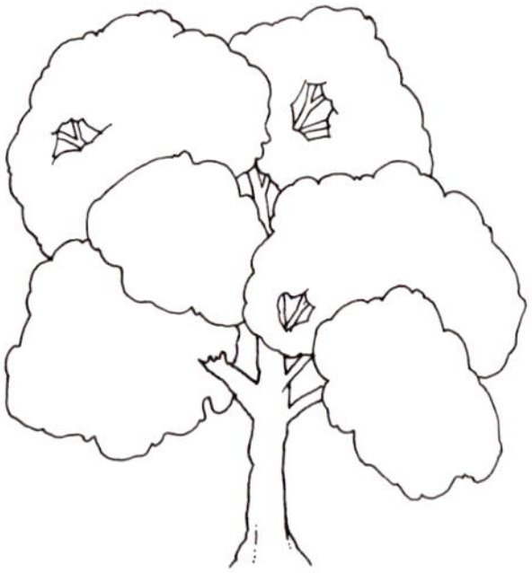

Simplifying the form

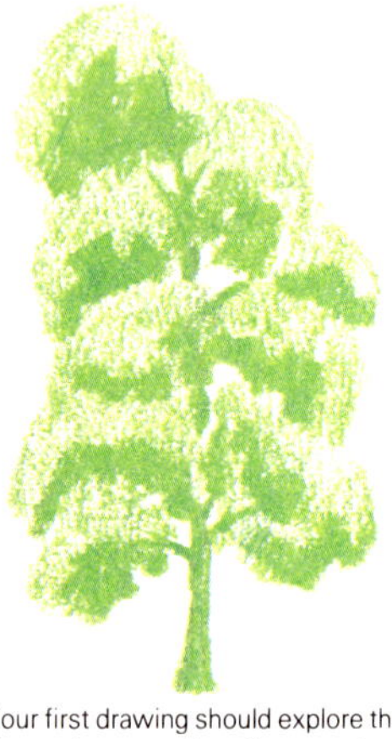

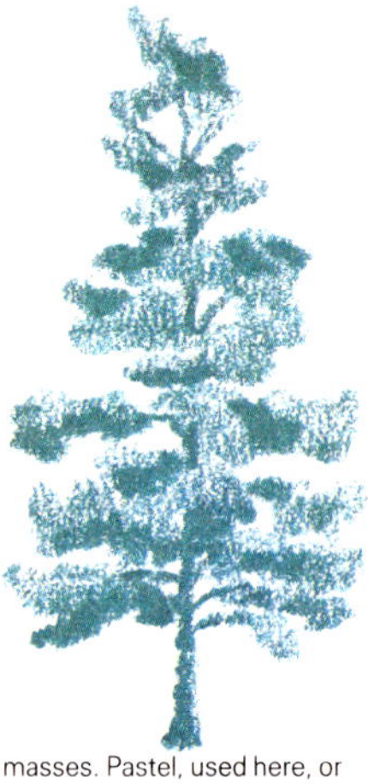

Your first drawing should explore the main masses. Pastel, used here, or charcoal, are good media to use for a bold approach. First plot in the trunk and main branches – the skeleton – getting the proportions right before you move on to block in the clumps of foliage, feeling for the direction of growth. Add a suggestion of three-dimensionality by building up lights and darks to suggest the fall of light. Use large sheets of paper for these drawings and develop the study to explore the contrast of the shapes of different species growing close together.

see also pages 18–19, 43, 87, 98, 100

Varying the medium

Some precision is possible with pencil; it can also be used to suggest atmosphere, and flickering light.

With wash, mark in the trunk, dark, then build up the clumps of foliage.

Pen and ink demands a more exact articulation of each branch. Shape the trunk, then follow out the branches, analysing them into leafy clusters.

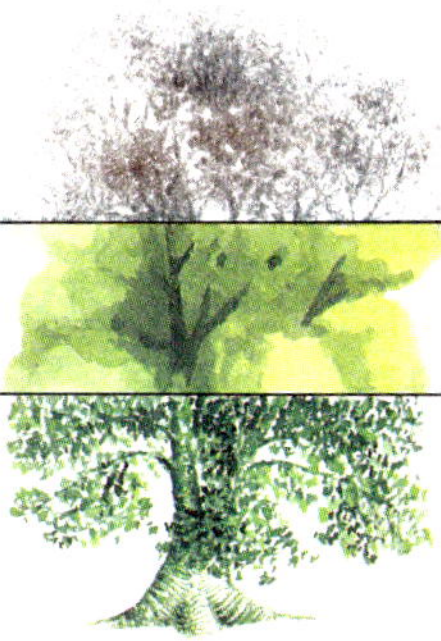

Studying the details: leaves, twigs and fruits

Having got to grips with the basic structure, you can explore the detail. Take a sprig of leaves and draw the outline in pencil, noticing the arrangement of the veins and how the leaves are attached to the twig. Now go on to refine details in pen and ink.

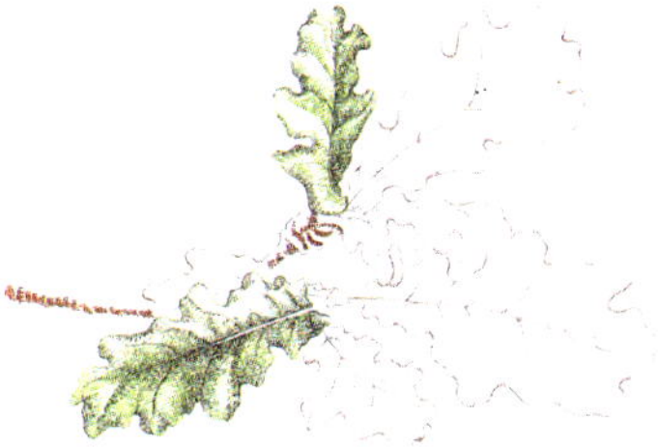

The undulation in the surface of the leaves has been modelled in pen and sepia ink in tight cross-hatching, and a green wash was then added. Such detailed drawings not only aid your knowledge of the subject but are attractive pictures in themselves.

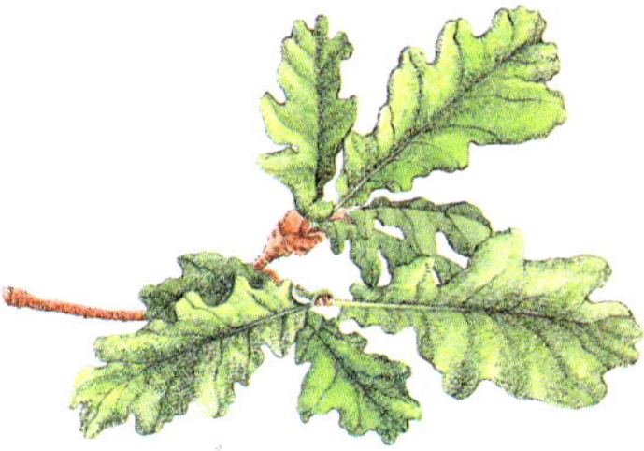

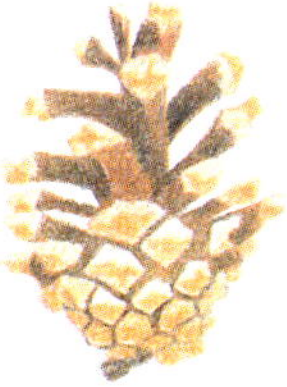

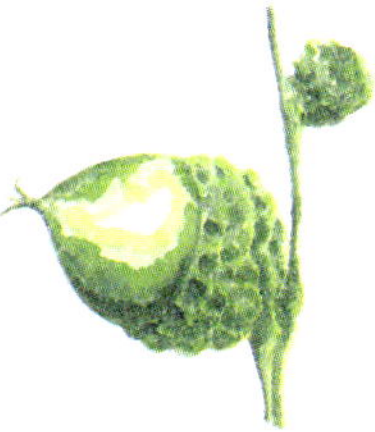

Collect acorns, pine cones, unusual fruits or leaves to take home and make detailed studies in various media. See how the texture is differently expressed in the crayon drawing of the pine cone on the left and that on the right, done in fibre-tip pen.

Seascape

The sea is a challenging and exciting subject to draw. Its colour, reflections, shape and mood are always changing, in turn affecting its compositional relationship to the land. Watercolour is a natural medium for this subject. Use it to evoke an impression of colour and mass and the swell of the waves.

If you have planned a long drawing session sit above high-tide level! Select a composition and sketch in the main shapes in pencil, starting with the horizon. The first wash should be the blue round the clouds. The white paper can be left to represent the clouds and the froth of the waves.

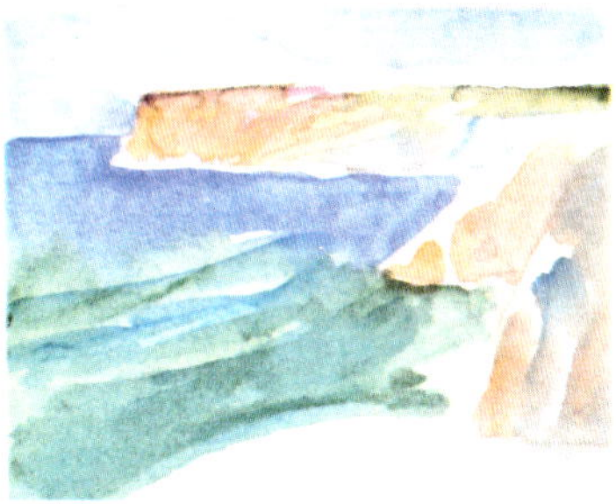

Mark in the land and then start on the layers of water, dividing it up into light and dark as it gets deeper and as the waves give way to swell. Now work (below) on the tonal relationship between the water and land, remembering that every new layer of wash will increasingly darken the picture.

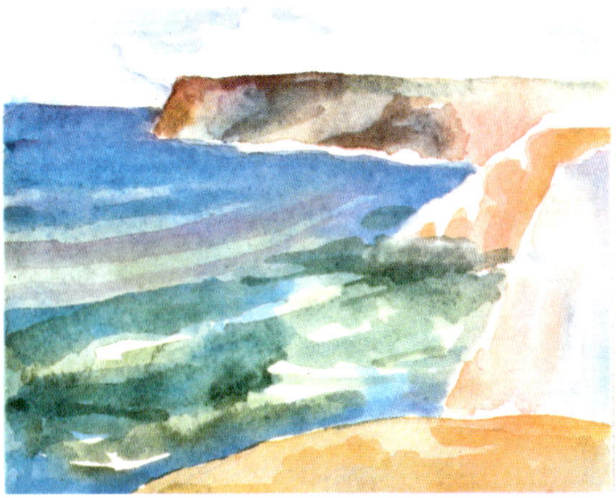

see also pages 18–19, 82–83, 87, 91

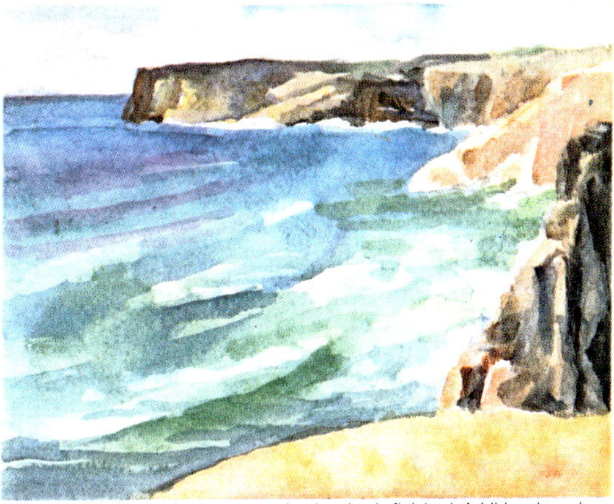

As far as the balance of colour goes, the drawing is finished. Additional touches to the water or sky will only darken them – possibly with disastrous results. However, having allowed the washes to dry, you could refine some areas of the sea by adding Naples yellow or a light purple. If you want to add grey to the clouds use a dry wash (see p88) to make sure that the colour does not spread. When adding detail to the land take care not to let the edges blur.

You can make final refinements with pastel, including any alterations in the balance of colours and of dark to light. A few crumbly pastel strokes will liven up light-reflecting forms such as the foreground rock, or a blue will add depth to the darker water at the horizon. Alterations to the sky can also be made in pastel. A few slight touches of colour here and there help to give an effect of movement, so that the clouds seem to scud in the wind. Resist the temptation of overworking the drawing and keep it looking fresh.

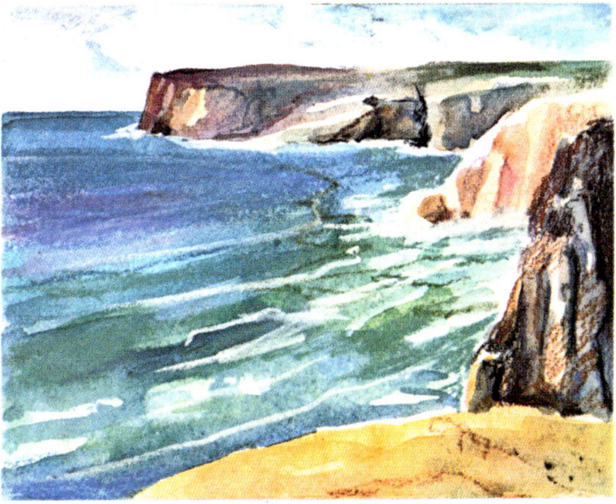

Collage

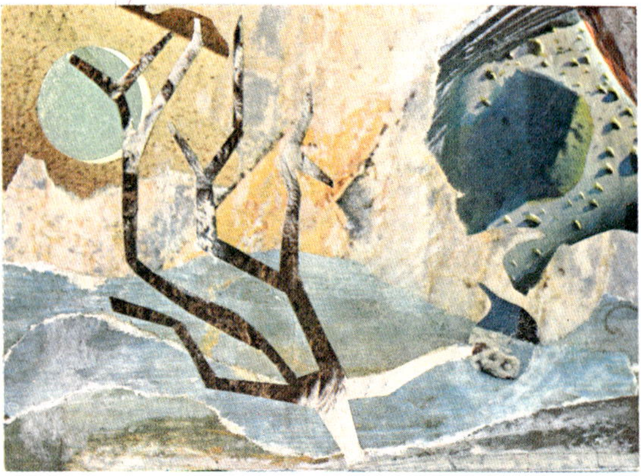

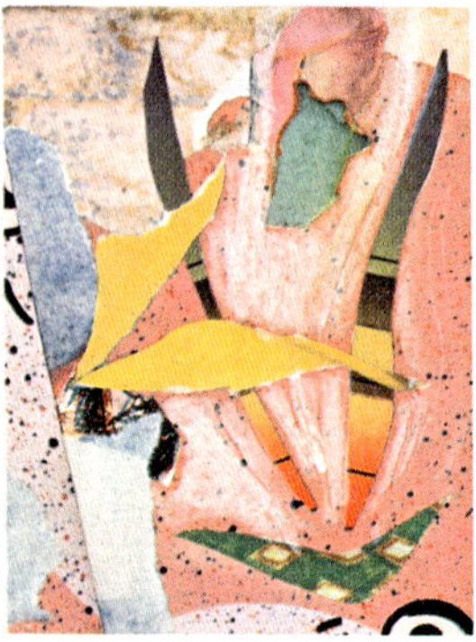

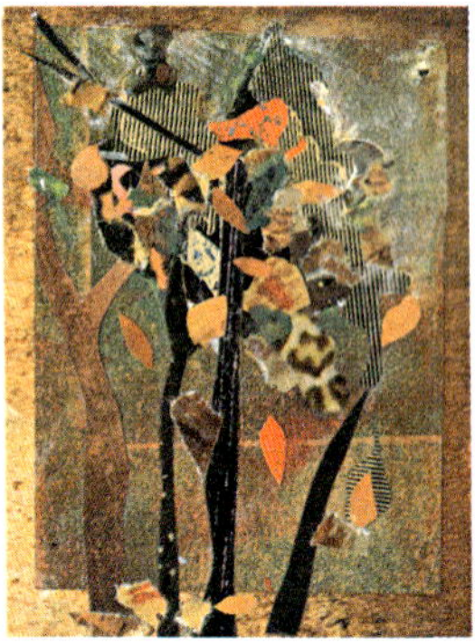

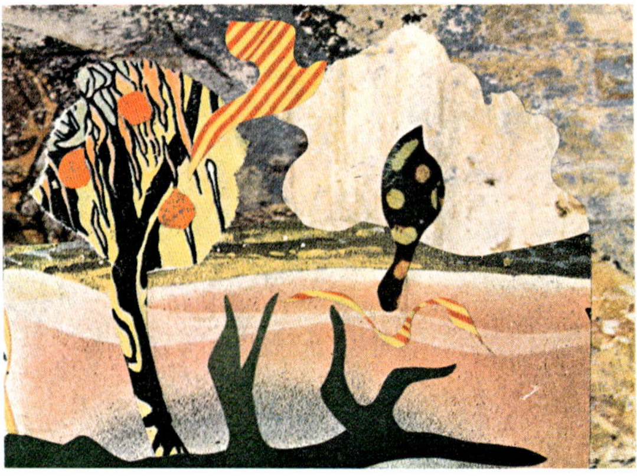

A drawing of a particular view seen at a particular time can be drawn so evocatively that it comes to represent a generalization of a scene – a summer's day, a quiet evening, a rough sea. It can be taken further to represent an abstraction of an idea or feeling of a landscape. Collage is one way of making a start into this approach. Creating forms from separate and tangible shapes that can be manoeuvred about will probably suggest to you other ways of using shapes that do not conform to your original ideas. Abstractions of natural forms tend to be easily identifiable – a simple horizon line or an outline of a tree will set scale and distance.

Collage can be used to reduce the depiction of a specific object to a simplified shape, as seen in works by Henri Matisse, or to let chance findings reveal new and imaginary forms.

Base your collage on a theme, such as the four examples opposite, which represent the four seasons, evoked by colour, shape and texture: top is winter with its cold colours and gaunt tree shapes. Spring and autumn are centre left and right. Summer, below, is depicted in warm colour and fervent pattern.

Making a collage

Build up a large collection of magazine cuttings from which you can select pieces for a collage, freeing your mind of the original purpose or function of the image before you and thinking only of its pattern and colour. Let the shapes suggest a composition to you or draw in some outlines on a sheet of paper first and cut or tear the pictures.

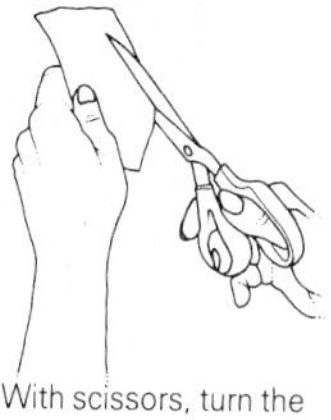

With scissors, turn the paper as you cut to form a free curve.

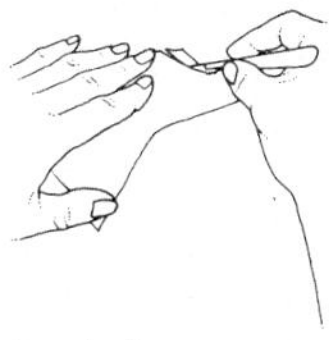

A scalpel is more accurate. Watch out for what is beneath!

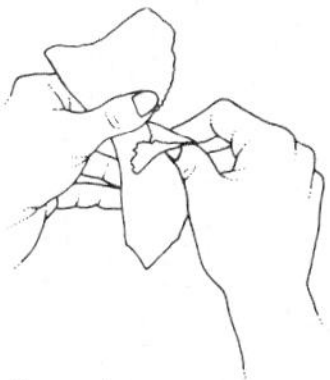

By tearing you get a rough edge, often tipped with white.

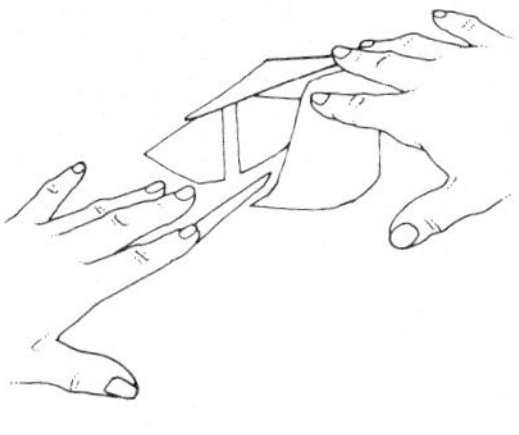

Lay out the cut and torn pieces on a rectangle of paper and see how they look. Choose a few to start with, then add to these.

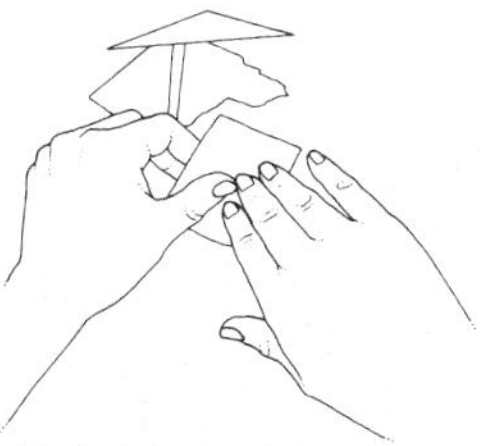

Stick glue is in a handy form and is good if used sparingly (it does not bubble or expand). Rubber-based glue dries more slowly.

Sketchbook drawings

Sketch as often as you can. If you carry a pocket-sized hardback book with you wherever you go you will not miss an opportunity to sketch something that catches your eye, and at the same time you will build up a visual diary which can be fascinating to look back on. You will gain valuable drawing practice, and also learn to be constantly on the look-out for subjects. These studies and impressions are working drawings, not finished pictures. Use them as reference material in the same way as you might collect magazine cuttings and photographs.

Natural objects and flowers

Make exploratory drawings of flowers, shells and stones to record details, building up from simplified contour lines without erasing any lines. Fill the page with studies of different parts of the flower seen at different angles. It is interesting to make a study of a plant over a period of several days to see how it grows – remember to date your drawings. Find out the names of plants and label them, if they are rare make notes of their colour on the drawing. If not, pick one and press it. Bring home shells and stones or almost any other interesting natural objects you find in order to study them in detail.

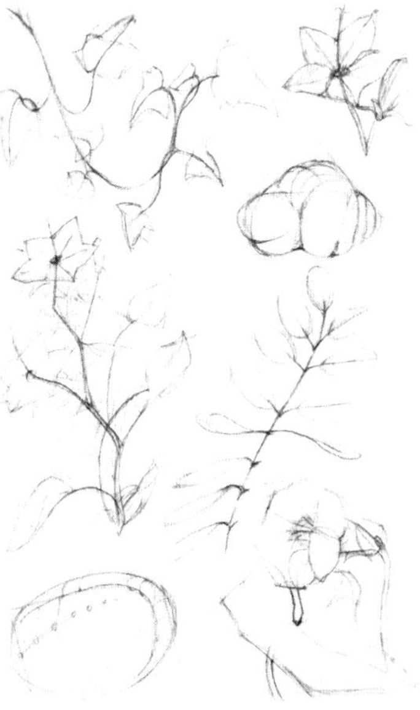

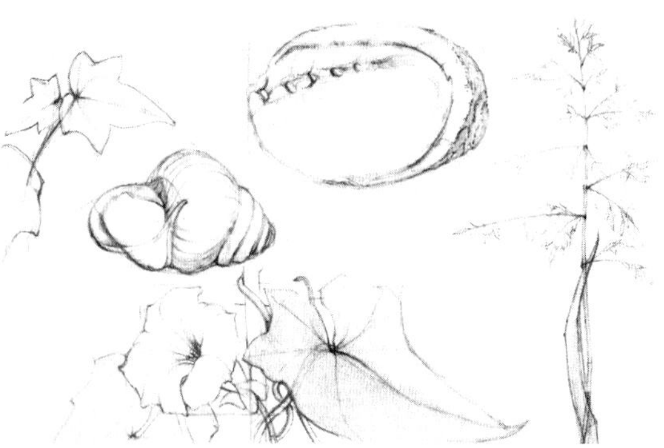

see also pages 48–49, 60–73, 133

Figures

People become very self-conscious when they know they are being sketched, so if you want your 'models' to pose naturally you will have to be inconspicuous. If you are using a small sketchbook at some distance, they probably will not notice. A larger sketchbook will be more suited to figure drawing but will soon be spotted, so sit somewhere out of view and pretend to be sketching something behind the subject, or to one side. Draw people reading, asleep or watching television for longer studies. Also do a series of quick line sketches of people in action to capture movement.

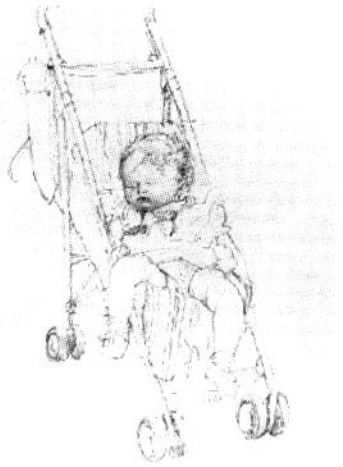

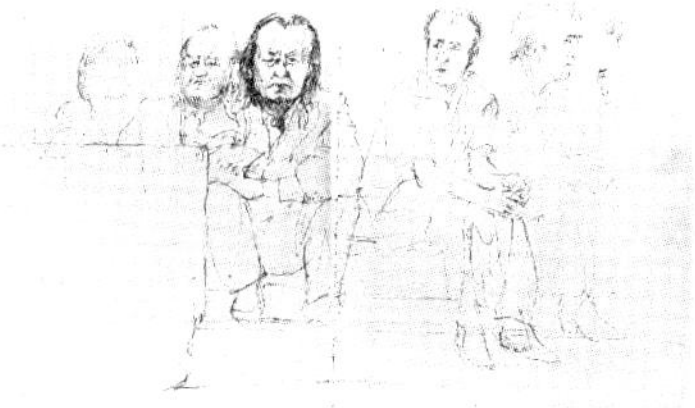

A lot can be said about character in the line you use, but this is also determined by the time available. The young child is drawn in curved, sympathetic lines; a simplified, clean line delineates the model; and the scratchy, broken line adds to the character of the old man. Different views build up a multiple portrait on the same page.

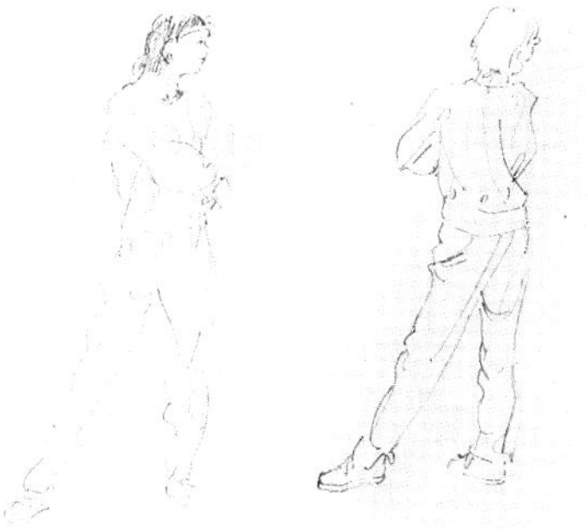

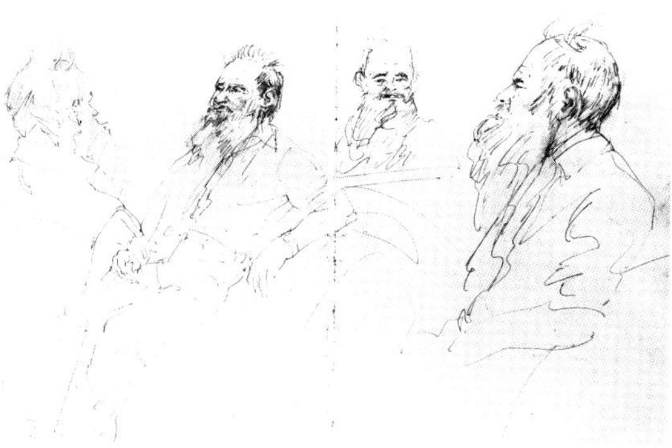

Sketching the countryside

The limits of the paper should not restrict your drawing. If the subject is a wide panoramic view use the double page of a sketchbook, and stick extra sheets on the side if you want to continue it. Find a place you want to draw and make several drawings of different views. If you can spend a whole day in one place try to capture the changing light by making drawings of the same view at different times of day. Return to the scene at a different time of year and see how it has changed. You will have to be selective – focus on a particular scene that interests you, or concentrate on one aspect, such as light and dark, or the shapes of trees or cloud studies. A wide scene can tend to break up into a series of small scenes – make sure it has cohesion.

Pencil sketches

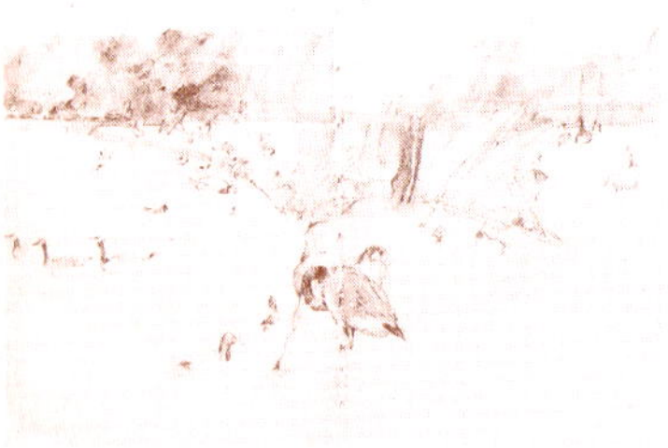

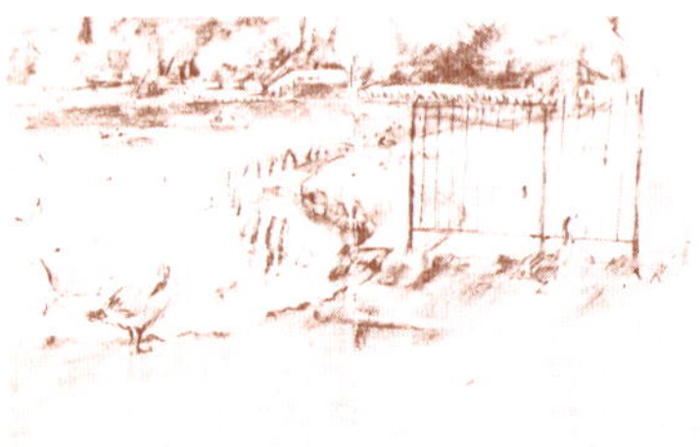

Make linear and tonal pencil sketches, picking out what attracts you about the scene and simply indicating areas that you are not interested in. Sketch in the main areas first, to establish a frame-work on which to add the detail. Superimpose drawings of nearer objects on top of things that are further back. If you stay still and quiet birds will get used to your presence and will come closer to you. Cows will be inquisitive at first, but will ignore you after a time. Try to settle into the slow rhythms of the countryside to find its real character.

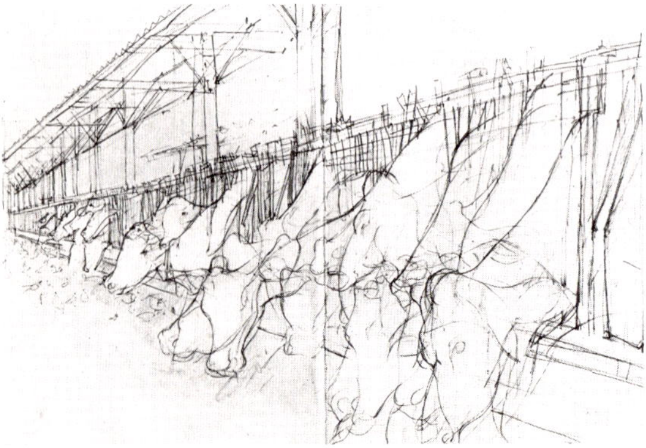

see also pages 78–79, 82–85, 108–111

Sketching in the town

The town provides a wealth of fascinating subjects for which you will need a certain amount of perseverance since you will not be left alone to your drawing; try to find a secluded viewpoint.

Railway stations can make unexpectedly evocative drawings. These dense, high-contrast studies made in soft pencil give a good impression of the grimy, smoky atmosphere. The architecture is given a monumental quality through this treatment.

Buildings generally demand a linear treatment which is more successful for the finer details but use your sketchbook to try out as many different materials and techniques as you can.

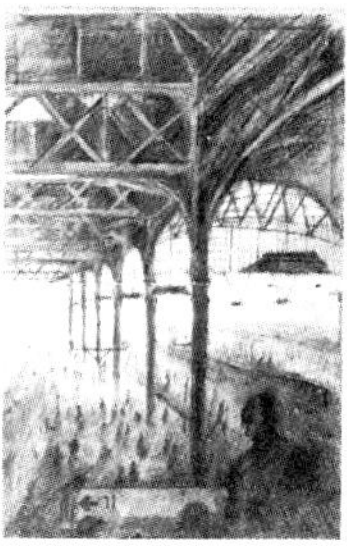

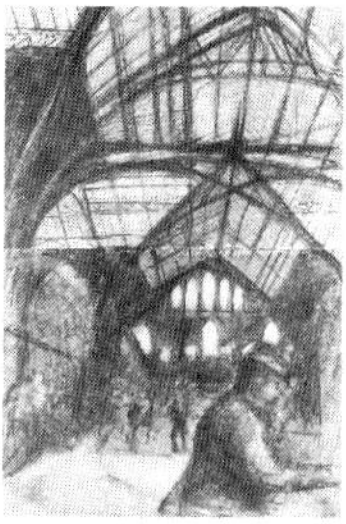

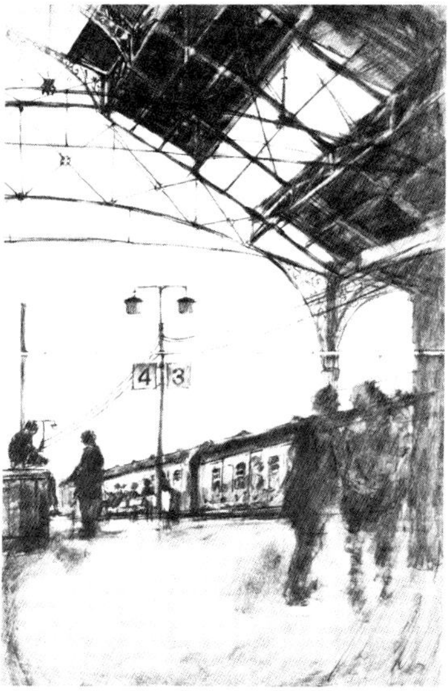

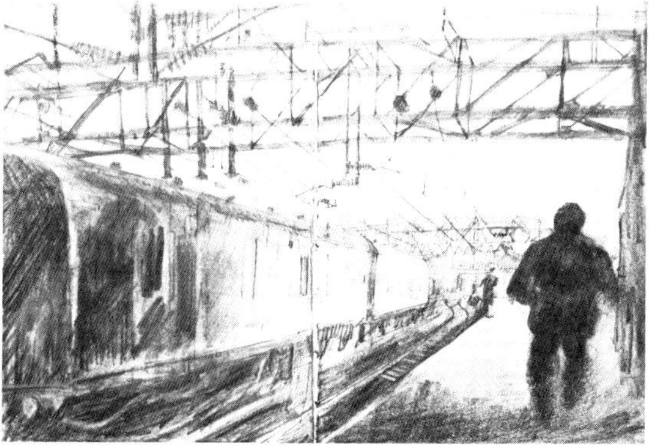

Perspective

Suggestion of spatial recession can be conveyed quite simply in most landscapes by drawing from accurate observation or by using one of the devices mentioned on page 83. However, greater accuracy is important when drawing a subject such as a straight row of trees or a building; then you will need a grasp of the basic principles of geometric perspective. This is a system based on the observation that parallel lines converge over distance towards a vanishing point on the horizon and all objects diminish on the same scale as they recede.

Simple methods of understanding perspective

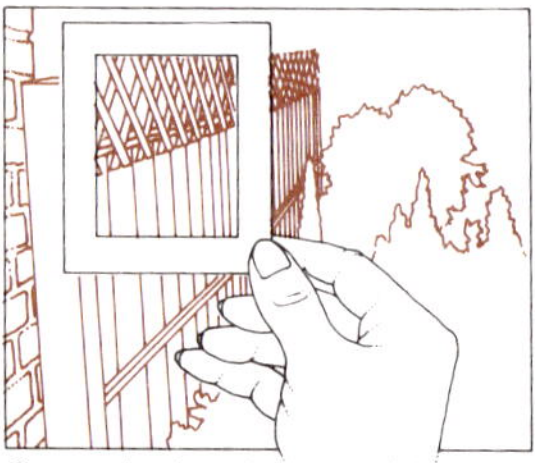

Converging lines (orthogonals) can be understood better if seen through a viewfinder (see p82). The frame will isolate the angles they make and will plot them on a small scale against a true horizontal and vertical.

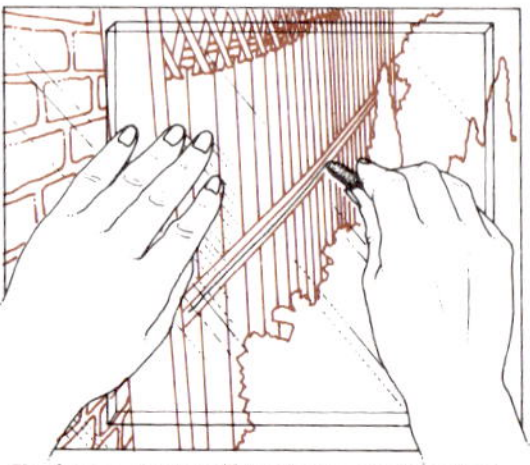

To force yourself to draw angles that the eye is unwilling to accept and that you find difficult to estimate, trace the image with a chinagraph crayon on to a piece of Perspex held up against a window.

Eye level

The eye level of the viewer determines the horizon line and the angle at which the converging lines recede until they meet at a vanishing point on the horizon. When drawing from a high viewpoint (as in this diagram) you will naturally tend to give the drawing a high horizon.

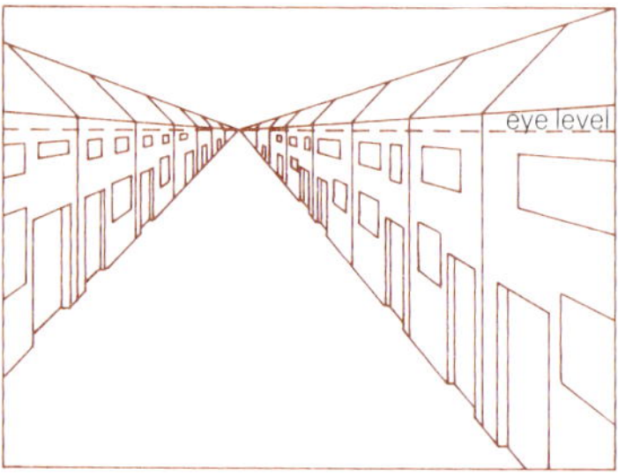

A low viewpoint tends to encourage drawing a low horizon on the paper. Notice how a different view of the subject changes the composition and how it creates a different mood. Remember that all receding lines above the eye level slant down towards it, and all lines below slant up to it.

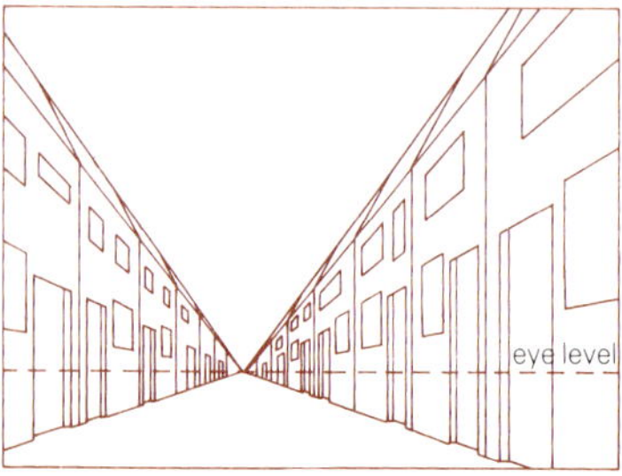

see also pages 38–39, 83, 107, 110

Constructing a drawing in perspective

Explore the methods of constructing an accurate drawing by making a study of a simple subject such as an empty hallway and introduce objects into it to develop the study. You will realize that you first have to be able to judge the angles of converging lines by eye before using the eye level and vanishing points to determine other lines. The vanishing point can be a visible point on the horizon, as in the street scene opposite, but it is more often a purely notional point which the receding lines would meet only if they were continued, and this often extends past the limits of the paper.

One-point perspective

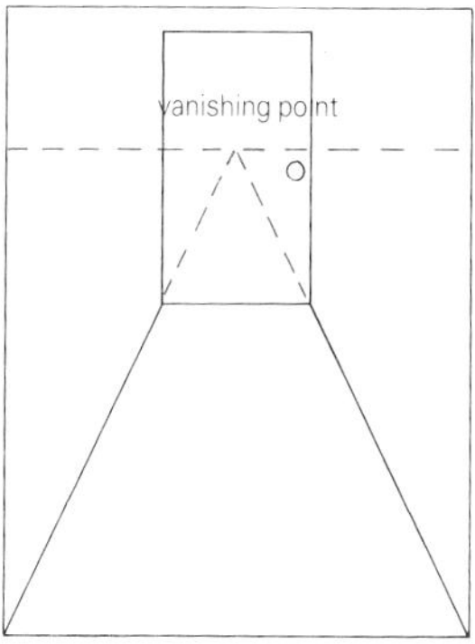

1 Draw in the verticals and then the horizontals seen straight on (these remain constant). Now draw in the receding lines and continue them until they meet a point on the eye level.

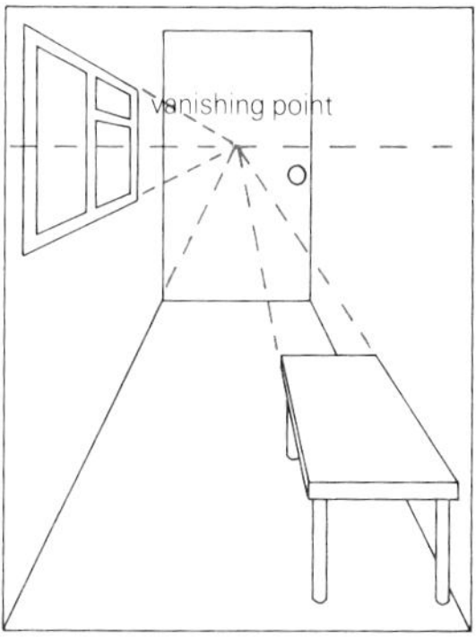

2 Draw in other objects that are parallel with the door (ie with the picture plane) or with the wall. Notice how all the converging lines recede to the same point.

Two-point perspective

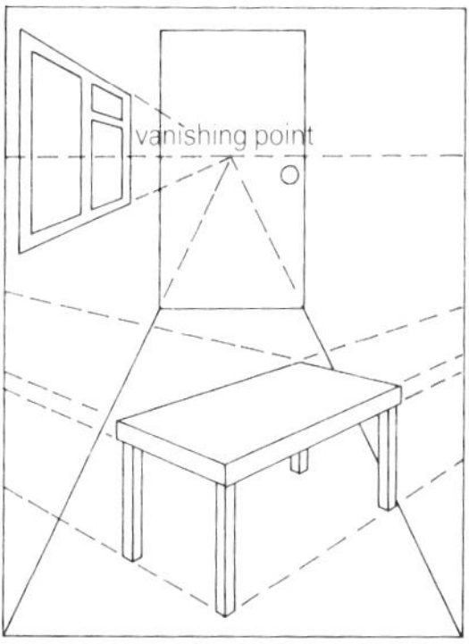

Move the table at an angle into a different plane. It now has two sets of converging lines and two vanishing points on the same eye level. The vertical lines remain constant.

Judging angles by eye

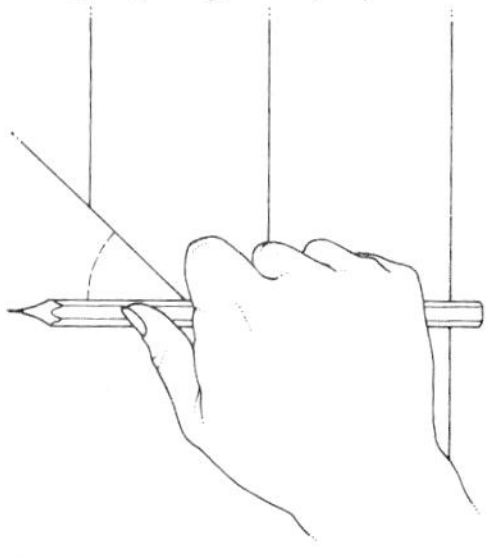

Geometric perspective can be used to make all the angles of receding lines consistent. The first angle, however, must be judged by eye. It can be read against an existing vertical or by holding out a pencil at full arm's length.

Curves in perspective

Straight-edged objects remain straight-edged in perspective, although their angles might change, but when curved objects are foreshortened the nature of their curves is altered. Circles become ellipses, which vary in depth the further they are from the eye.

Drawing a circle in perspective

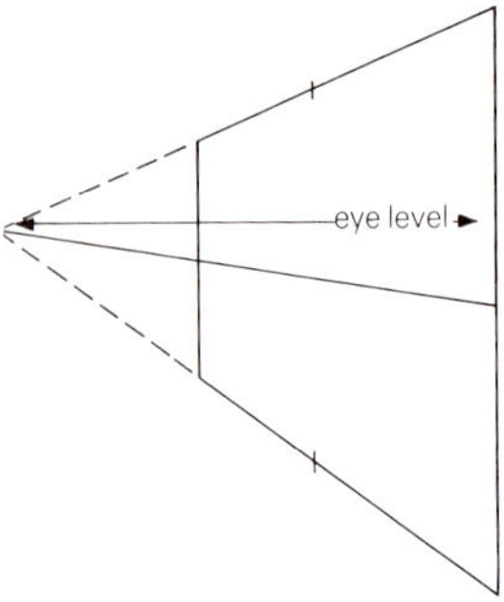

1 Drawing a circle can be made easier by first drawing a square in perspective and then marking the halfway point of each of the sides.

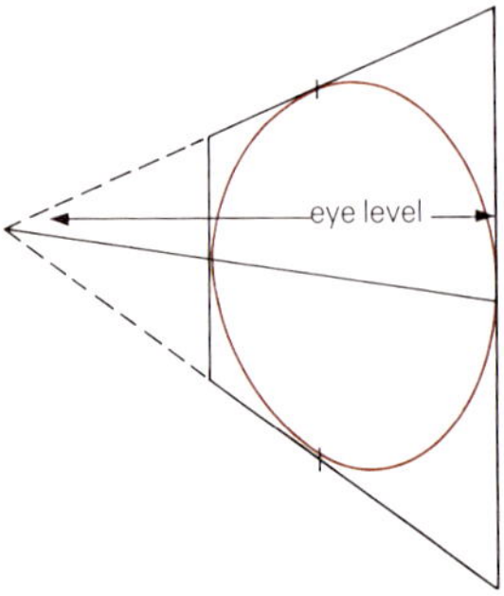

2 Join up these halfway points freely by drawing arcs between them. The circle will appear to lie in the same plane as the rectangle.

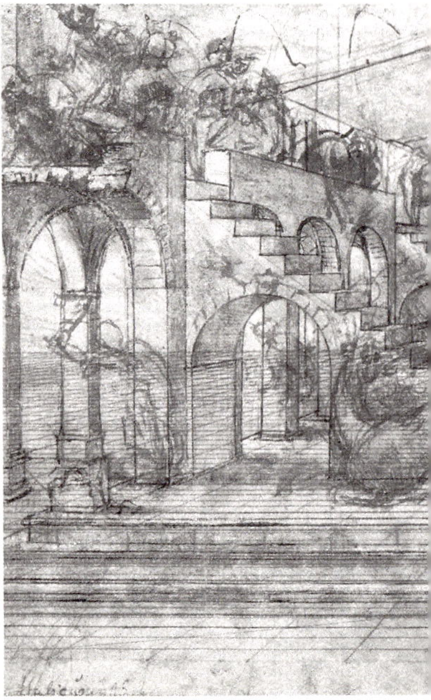

Leonardo da Vinci
Perspective Study for The Adoration of the Kings
This famous drawing demonstrates that perspective should be used as an aid, not a rule. There are several places where Leonardo has paid no attention to it. He has used the grid of perspective lines as a platform on which to set these gesticulating, almost spectre-like figures, running and rushing, defying mathematics or even gravity. In fact the true use of all these lines seems to be to add to the drama of it all: they seem to shoot the ground out from under the feet of the figures, while at the same time establishing the three-dimensional space they occupy.

Edges in rounded objects

When drawing cylindrical objects, such as jugs or vases, note that the elliptical curves become deeper the further down from the eye level they are. This determines the shape of the base – a fluent curve without an angle.

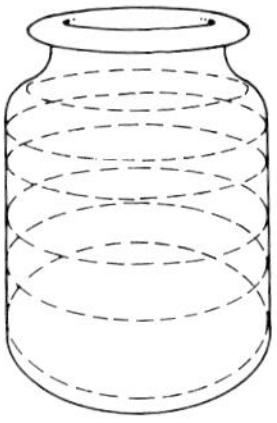

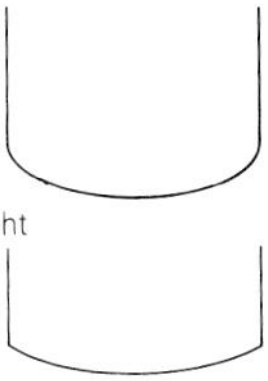

Analysing cylindrical forms in perspective

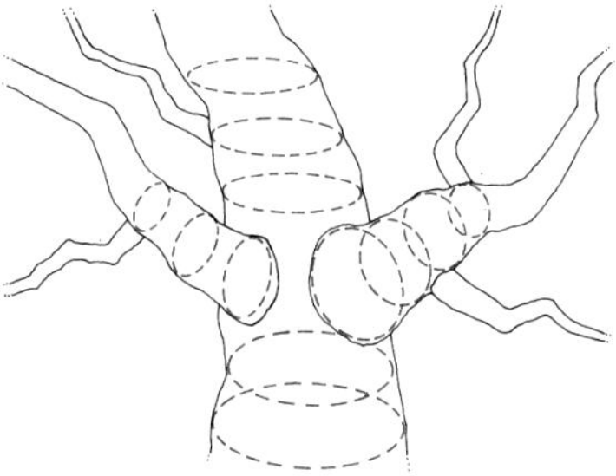

Tree trunks and branches and other cylindrical forms can be thought of as a series of encircling contour lines which become less or more shallow depending on their distance from eye level. Preliminary drawings done in this way help an understanding of volume.

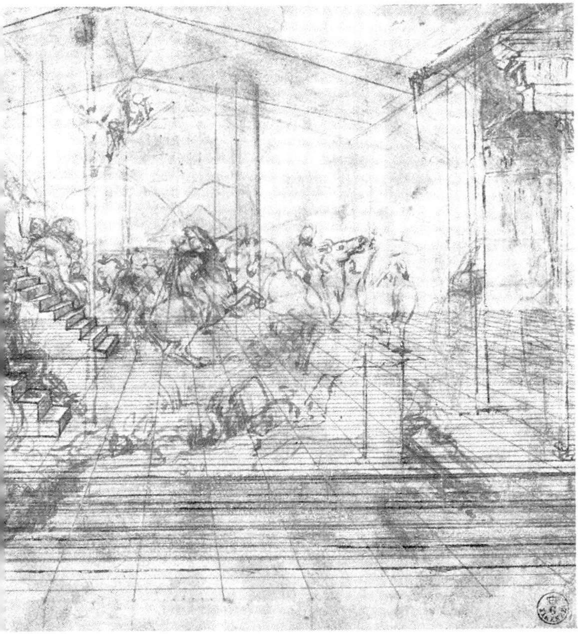

Figures in the landscape

A landscape can be given extra compositional interest by the introduction of human figures or animals. They can help to identify the scene and perhaps introduce a narrative element. They will also reflect what is happening in that landscape and can provide the focal point of a composition, since the eye is easily attracted by the human element in a drawing. One important consideration when adding figures to a landscape is keeping them to the right scale.

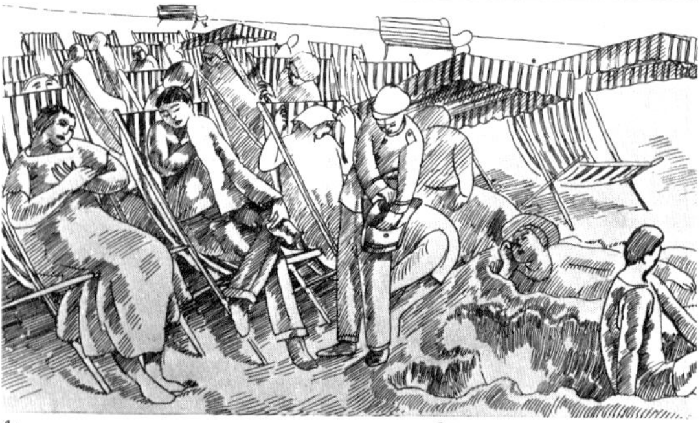

1▲

2▼

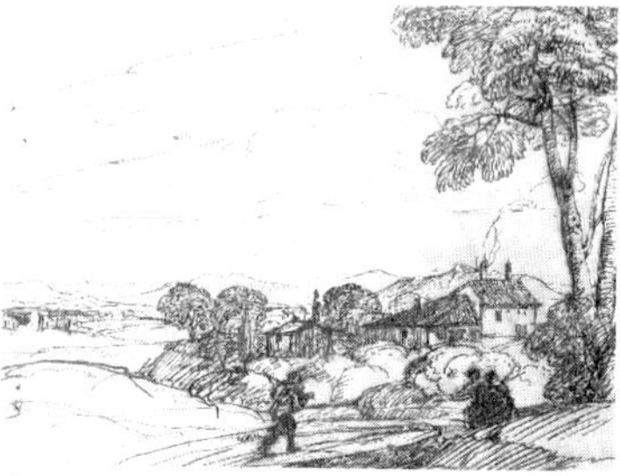

On a Beach in Deck-chairs **1** by Stanley Spencer shows strong characterization of the dominant figures. The figures provide a focal point in the landscapes by Claude Lorraine **2** and Georges Seurat **3**, but in J.M.W. Turner's *Transept of Tintern Abbey* **4** the figure sets the scale.

3▼

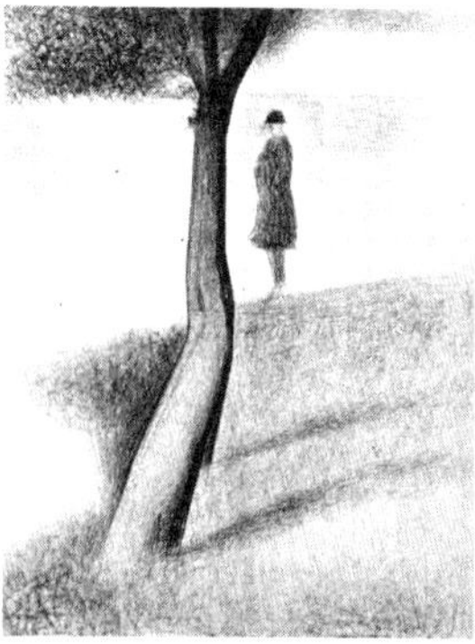

4▼

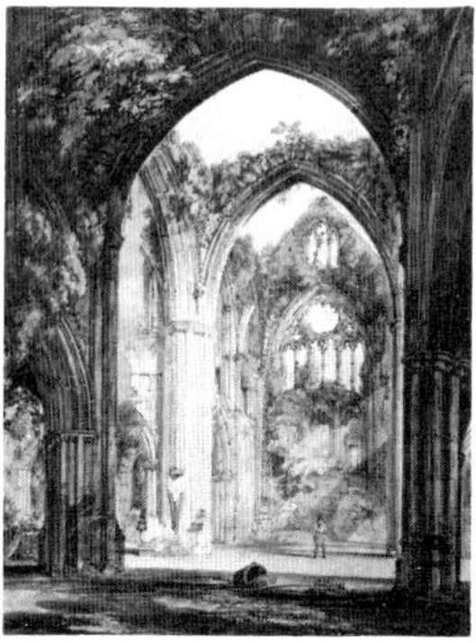

see also pages 66–67, 69, 103–104

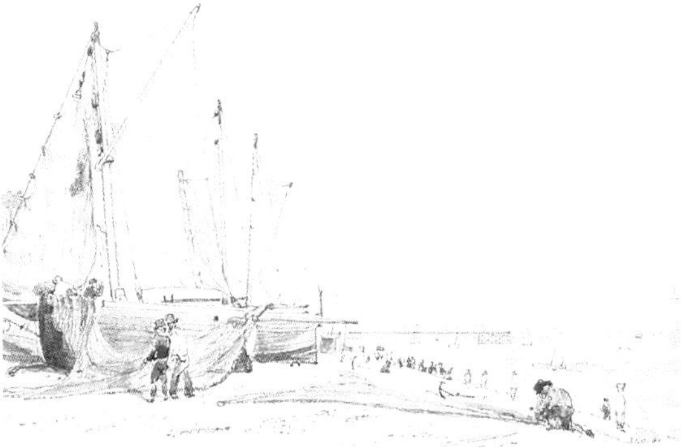

5▲

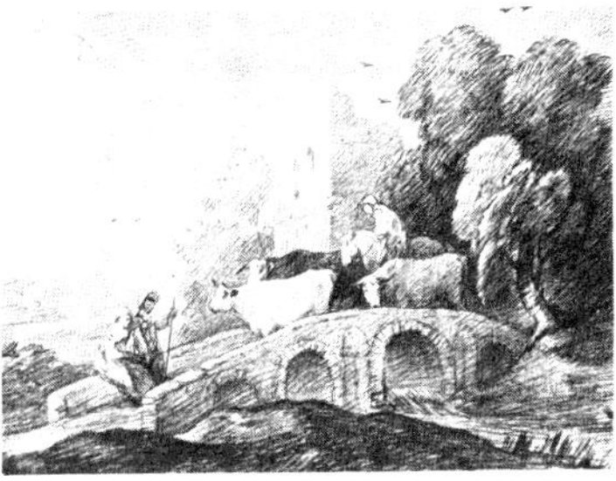

6▼

John Constable's figures are rather smaller than life in *Brighton Beach* 5, and play little part in the composition. Thomas Gainsborough 6 exaggerated the size of the figures and animals so that they became the dominant feature of the composition.

Drawing figures to scale

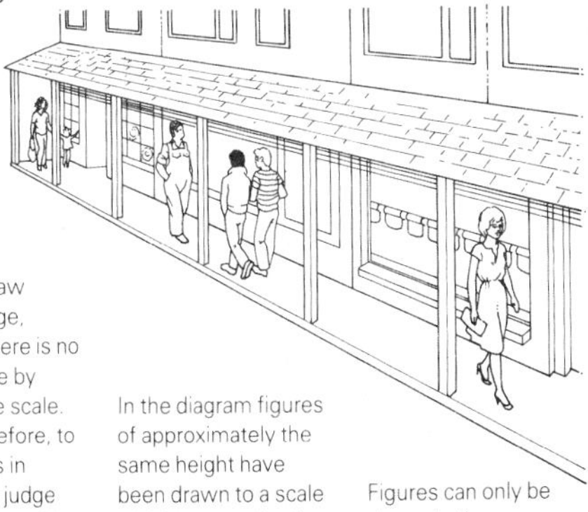

It is easy to draw figures too large, especially if there is no landmark close by which sets the scale. It is best, therefore, to put the figures in when you can judge the size they should be in relation to the surroundings.

In the diagram figures of approximately the same height have been drawn to a scale which was set by the converging parallel lines of the building.

Figures can only be drawn to the same size if they are in the same lateral plane.

Drawing Buildings

Townscapes demand a knowledge of perspective, and are natural subjects on which to practise it. Perspective, however, should not be the only ingredient of your drawing – tonal and textural variations are needed to give real conviction to the web of neat lines. The usual way to proceed is to introduce light and shade over a grid of perspective lines. The lines generally are left intact, but with a medium such as crayon or pastel you can dissolve the edges and seek dramatic effects, even though you retain an invisible perspective structure beneath.

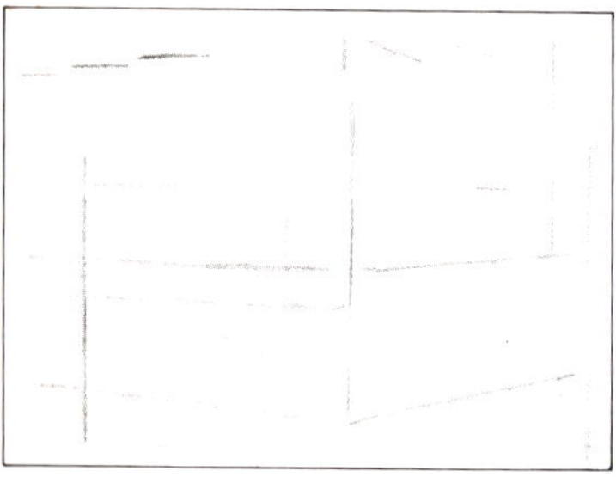

Begin with a simple sketch, using line to identify the main angles. Remember that vertical edges remain so in the drawing, it is only the other angles that change. With the verticals established, plot in the directions of the main features – the roofs and bases of the buildings.

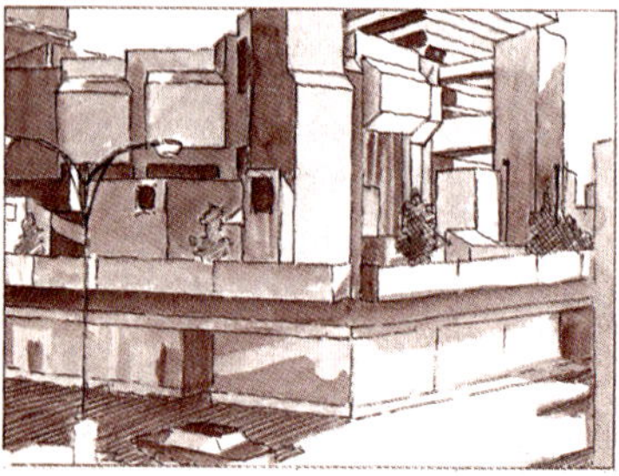

Over the simple perspective sketch, add the main shadow areas and pick out significant details. Here, wash has been used for the main shadows with pen and ink hatching on top. In the finished drawing (below), elaborate tones have been established, accurately defining the complex architecture.

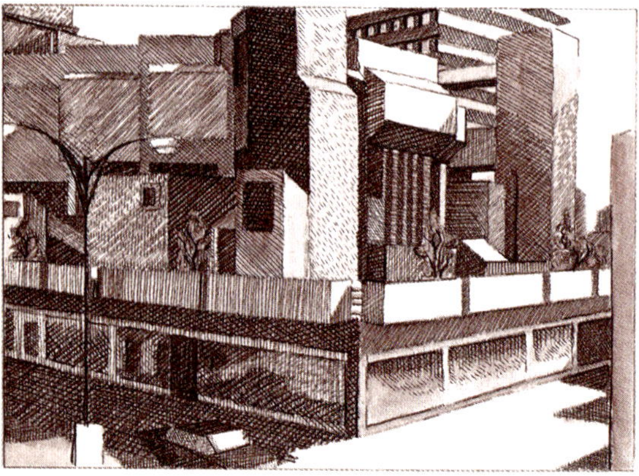

see also pages 40–41, 88, 102–105, 110–111

Using other media

Using **charcoal** and **conté crayon,** together or separately, gives considerable scope for tonal variation and the introduction of texture. Detail, however, is not easily dealt with. In this drawing, the tones were first laid out in charcoal and were subsequently deepened in conté.

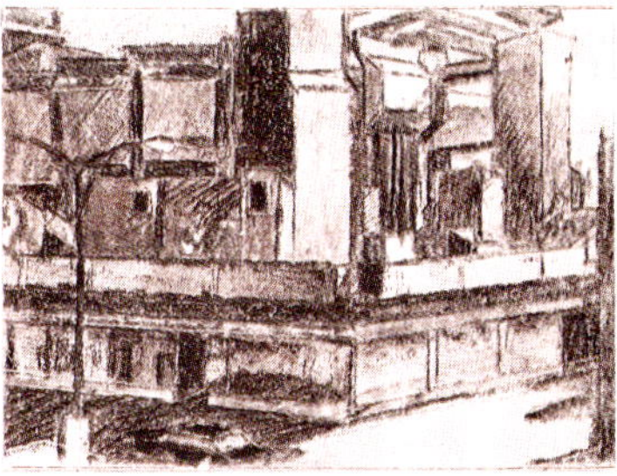

Fibre-tip pen has advantages but also limitations. It is a highly fluent medium, good for sketching out the bones of the scene quickly. But it has almost no tonal variation and, without carefully planned hatching, it may merge into a solid mass of black with no middle or light tones.

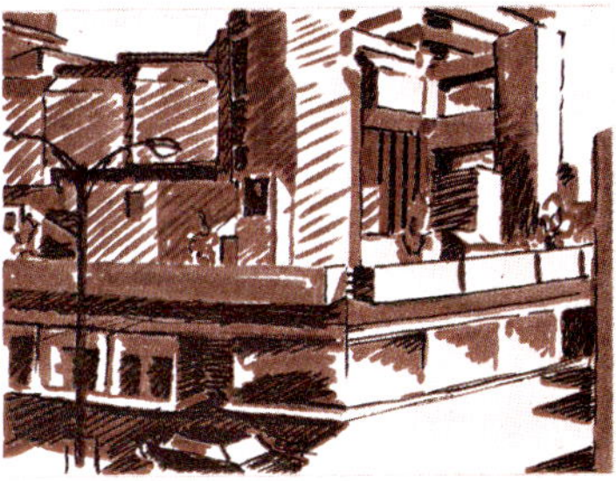

Free drawings of buildings

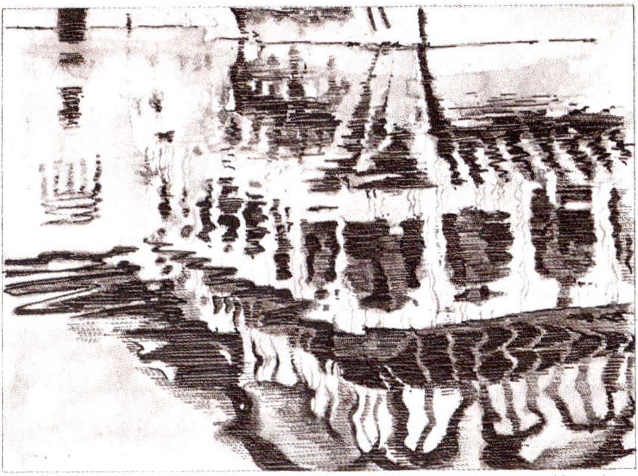

There is no need for buildings to be drawn so precisely in every case. Here, by choosing the reflection of a building in water it is seen as a design of interesting patterns and shapes. An impressionistic approach to buildings can often produce effective results. This drawing was begun with a preliminary pale wash, which was then built up into darker tones. Some tones were enriched with pen, the added detail establishing the rhythms running through the groups of broken shapes. The pen does not outline the shapes, but defines them as tones and textures.

Architectural details

Buildings are often rich with details, and in some cases it is the details that give a building its individual character and make it an interesting subject to draw. Occasionally, the regular repetition of architectural mouldings will need to be shown. Avoid unnecessary elaboration – learn to suggest details with a few strokes indicating a firmly grasped structure.

A roof study

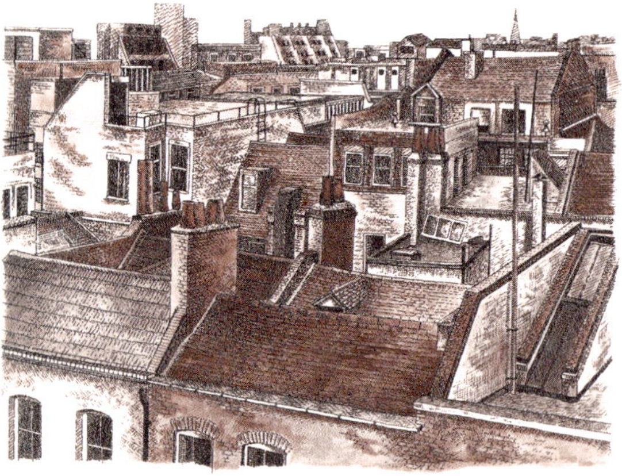

When drawing complex and detailed groups of buildings, first find the underlying structure of the composition. Here, the view is divided into thirds by the main verticals, while the perspective converges in two opposite directions, giving rise to quite complex problems.

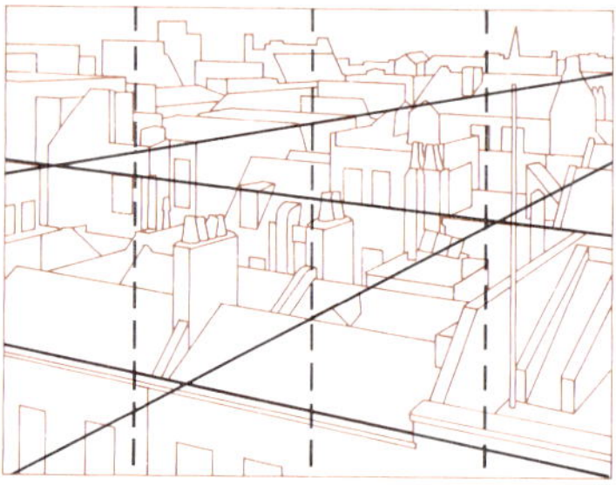

Texture in buildings

Although you must start with the main shape of the building, draw textures as you progress rather than leaving them for the end. Having outlined the pattern of these tiles, for example, the differing textures could be developed and contrasted with the foliage of the tree.

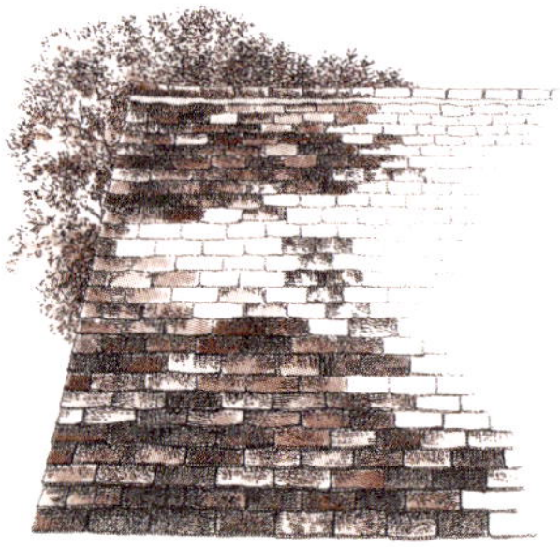

see also pages
108–109, 102–105, 88

Stairs

Both of these studies of stairs were done by sketching in the basic geometric shape – a cube and a cylinder – in which each form is enclosed. The main lines of the straight stair, converging to a single vanishing point, came first to form a rectangular box. The addition of diagonals gave the line of the stair and the banister. In the same way, a drum was drawn for the curved stair and the outer and inner rails were then added. In both cases, the steps themselves came last. Notice how less of each step becomes visible as the stair rises towards and above the eye level of the drawing.

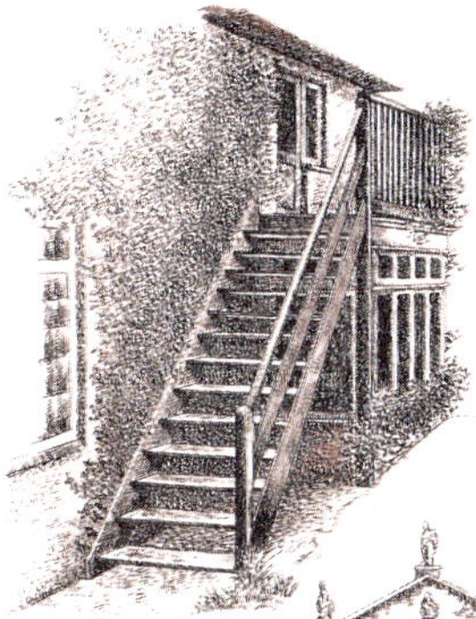

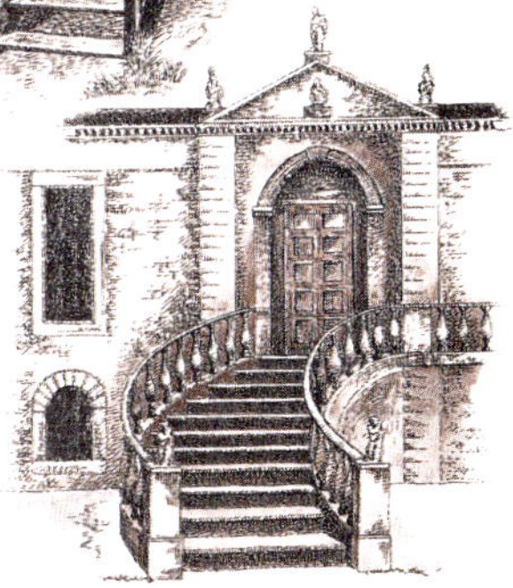

Curves – bridges and arches

Because the portico is set at a slight angle, the curves of the arches are not quite true. Even more important, they are smaller as they are further away, and consequently less of the background is visible through each of the arches.

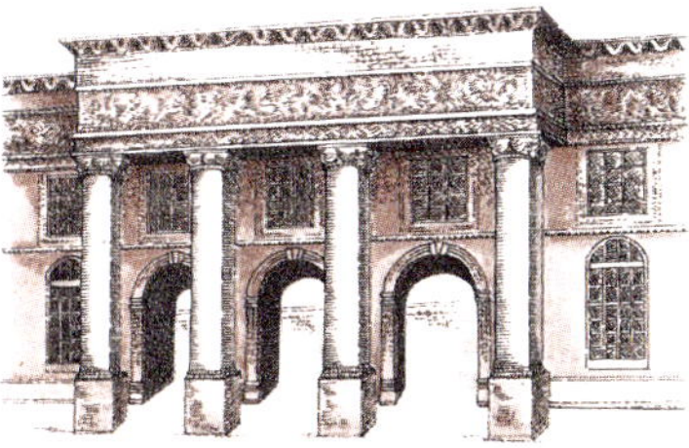

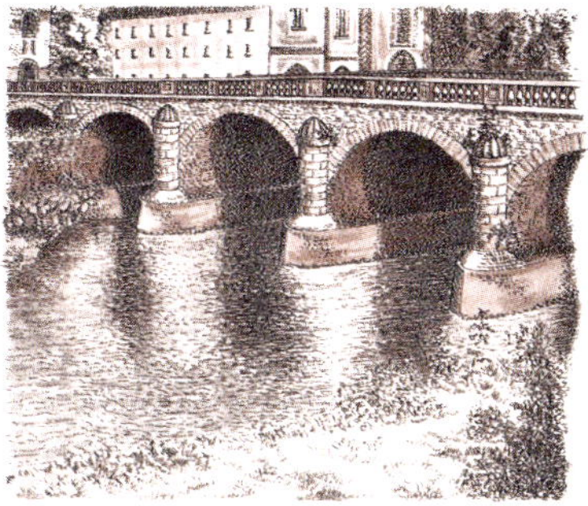

The perspective of a bridge is complicated by its rise towards the centre and the elliptical curves of the receding arches. Draw in the main lines of the perspective and add the arches as freely drawn curves. Develop the reflections at the same time as the light and shade on the bridge itself – they are as important to the scene.

Composing from sketches

It is not possible to draw constantly changing scenes from the life. You must make studies of the essential forms and telling details, and then develop them into a composite view – often making adjustments to suit the final design. It is important to keep a sense of place, however, so do not neglect the setting when making your preliminary sketches.

Preliminary sketches on a small scale

Make quick sketches of the aspects of the scene that strike you – both people and objects. Use pencil or a convenient pen such as a fibre-tip.

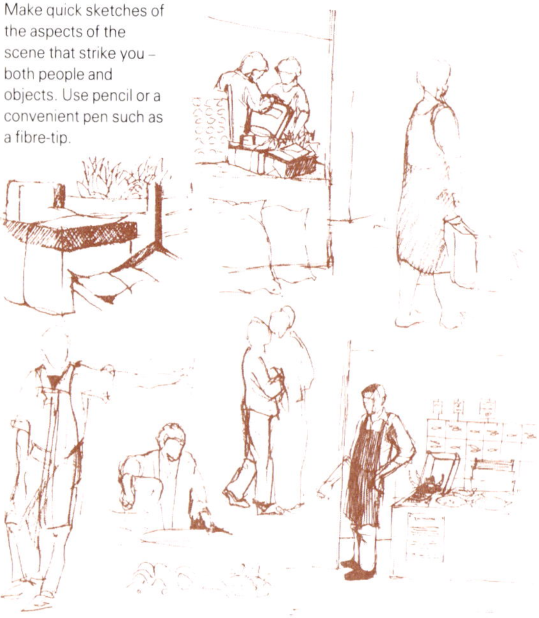

The basic composition

The next stage is to use the sketches to construct a composition. Start with the underlying design, indicating the perspective and the rough shapes of the people or any other elements you will include. For this it is advisable to use charcoal or crayon to register the distribution of light and dark sensitively. Try various compositions until you find one that fulfils your intentions, moving people and objects until you establish a satisfactory overall arrangement of the shapes.

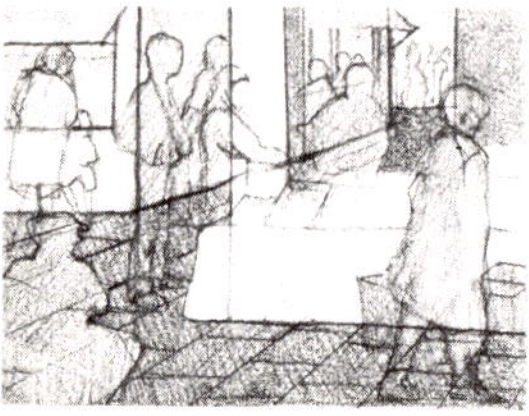

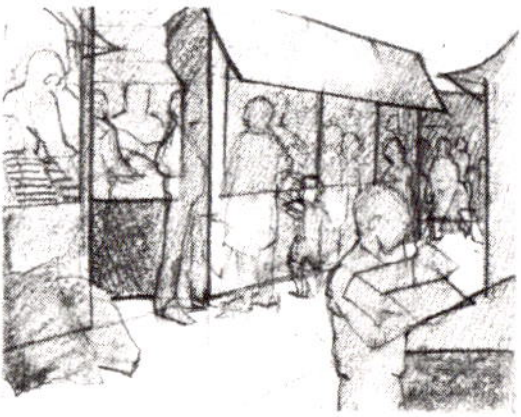

see also pages 68–69, 98–105, 108–109, 114–115, 116–117

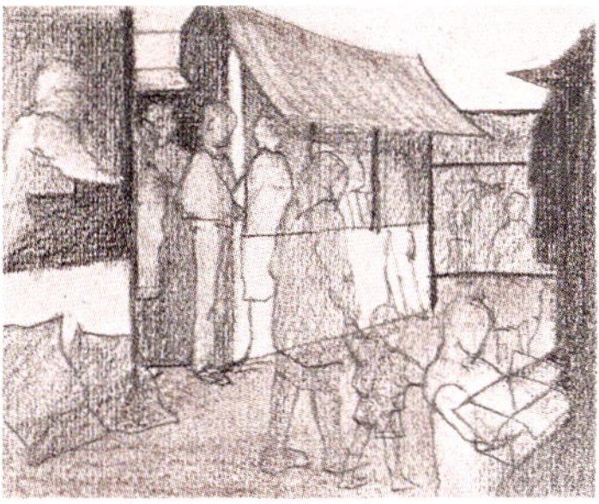

When you have settled on a composition (left), include all the elements of the final drawing. Here, a toned Ingres paper has been chosen, with the lighter tones heightened with white conté. Work on the whole drawing, darkening and lightening passages over the whole area of the paper.

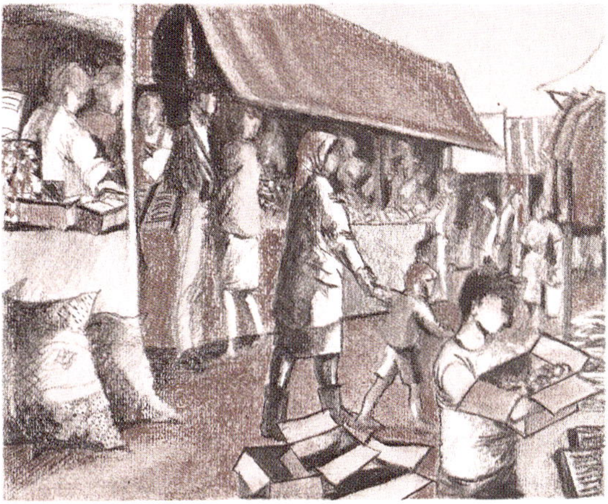

Experimenting with tracing paper

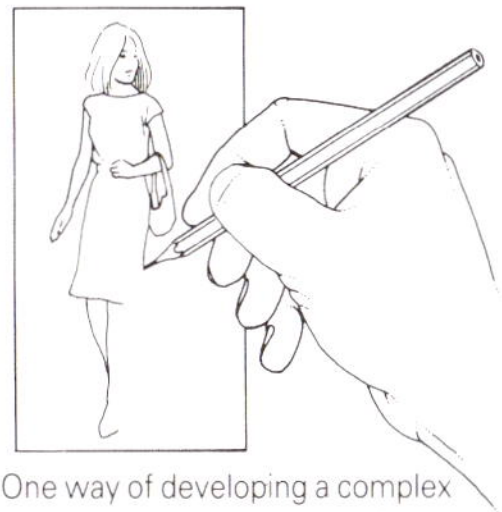

One way of developing a complex composition is to rough out the design and then sketch the figures on separate pieces of tracing paper.

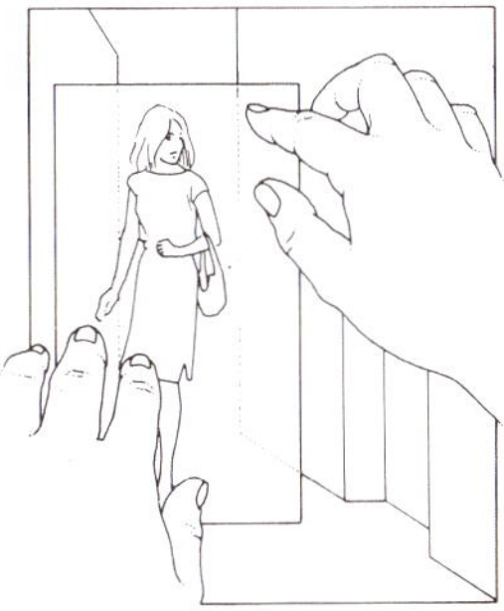

You can then try them in varying positions and adjust as necessary.

Enlarging and reducing

If you want to enlarge a finished drawing to a particular size in preparation for a painting, or if you need to enlarge or reduce an image you have drawn by a given proportion, the methods given here will help you.

Squaring up

By drawing a grid over the drawing and then reproducing that grid at a larger scale, the lines and shapes within each square can be plotted by eye in the corresponding square on the larger grid. The size of each square will depend on the size of the picture, but smaller squares will increase accuracy.

Marking out the paper

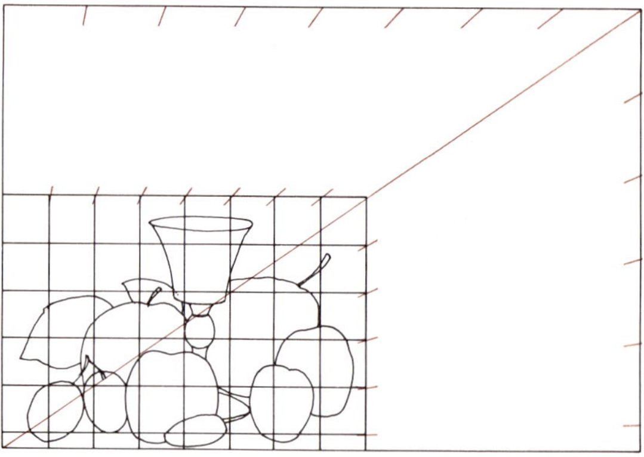

Use a T square and set square to draw an accurate grid over the drawing and then tape it to the bottom left-hand corner of a larger sheet of paper and accurately align the grid again with the T square. Extend the bottom line to the required width of the enlarged drawing and draw a line at right angles to it. Extend the diagonal of the original grid to intersect this vertical line. This marks the height of the enlargement from which you can draw the rectangle. To plot the grid on the enlargement, align a straight-edge ruler to pass through the bottom left-hand corner of the rectangle and the furthest point of each vertical and horizontal line of the grid. Mark where the ruler meets the edge of the larger rectangle and draw a new grid using these points.

Drawing accurate lines

Use a T square for the horizontal lines and a set square for the vertical ones. Stick the paper down on a drawing board, taping the corners diagonally so that the paper is stretched tight. Ensure that the pencil point runs against the straight edge – if it is held incorrectly the point may be deflected away from the intended line.

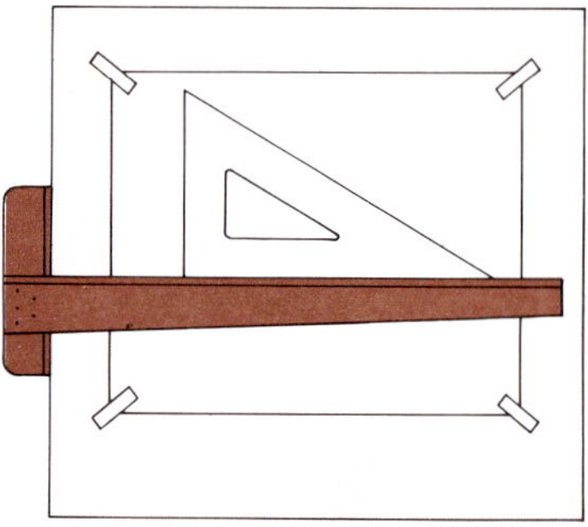

see also pages 112–113, 122–123

Other methods of enlarging and reducing an image

Dividers If you want to enlarge or reduce your drawing by a simple proportion, such as two or three times, use a pair of dividers to step off the measurement. Having set the dividers to the length of a line on the original, 'walk' them the required number of steps along a line on a new sheet of paper.

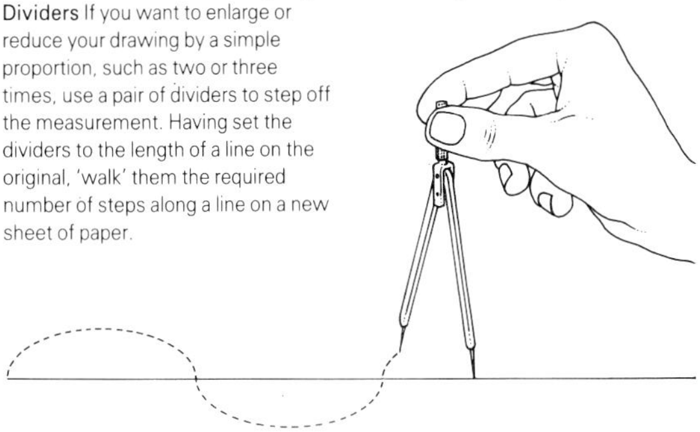

Proportional dividers The sliding pivot of proportional dividers can be adjusted to arrive at a number of set proportions. If set to a proportion of one to three, the distance between the points of the longer legs is exactly three times larger than that between the shorter legs. Measurements can be made with either end – the shorter legs giving enlargement, and the longer legs automatically giving reduction.

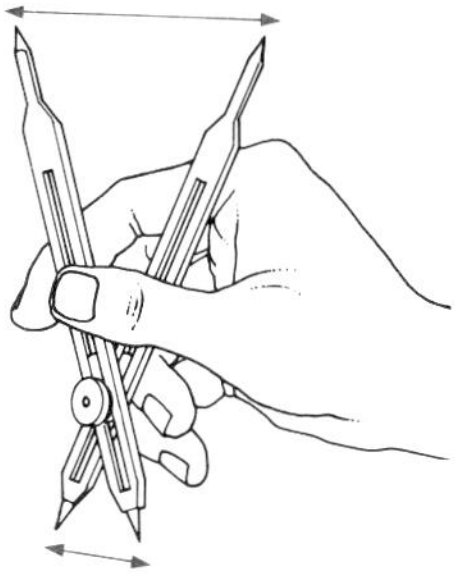

Pantograph As the point of a pantograph is guided over the original, the pencil at the end of the arm draws a proportionally larger image. If the point and pencil are interchanged, the image will be reduced. Although very easy to use, a pantograph will not produce very accurate enlargements. Some models can be set to work to particular proportions.

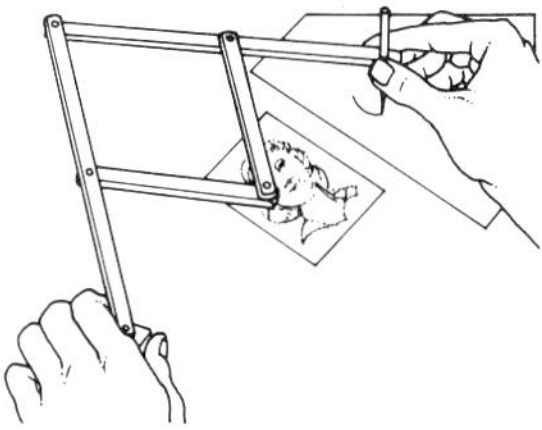

Projector A photographic transparency can be projected onto a piece of paper taped to a vertical board. Move the board and focus the lens until the image is the size you want. Plot the major components of the image onto the paper lightly with a pencil, switching off the projector occasionally to look at your work.

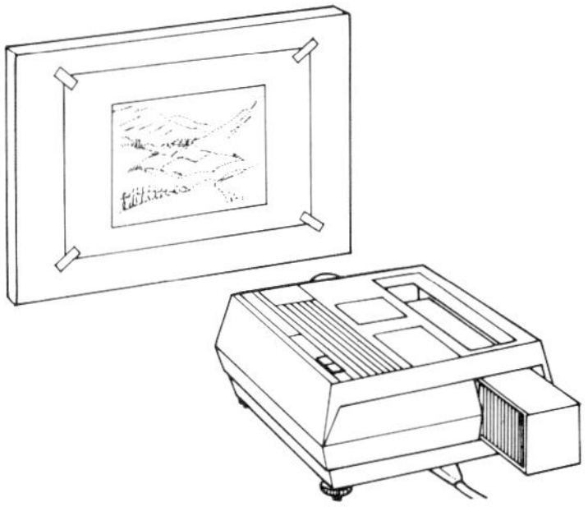

Tracing

Tracing always tends to imply the idea of straight copying. Try to avoid this as it will limit the individuality of your drawing. Instead, use tracing as a means of adapting information from various sources or simply of transferring the bare structure of a sketch or drawing onto a new sheet of paper.

Methods of tracing

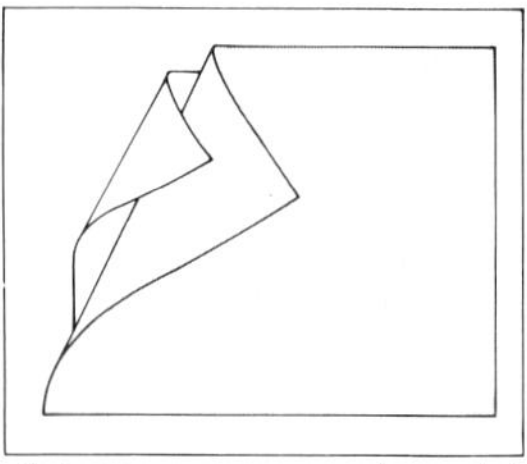

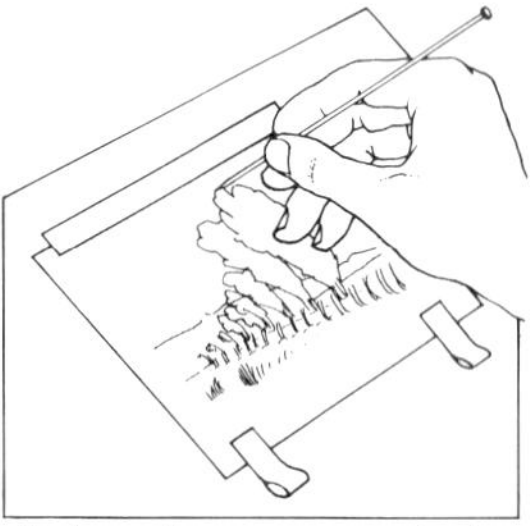

Carbon or rouge paper can be sandwiched between the source you are tracing and the sheet of paper you want to use for you drawing. By tracing over the shapes with a used ball-point pen or knitting needle, a line is transferred onto the paper and directly reproduces the image. A carbon line cannot be erased, but the fine red powder deposited by the rouge paper can be removed with an ordinary pencil eraser and is suitable for more delicate work. To produce a traced pencil line, make your own image-transfer paper by rubbing soft pencil over one side of a sheet of paper and use in the same way as carbon paper. It is essential that neither the tracing nor the drawing move while you are working. Having taped both to a drawing board, fold masking tape tabs and attach them to the bottom edge of the tracing so that you can look at the work from time to time. Do not rest your hand on the drawing or it will smudge.

Graphite

If you cover the back of the drawing or a tracing of it with soft pencil, the graphite will be transferred as you retrace the lines with a pen or knitting needle. But using a separate sheet of paper as described above is less messy.

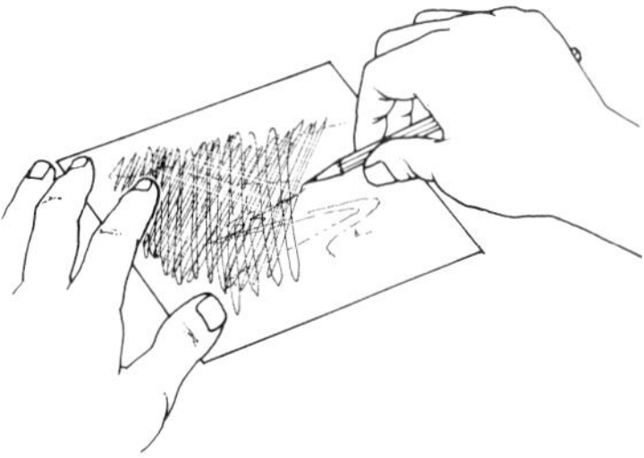

Daylight

Tape the tracing to a window and cover it with the paper. The strong back lighting will show the design clearly through even thick drawing paper. A 'light box' can also be used in this way. It is a box with a Perspex top, lit from below by fluorescent tubes.

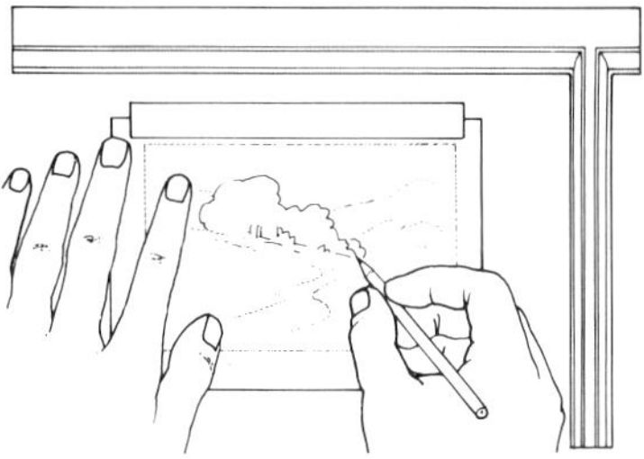

Developing an image

Tracing paper can be used as an ideal means of building up a design, perhaps for a Christmas card, if you are using a subject that is unfamiliar to you or if you want to take various elements from different sources and adapt them to create a unified image.

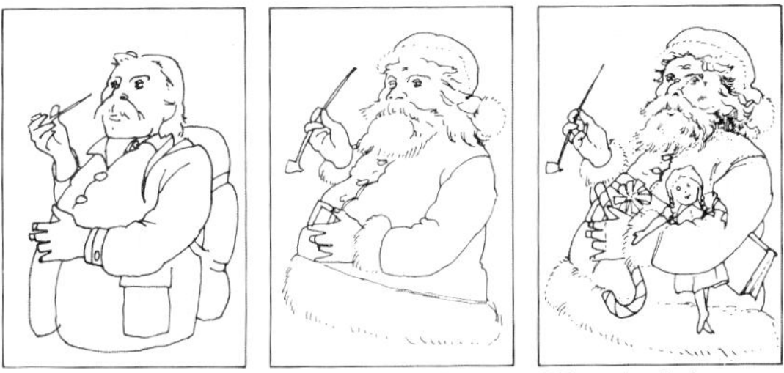

1 Decide on the main theme of your design and find an image that will form the basis of it. Trace the outline onto a sheet of tracing paper in pencil.

2 Adapt the drawing to your needs, using new sheets of tracing paper rather than erasing each element. In this way you can keep the tracings for further use.

3 Trace details from other sources on separate sheets and superimpose them on the design. Do a final tracing of the whole picture on one sheet.

Symmetrical designs

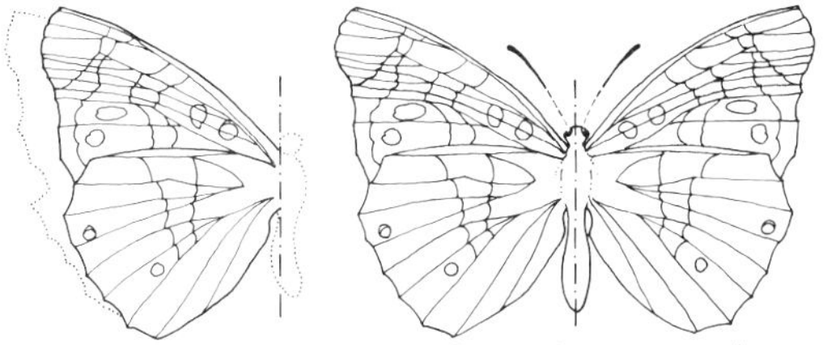

Tracing paper can be used as a short-cut when drawing a symmetrical object. Draw one half of the object and then fold the paper along the central line. Now trace the image again.

Open up the paper to see the complete image and transfer it onto a sheet of paper using one of the methods shown opposite. To produce a symmetrical design reverse and transfer it as a mirror image.

Rubbings

Using the tracing principle of transferring an image through paper, interesting textures can be added to your drawing by rubbing areas with a pencil over wood, canvas, or even a comb.

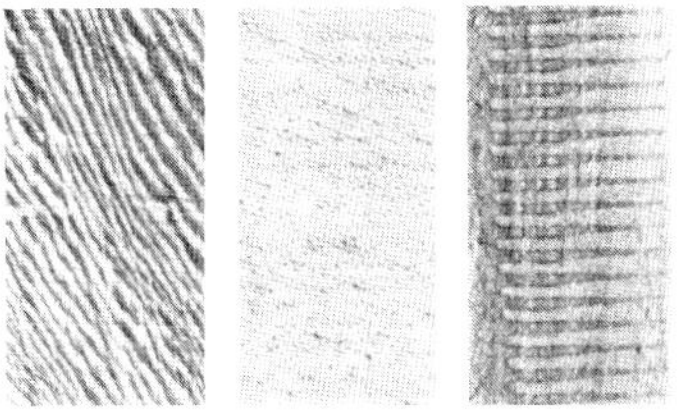

Masks

Masks provide the means of defining interesting areas of texture or pattern in a drawing, which would otherwise be a difficult or laborious process. A mask can be made from card, film, wax-coated stencil paper, or found or bought ready made. It will protect areas of paper from ink sprayed onto it, or pencil rubbed over it, to give a sharp edge.

Drawing up to a straight edge

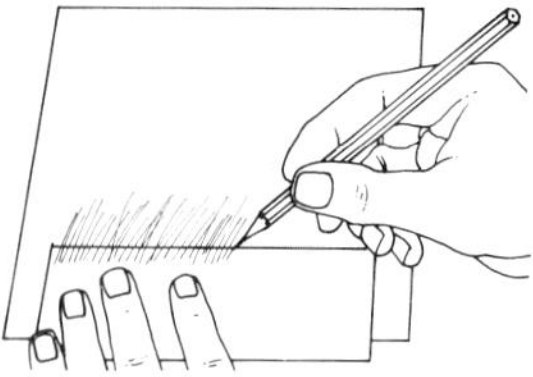

A striking effect can be produced by masking off an edge with a straight piece of paper. Holding the paper firmly down on the surface draw the pencil across the mask in short strokes, always working away from the edge, never towards it. It will leave a crisp edge.

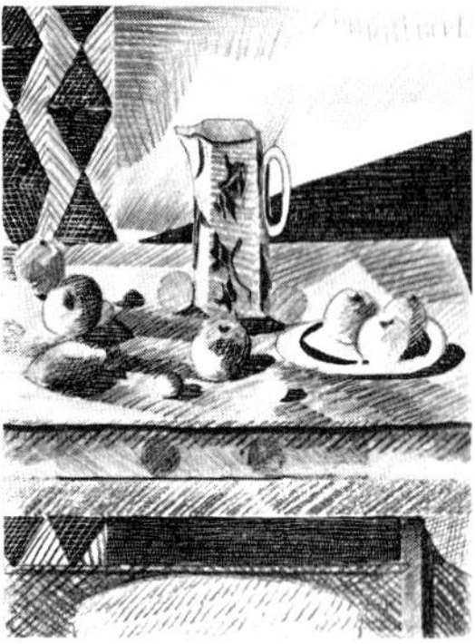

Erasing with a mask

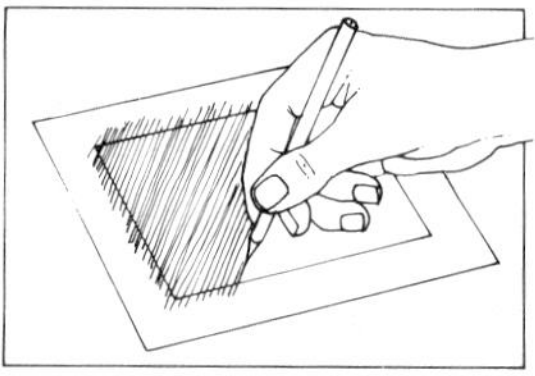

1 A freely drawn texture cannot be stopped abruptly at a definite edge. To achieve this effect mark in lightly the intended edges of the drawing and draw the texture over this line.

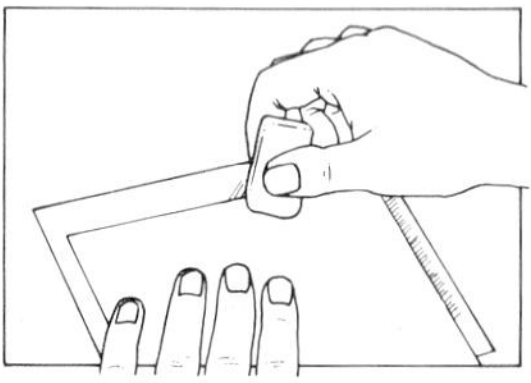

2 Lay a piece of sharply edged paper over the drawing to align with the marked edge and use a plastic eraser to remove the part of the drawing outside the line, leaving a crisp frame.

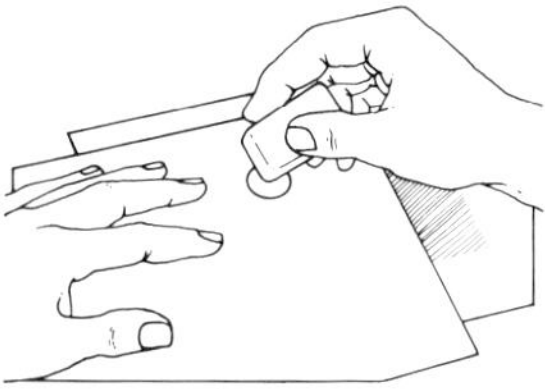

Areas of texture can be taken out of the background by cutting the shape out from a sheet of thin cardboard. Position the cut-out and carefully erase the pencil from the paper within this area.

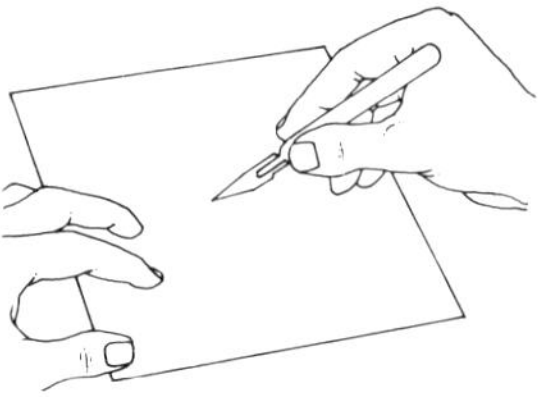

If the drawing has been made on paper with a hard surface, grass-like textures can be scratched into a solid pencil background with the point of a scalpel blade to reveal the colour of the paper below.

see also page 87

Masking fluid

Areas of paper can be effectively masked out with masking fluid when watercolour wash is being used. **1** Apply with an old brush and allow to dry thoroughly. **2** Remove by rubbing off with the finger or a putty rubber when the wash is quite dry.

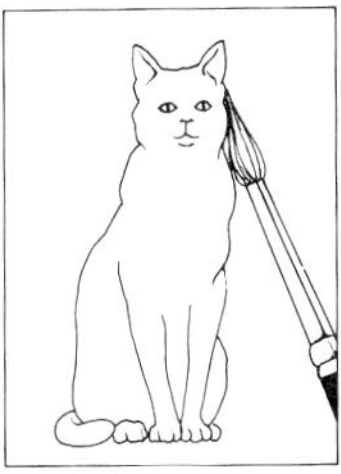

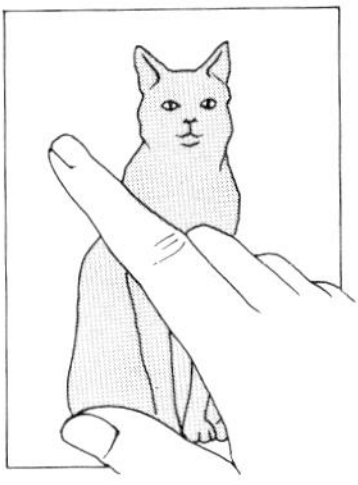

Spraying over a mask

Ink or thinned paint can be sprayed using a miniature spray gun or airbrush. An airbrush is an expensive item that is most commonly used by commercial illustrators. It will produce flat areas of colour and slick tonal gradations and can even be adjusted to spray fine lines, but where such accuracy is not needed, a small spray gun will give results that are just as effective and much more economical. Both instruments need a supply of compressed air, which is most easily provided by using aerosol cans of propellant. Wash the spray often, particularly when changing colour.

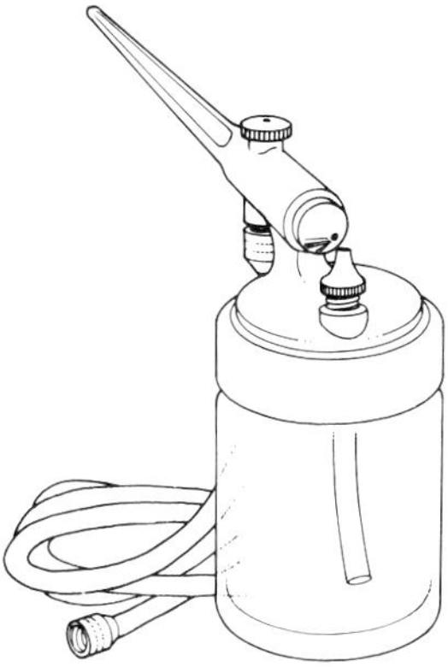

A hard edge

A hard, straight edge can be produced when spraying by the method already shown of masking with a piece of paper, but it must be weighted or stuck down to prevent it being blown away by the jet of compressed air.

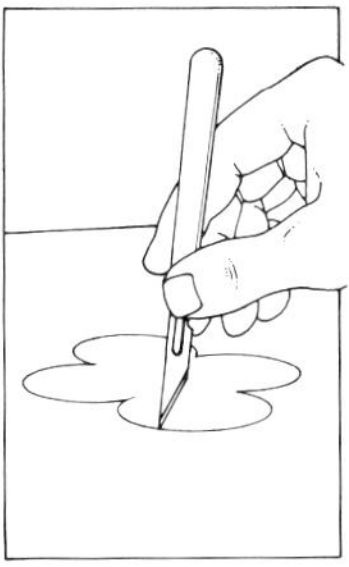

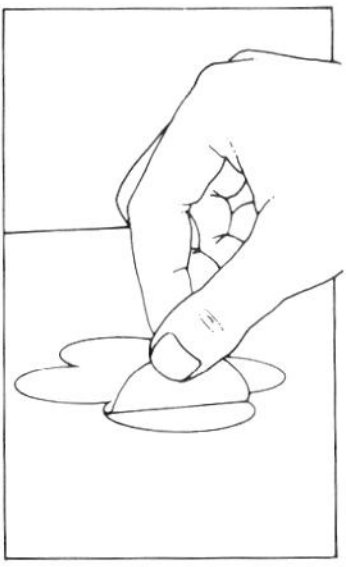

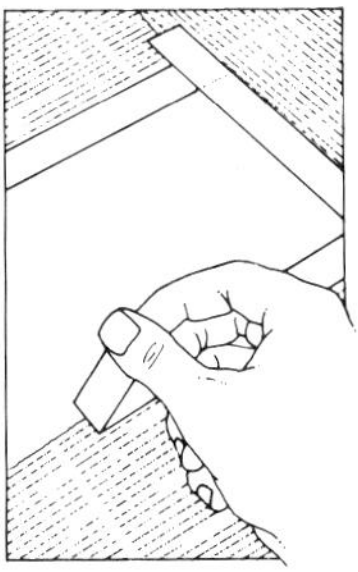

Curved or irregular shapes should be cut from adhesive-backed masking film. Lay a sheet of film over the whole drawing and carefully cut out the shape you want to spray with a scalpel blade. Lift out the cut shape and rub down the rest. The adhesive will not lift ink off the paper, but fix any other medium, particularly pencil, crayon and pastels before starting.

Straight edges Stick masking tape down firmly along the edge you want to mask and protect the outer areas with newspaper. Spray and remove tape carefully without delay.

A soft edge

To produce a soft edge when spraying tonal areas using a mask, hold a piece of card just above the surface of the paper. When the ink is sprayed across the edge of the card, enough will fall under the mask to soften the edge of the sprayed area and blur the definition. The degree of softness can be varied by altering the height of the card from the paper and the angle at which it is held.

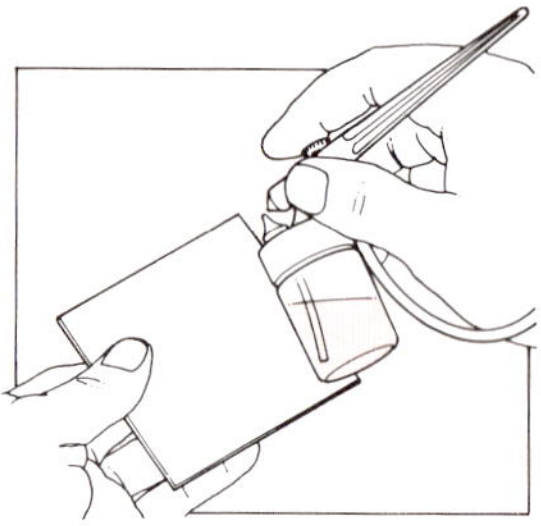

Varying the edges

For an edge that runs from hard to soft, use transparent masking film, partially rubbed down onto the paper, while holding one area of it away from the paper to allow the spray to diffuse the edge. The angle at which you hold the film will determine the smoothness of the transition.

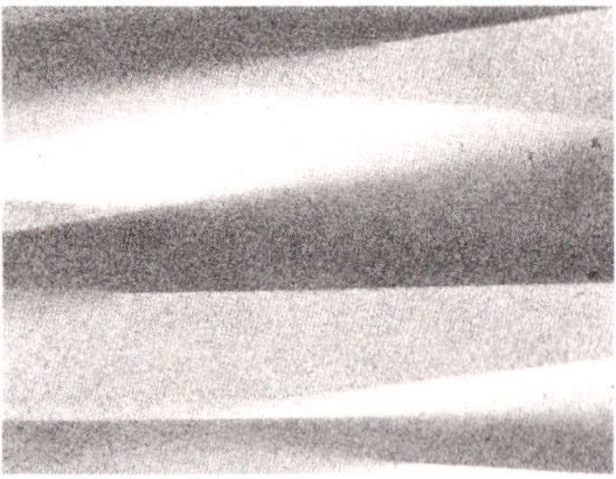

Ready-made masks

Masks do not have to be cut out from card or film. Interesting patterns and textures can be made by spraying over objects that you have collected. Dried flowers, leaves, paper doilies and loose-weave cloths are just a few ideas. You will soon discover a wide variety of masks to use.

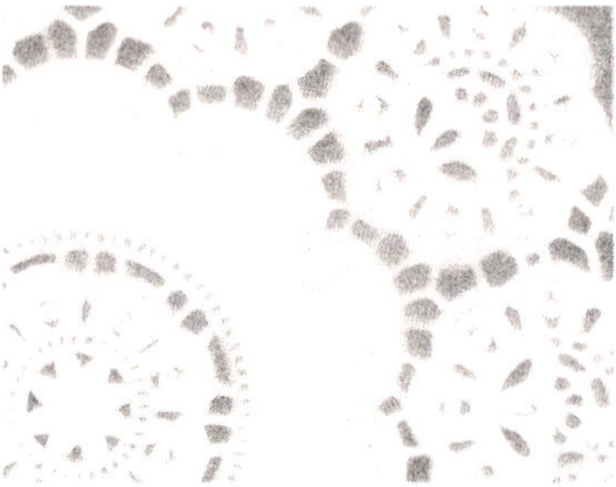

Repeating a pattern

A repeated pattern can be built up by moving the mask a little to the side of the first sprayed shape, being careful to wait until the colour is dry first. Where sprayed areas overlap, the colour will be stronger and interesting tonal variation will occur. Keep to simple shapes for the mask.

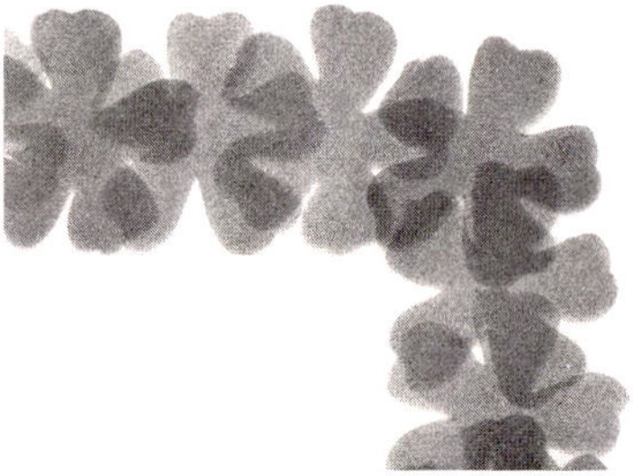

Guides

Templates and stencils

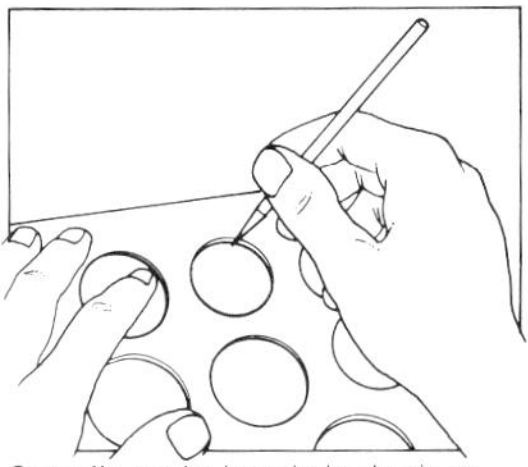

Stencils can be bought in plastic or thick oiled paper. They will guide the point of a pencil or pen around the outline of shapes such as circles, ellipses or letters, which would be difficult to draw accurately freehand.

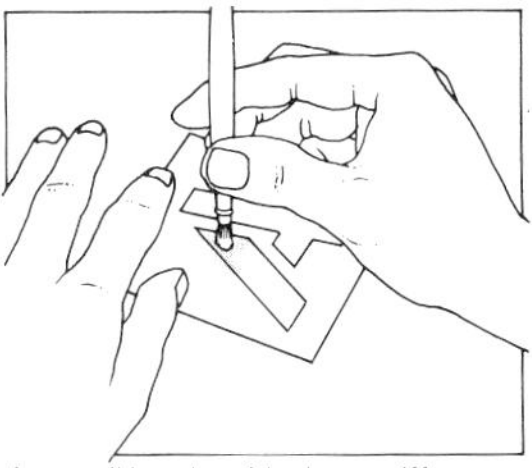

A stencil brush, with short, stiff bristles, can be used to fill in a shape by stippling, or dabbing the brush on the surface of the paper. Excess paint should first be brushed onto a piece of scrap paper.

French curves can be used for drawing complex curves when accuracy is required, or when copying a photograph. Having drawn part of the curve, move the guide around to find another part of it that matches up and continues the curve smoothly.

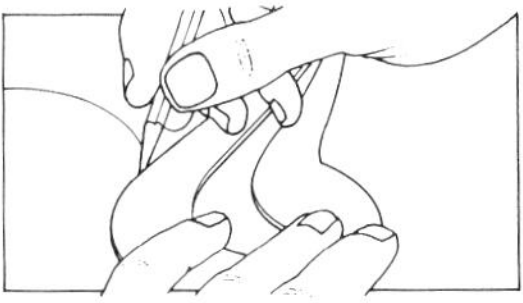

Flexible rules are plastic-covered guides which can be used to copy awkward curves from a drawing or photograph. Lay the rule flat on the original and bend it to follow the curve. Transfer to your paper and draw along the bevelled edge.

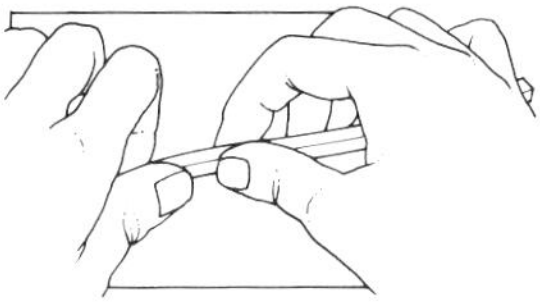

Drawing large curves and circles

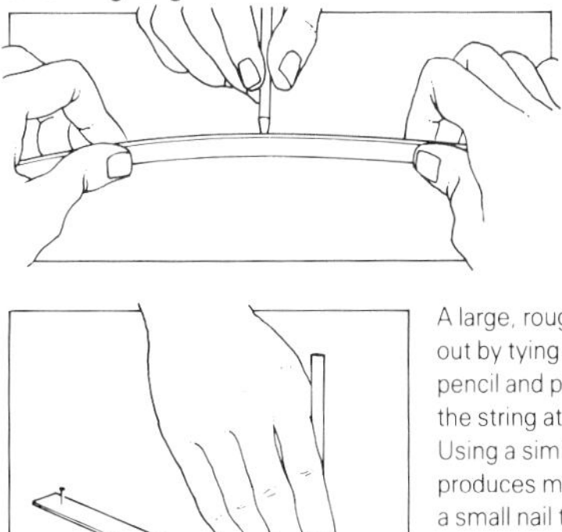

Most commercially available templates are small. Rather than cutting out a large one ask a friend to hold a flexible strip of wood to the curve you want and draw along it.

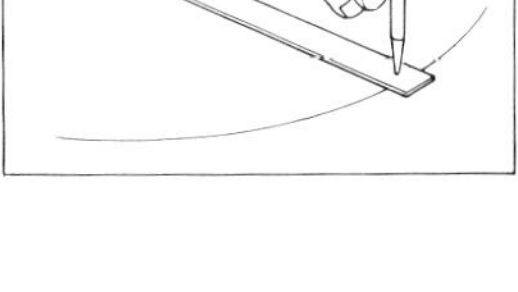

A large, rough circle can be marked out by tying a piece of string to a pencil and pinning the other end of the string at the centre of the circle. Using a similar principle, which produces more accurate results, drive a small nail through a strip of cardboard. Measure the length of the radius required from the nail and punch a small hole, large enough for a pencil point. Swing the card strip around the nail to draw the circle.

Reproducing drawings

Any drawing you make can be reproduced. The number of copies or prints you require will largely dictate the process you choose, which will, in turn, determine the medium you draw with. The quality of the printing can differ greatly. Line reproduction, which can be done by all the methods listed opposite, will cope with any solid line. Tonal reproduction is achieved photographically and is a more complex procedure. The pencil drawing reproduced below in line, tone and colour shows the different effects produced by these processes.

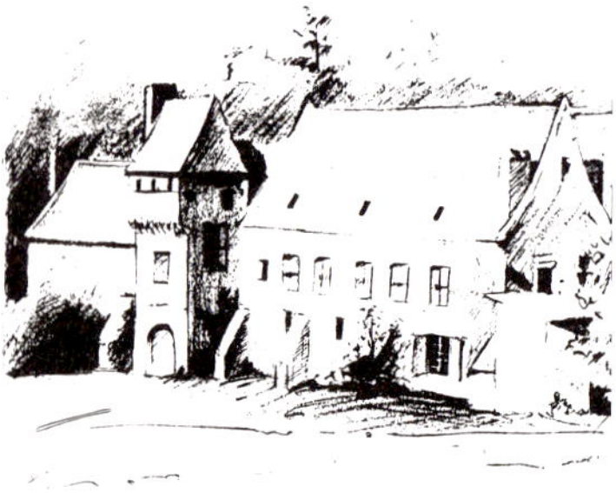

Line A solid, well-defined mark on white paper will print by line reproduction. Tones can only be reproduced if they are hatched or stippled. An ink line is ideal, but faint pencil lines disappear and even darker lines break up, although this can look effective. Only dark marks show, so mistakes on the original can be whited out.

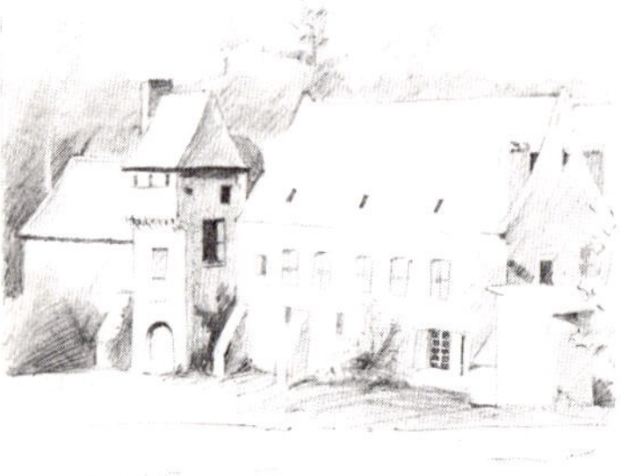

Tone The graded tones of a pencil drawing are broken up and printed as a series of small dots, which vary in size depending on the density of tone. A solid line will also be broken up into dots and be less well-defined. This process is done photographically and is more expensive than printing by line reproduction.

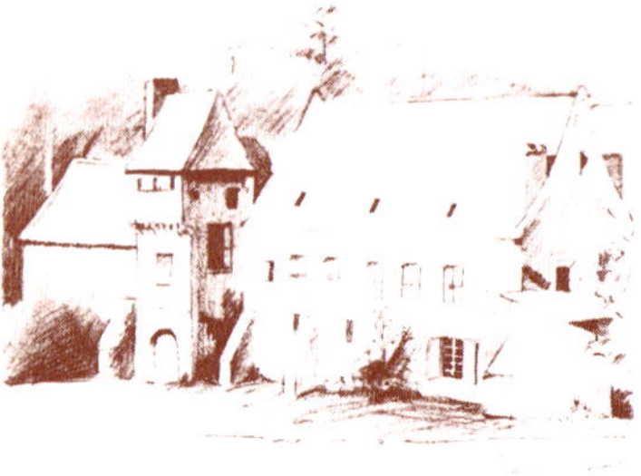

Colour Any black drawing on white paper can be printed with coloured ink onto coloured paper if you wish. Black on white produces the strongest images, however, and any other colour you use will reduce the impact of the drawing to some extent. The colour you choose will affect the mood of the original image.

Methods of printing

Photocopying This is the fastest and most economical way of reproducing small quantities of a drawing – most printers and public libraries have photocopying machines. It is suitable for reproducing black line work but will also cope with tone reasonably well. The print is normally the same size as the original, although some copiers will reduce the image by set proportions. Most machines only work with special paper, but an increasing number will print onto a paper of your choice. Colour photocopiers are now more widely available but are more expensive to use.

Dyeline printing The original drawing must be made on tracing paper to reproduce as a black and white same-size copy. Ink and pencil line can be used for the original, but for the best results, producing a crisp line on a white background, ink should be used because the background darkens as the contrast of the drawing decreases. This is a good method for producing posters as it will make enlarged prints.

Photographic printing Drawings can be reproduced as line, tone or colour photographs. The original can be enlarged or reduced, although the price increases according to size and becomes too expensive if you need large numbers of prints. Glossy or matt paper can be used.

Block and plate printing A printer can convert a line or tone drawing photographically into a block or plate which transfers ink to paper. The main expense is in making the plate and therefore the more you have printed the cheaper it becomes. Almost any card stock or paper is available, but it is worth discussing this and other aspects of your proposed project with the printer before embarking on the finished drawing as it may affect your technique.

Preparing a drawing for reproduction

Having chosen your subject and medium, discuss the project with your printer, telling him what you can afford, how many copies you need and the kind of paper you want to use. Consider, too, the size print you want – reducing will tighten the image but may mean loss of detail, enlarging will exaggerate the quality of the line and may cause distortion.

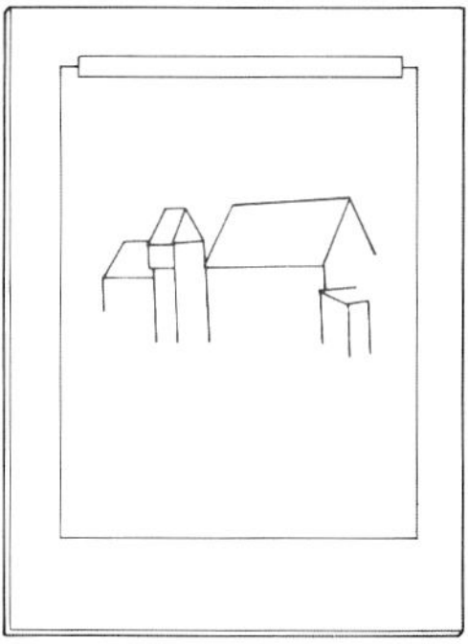

If your drawing is well presented there will be less chance of it being damaged. Attach the paper to a sheet of stiff cardboard, taped at the top with masking tape, so that it can be detached.

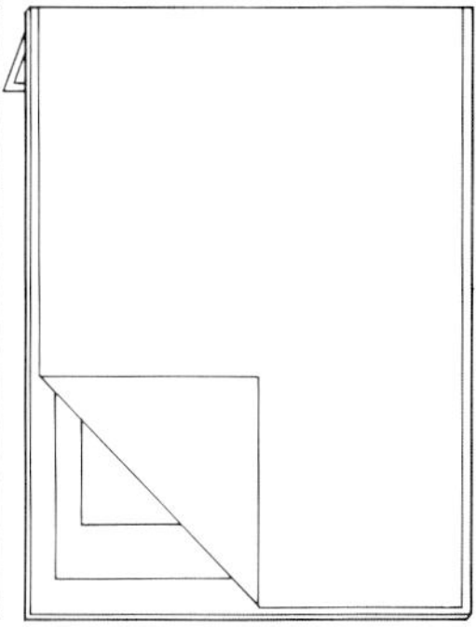

Tape a sheet of tracing paper over the drawing. This will protect it and will enable you to write instructions to the printer over the drawing, such as where marks should be masked out. Finally, cover with thick paper.

Monotype print making

Monotype printing, a technique revived in popularity by Degas in the nineteenth century, is the simplest and most direct form of print making, which encourages experimentation with a wide variety of materials and techniques. A monotype is produced by printing from an image created in ink or paint on a hard surface by an 'additive' or 'subtractive' method. As the word monotype implies, generally only one print is taken, but many artists will take up to three or four. Results can be unpredictable and you will never get two identical prints, making this a very spontaneous technique. Monotypes can be made simply by hand, or with metal plates, such as aluminium, zinc or copper, printed under greater pressure in a press. Altering the pressure applied will produce a different image.

Equipment

Little basic equipment is required. You will need a smooth, hard, non-porous surface on which to create the image – a sheet of glass or metal is ideal. Good mediums are oil- or water-based printing inks, but exciting and often very sensitive results can be achieved from using oil paint, tempera and watercolour. You will need a palette knife and roller or a brush to apply the ink, other instruments to incise images, plenty of rags both to draw with and clean up with, and turpentine for diluting and cleaning oil-based ink.

Subtractive method

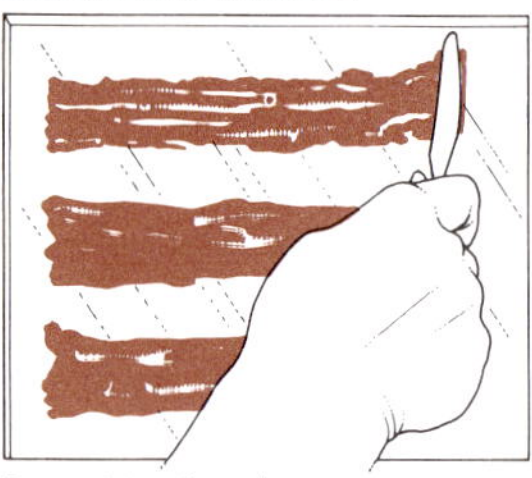

Brown ink will produce a strong image and is a good colour to start with. Squeeze out some ink on one side of the glass and spread it across in bands with a palette knife.

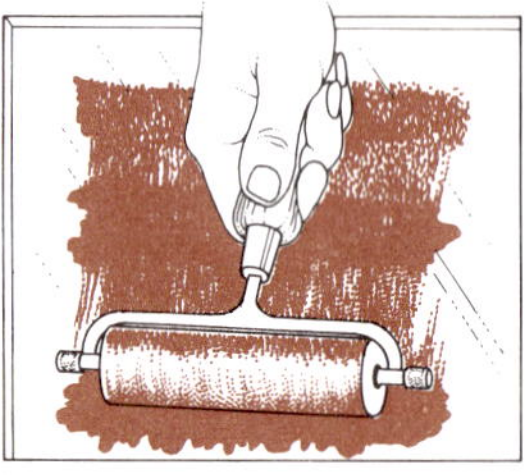

Use a lino-printing roller to spread the ink into an even layer over the printing surface. Make sure that the roller is quite clean and smooth. Clean with turpentine or water after use.

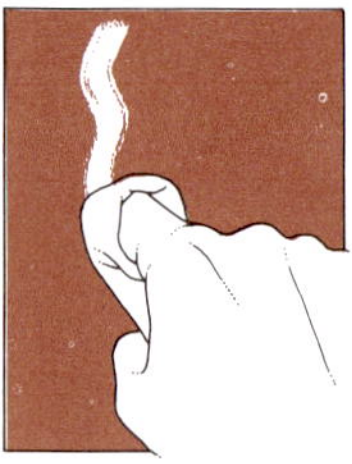

The image is taken out of the ink. A cloth will remove broad areas, or if dabbed on, will create textures.

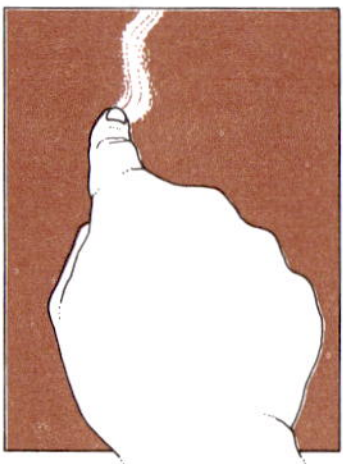

Drawing with a finger is messy, but will produce smooth, curved lines and traces of fingerprint patterns.

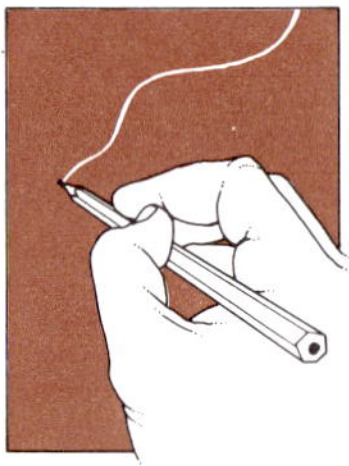

A pencil makes a sharp, thin line. Also try drawing with wooden tools such as the ends of brushes.

Additive method

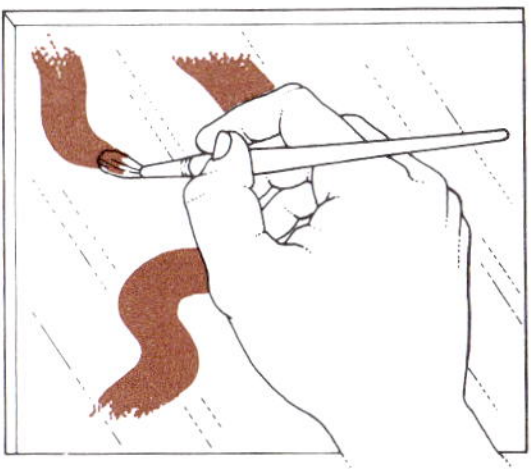

With this method you will work on the clean surface of the glass, drawing with ink applied by brush. Different colours can be used and the ink can be diluted to any viscosity. When highly thinned it will resemble a watercolour wash. This process can be applied to areas of a plate that have been wiped out when using the subtractive method already described.

Taking a print

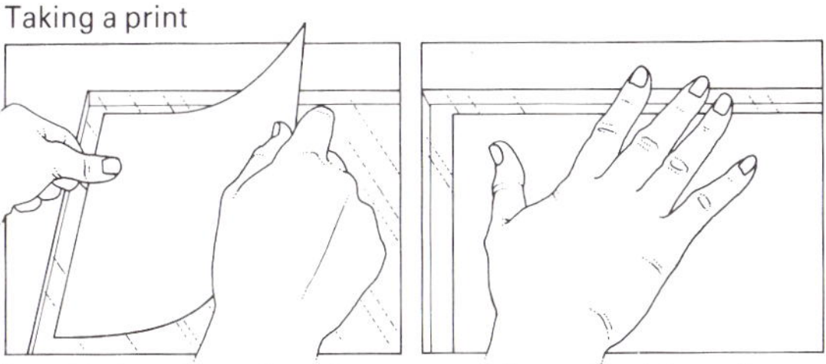

Lay a thin sheet of smooth cartridge paper carefully over the printing surface, avoiding any movement once the paper has touched the surface. Apply consistent pressure with the palm of the hand or the back of a spoon, or gently and evenly run a clean roller over the surface. Carefully pull the print up by lifting it slowly from the near right-hand corner of the paper.

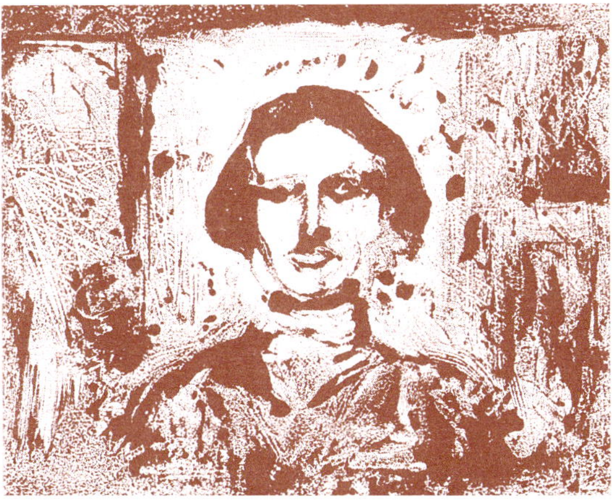

In this example both the subtractive and additive methods were used. Water-based ink was rolled over the entire surface and large areas wiped out with a cloth, more thoroughly in some areas than others. Texture was drawn into the mid-tone areas and details around the mouth and eyes were drawn with a pencil. Finally, ink was brushed onto the clothes and background.

Reference

Top: mixing the ingredients and shaping pastels. Middle: stretching paper on a board and cutting off the finished drawing. Bottom: making paper at home.

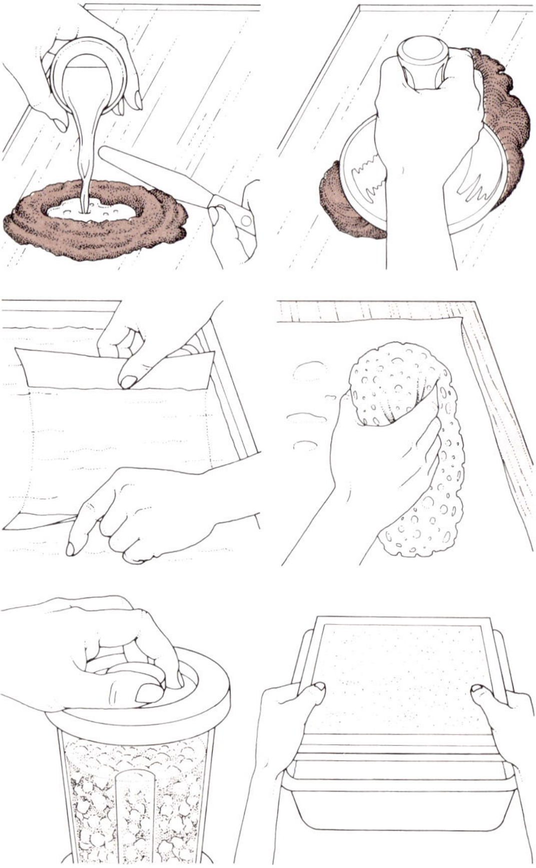

Drawing is a very personal art, a spontaneous and direct visual realization of one's response to an object or emotion. Therefore the more sympathetic the materials used, the more personal the image becomes. Having chosen your materials, their preparation is then part of the act of drawing. For instance, to tint your paper or, to take it one step further, make your paper, gives you a surface that you have determined.

The traditional method of quill-cutting is described here, a method easily adapted to cutting any hollow twig or cane. Homemade pastels have advantages over bought ones: they are brighter, and you will have exactly the colours you want, or the ones you cannot buy. There are also practical hints on fixing drawings, making sketchbooks, a portfolio, mounts and frames, all economical measures as well as being satisfying to do.

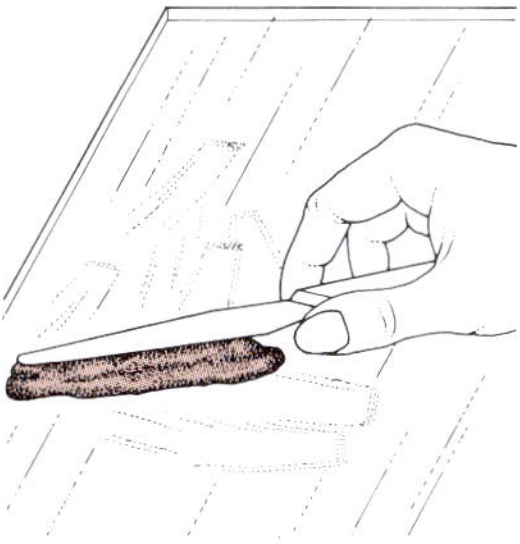

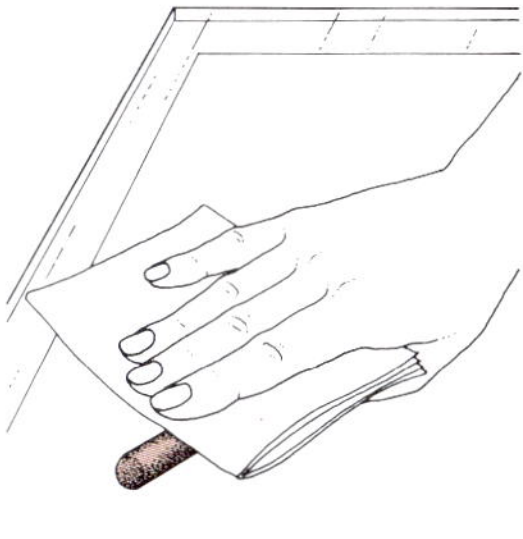

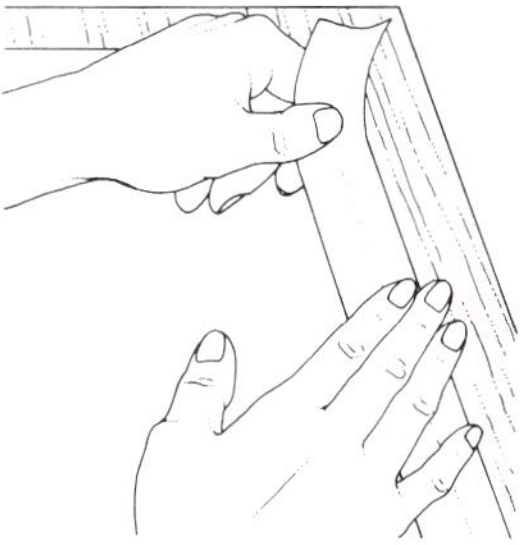

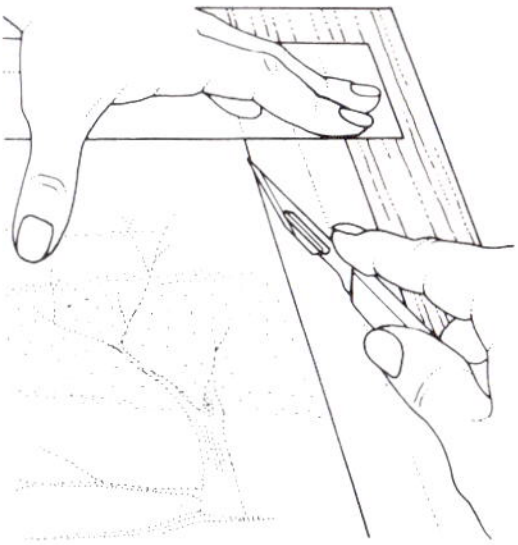

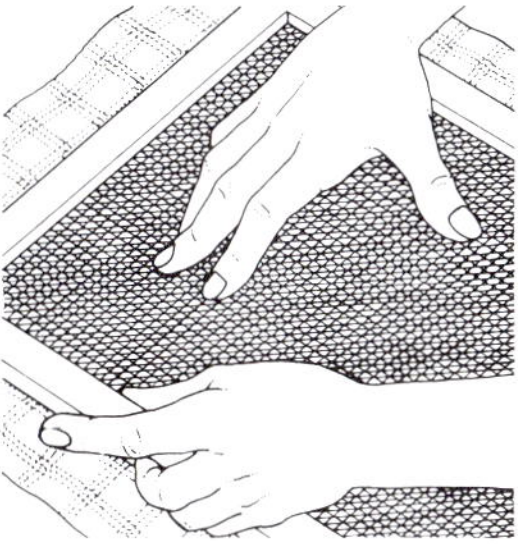

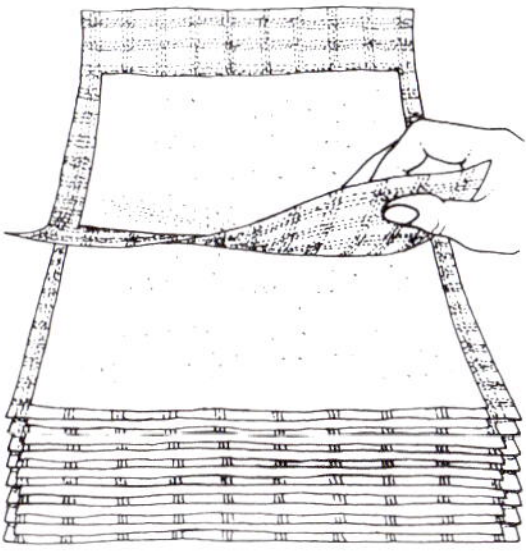

Making drawing tools

If you find that you have gone out sketching without a pen, pencil or piece of charcoal try improvising by whittling down a twig and dipping it into ink; even matches will make some kind of mark. Then you could also shave the end of your paintbrush into a sort of pen. Some exciting and unexpected results may come of this potential disaster. A reed pen can be made from a piece of bamboo or other hollow twig in a similar way to the traditional method of cutting a quill.

Cutting a quill

The flight feathers of a turkey, swan, goose or crow can be cut to make a strong, flexible and yet delicate pen. To cure the feathers either hang them in a dry, airy place for about one year, or cut off the end, soak in water and plunge into fine sand heated in a pan, for about 30 seconds, spooning the sand into the barrel; then rub with a cloth.

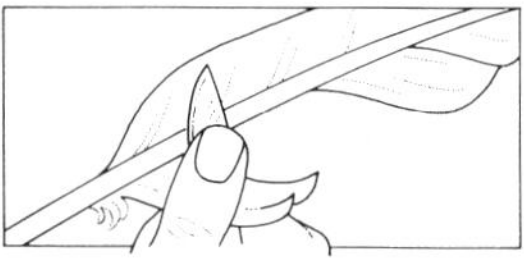

1 Strip the barbs off the feather and scrape the barrel to remove the horny skin.

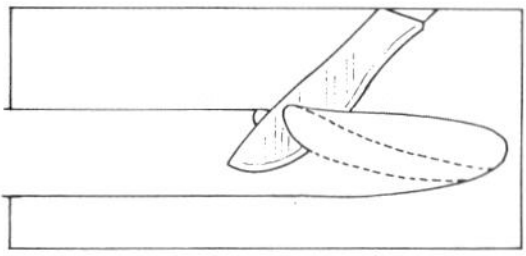

2 Find the natural curve and make an oblique cut on the underside with a thin blade.

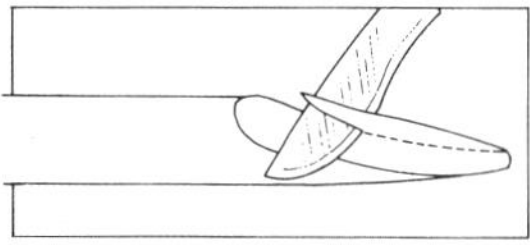

3 Make two more cuts to hollow out the sides (this gives the quill its spring).

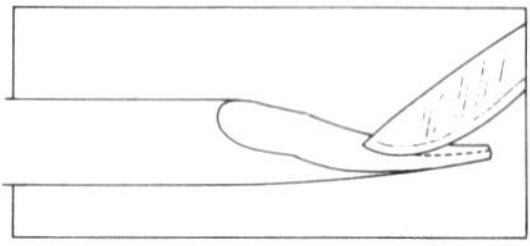

4 Now (or after step 2), cutting on a hard surface, make a slit at the end of the nib.

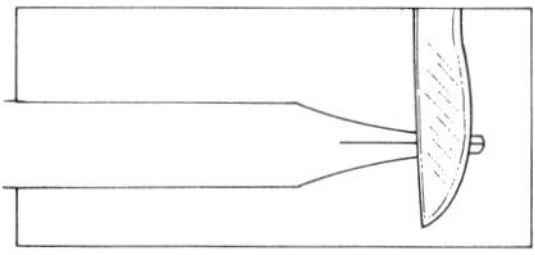

5 Cut off the end to any shape with the blade at an oblique angle. Trim the end with a vertical cut.

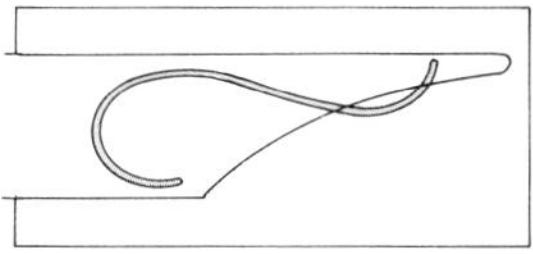

6 Bend a 2mm×3cm strip of thin metal such as tin into a spring. This acts as a reservoir.

Grinding Chinese ink

Grind the inkstick in a few drops of distilled water against the ink stone. A range of tones from light grey to dense black can be produced. Dip the pen into the ink or load the reservoir with a brush. A delicate, very fine line can be achieved with Chinese ink. Grind fresh each time.

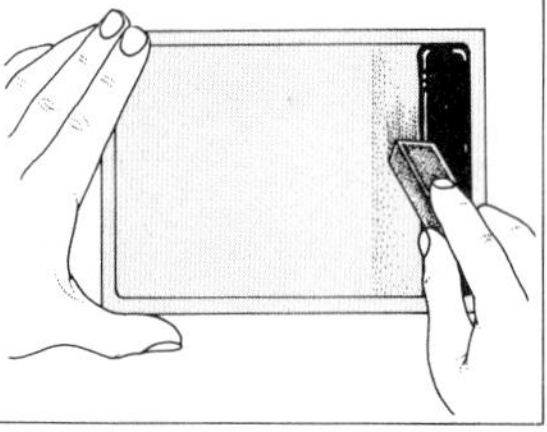

see also pages 18–21

Making soft pastels

Pastels can be made very economically and you will be able (with practice) to make exactly the colours you want to use. You will need a ground glass slab and muller (or a mortar and pestle, or simply a spatula and a hard surface), a palette knife, pigment, whiting and gum tragacanth.

First mix up a binder for the pigment. Add 3g gum tragacanth to one litre cold water. Cover and allow to stand overnight in a warm place. Divide into three parts: put one part aside; mix one part with an equal part of water; mix one part with two parts water. Pigments require different strengths of binder (ie burnt sienna needs medium strength, raw umber needs only a very weak binder). The strongest mixture is seldom needed.

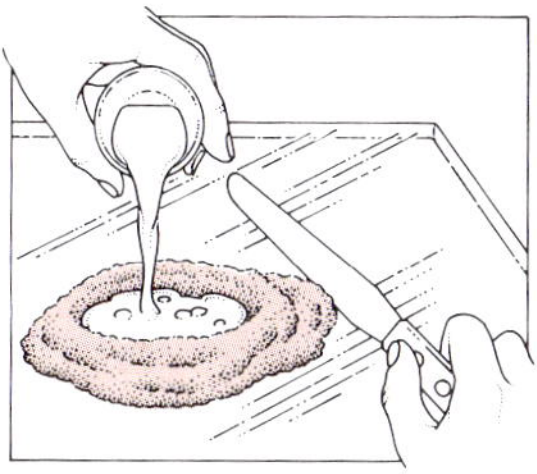

1 Measure equal parts of pigment and whiting. Mix to a paste with a palette knife on a glass slab adding binder gradually.

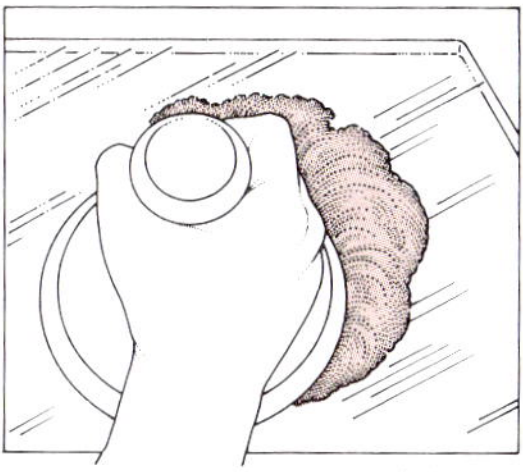

2 Grind well with the muller. If the mixture becomes too dry add some water; if it is too wet add some whiting.

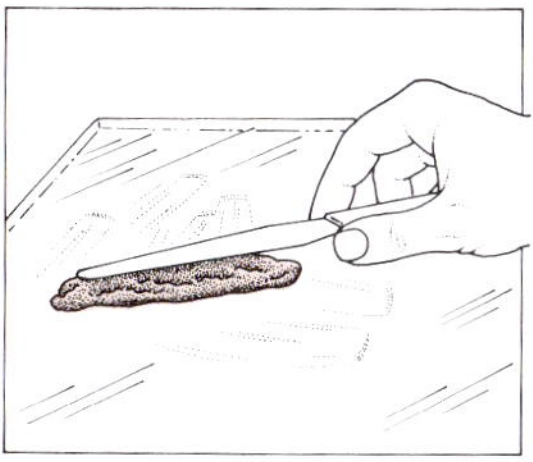

3 Shape into a stick with the palette knife. Do not make too thin (this is a drawback of many brand-name pastels).

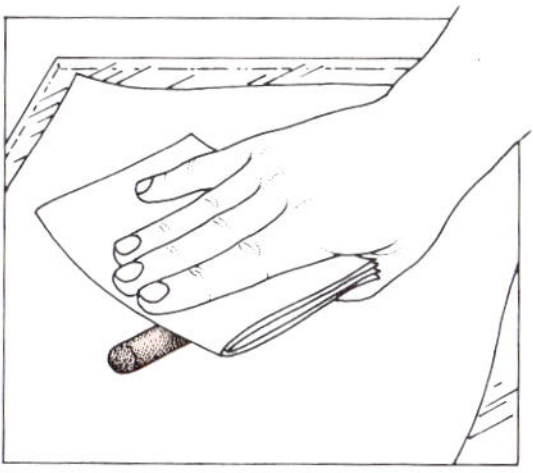

4 Transfer onto newsprint. Roll out with the hand or card covered in newsprint to take off some moisture. Allow to dry naturally.

Graded tones can be mixed either by using the raw pigment or the paste. Start with a measured amount of half pigment, half whiting (the darkest tone), and a measured amount of white (either whiting or titanium white). Divide the full-tone powder or paste in half, make pastels from one half and add the same quantity of white to the other half. Repeat, replacing the same proportions each time until it becomes as pale as you want it.

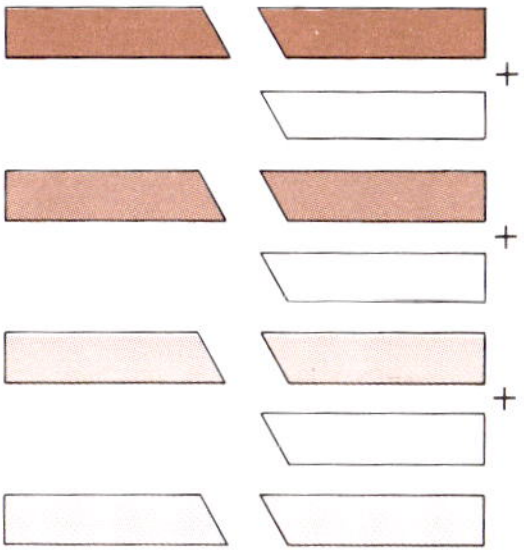

Paper

Stretching paper

It is worth taking the trouble of stretching paper for a finished drawing to prevent it from cockling. This is essential if you are going to use a watercolour wash, unless you are using a heavy watercolour paper which will withstand the expansion and contraction caused by moisture. It is best to stretch on a hardwood board that will not warp and use brown gummed strip to secure the paper. Paper can be run through water before stretching, and it can also be dampened on both sides with a sponge.

The paper should be left on the board while you are drawing, and cut off with a sharp blade when finished. The board will become heavily scored so try to use paper of the same size to avoid carving up the drawing surface and risking tears and bumps.

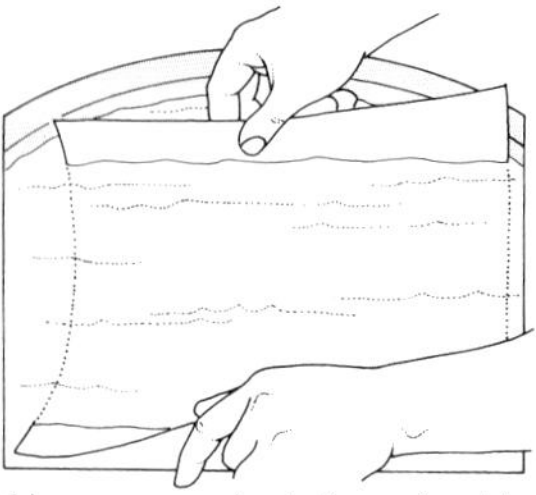

1 Immerse one sheet of paper in cold water. If you want to tint the paper colour the water with ink or watercolour. Wet paper tears and creases easily so handle with care. Allow to soak for a minute or two.

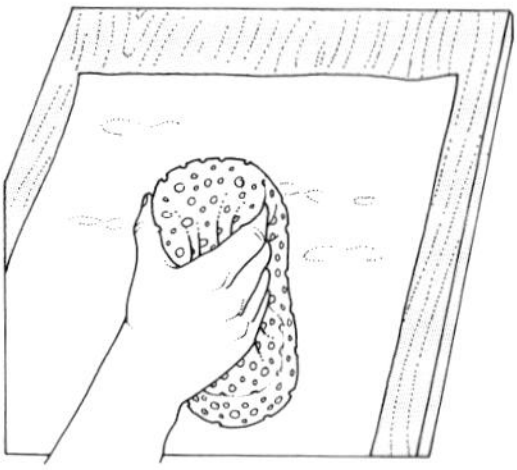

2 Take out of the water, allow to drip dry at an angle for a few seconds. Lay on a flat board and smooth out from the centre with a clean sponge or cloth to remove air pockets and excess water.

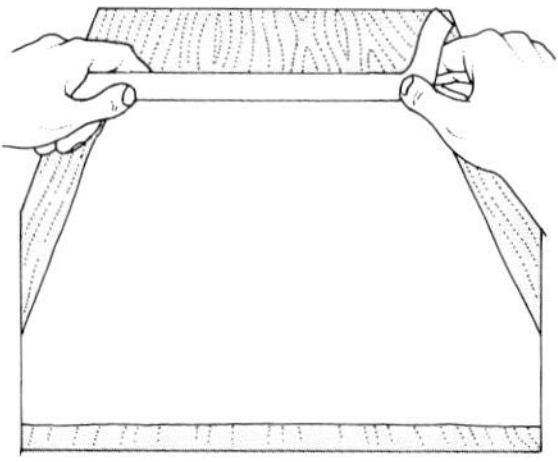

3 Wet some gummed brown paper strip and stick down the edges, overlapping the paper by about 1cm. Add an outside layer of strip to mask off the board. Masking tape does not adhere to wet surfaces.

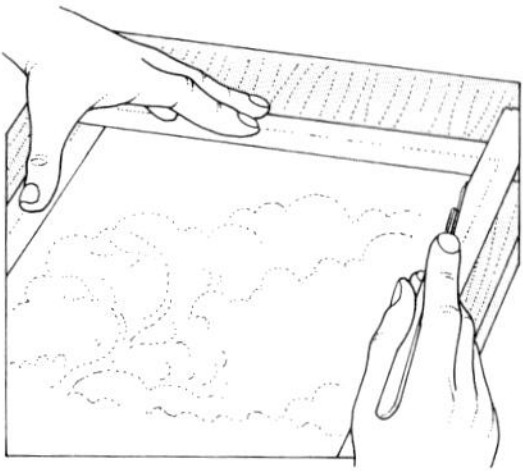

4 Allow to dry flat naturally. When quite dry the paper can be used on the board. Cut off with a sharp blade against a steel ruler. The paper will remain stretched once it has been cut off the board.

Uncrumpling paper

A crumpled piece of paper or drawing can be ironed flat. Cover a table with some clean cotton, a layer of damp white blotting paper and a dry piece of white paper. Place the crumpled sheet on top and another dry sheet above that. Iron carefully with a moderately hot iron. Remove damp cotton and paper. Iron again through dry paper.

Making paper

An ingenious method of making paper at home uses old newspaper as its main ingredient. Liquidize some soaked newspaper in warm water for ten to 45 seconds, depending on the coarseness you want. The mould and deckle, the frame on which the paper is formed, can be bought or made at home.

1 Mould and deckle
Make the mould from strips of 50×25mm wood, with mitred corners (see p134). Reinforce the corners with brass L-shaped braces. Stretch material, eg cheesecloth, over the frame and staple halfway down the width on the outside, ensuring even tension. Make the deckle from 25×25mm strips, to fit on top of the mould exactly.

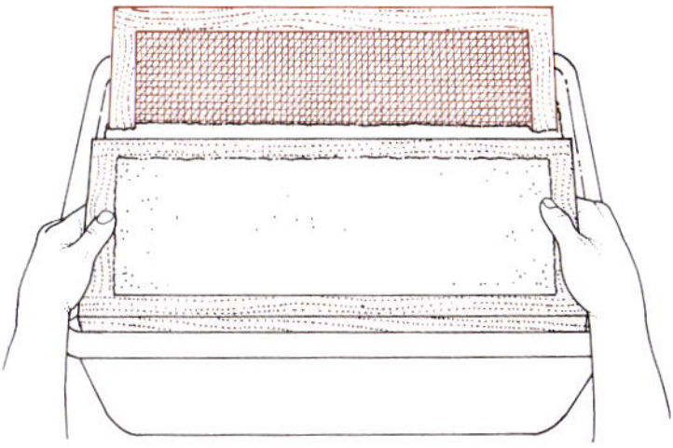

2 Pour about five loads of pulp from the liquidizer into a basin of warm water. Stir frequently. Fit the deckle over the mould and sweep into the water towards you; level out below the surface; lift out horizontal. Tilt at an angle for five seconds to drain off surplus water.

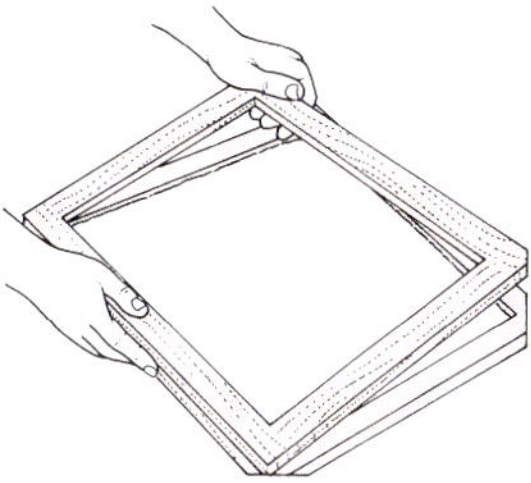

3 Take the deckle off the mould with a swift movement. Wet some absorbent cloths, eg J-cloths, and lay one flat on a board.

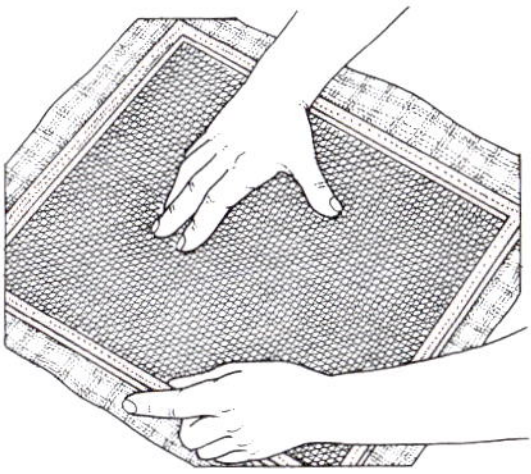

4 Quickly place the mould on the cloth, press on the back of the mesh to loosen the paper and remove the mould sharply.

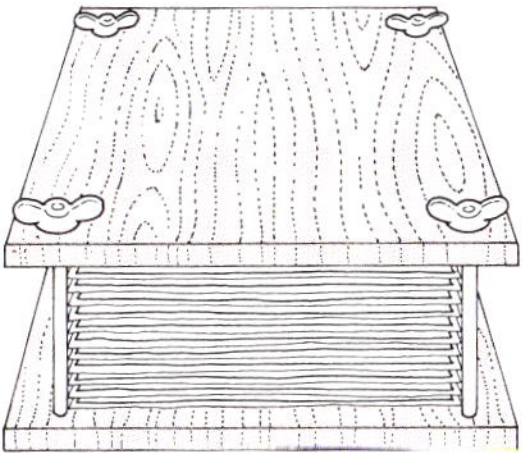

5 Repeat the process and build up a pile of wet paper sandwiched between cloths, finishing with a cloth. To remove excess water weigh down or clamp between boards for about ten minutes.

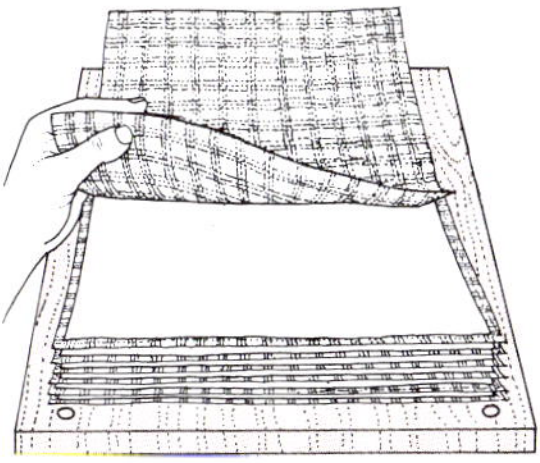

6 Gently peel off the cloths from one side of the paper and allow to dry for a few hours. Remove the other cloth and dry out completely between blotting paper or separately on a board.

Tinting

Coloured paper tends to have a uniformity about it that is not very sympathetic. Hand tinting will get over this problem. Paper can be tinted when being stretched by colouring the water with watercolour or ink, by laying a watercolour wash, by wiping colour on with a rag, or, if you are making paper at home, by adding colour to the pulp (see p131).

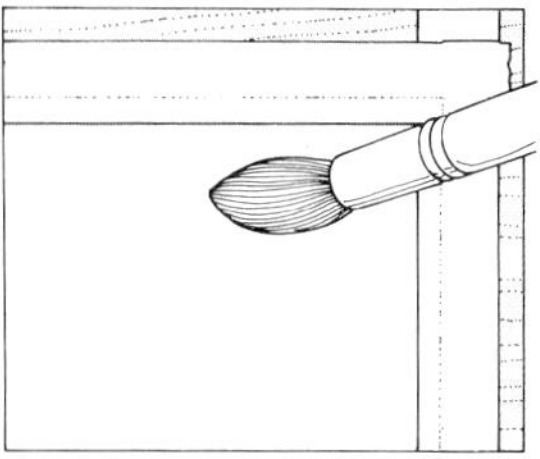

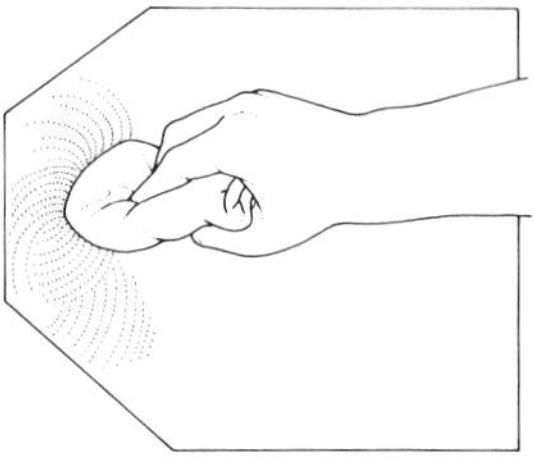

Laying a wash Stretch the paper (see p130); while still damp tilt the board at an angle and mix a large quantity of dilute watercolour. Load a large, soft sable and brush in long, even sweeps across the paper, going over the edge of the paper at each end and catching the tear of colour from the previous stroke.

Wiping on tints Grind up some broken pastels finely, dab a damp cloth into the colour and wipe over the paper. Apply evenly or create patterns with the colour. Tea and coffee bags can be rubbed onto paper (use already brewed bags); they will give interesting and subtle tints and can be varied tonally.

Fixing drawings

Pastels, charcoal and soft pencil drawings should be protected or they will smudge. Framing and glazing is the best method, but not always practical. Fixing will stabilize the medium and is useful for charcoal and pencil, but it tends to spoil the freshness of pastels, darkening the colours, dulling white highlights, fusing the marks and thus losing crispness. Whenever possible avoid fixing pastels, but with care they can be fixed through the paper from the back. Charcoal can also be treated in this way, but it is not necessary for pencil.

Fixatives can be bought in aerosol cans but it is better to buy it in bottles and spray on with a spray diffuser. Proprietary brands are generally resin based, dissolved in alcohol, but casein can also be used. Skimmed milk has a high casein content and can be sprayed on a drawing in a spray diffuser.

Always fix drawings in a well-ventilated room; the fumes given off by alcohol-based fixatives are highly dangerous if inhaled.

Spraying fixative

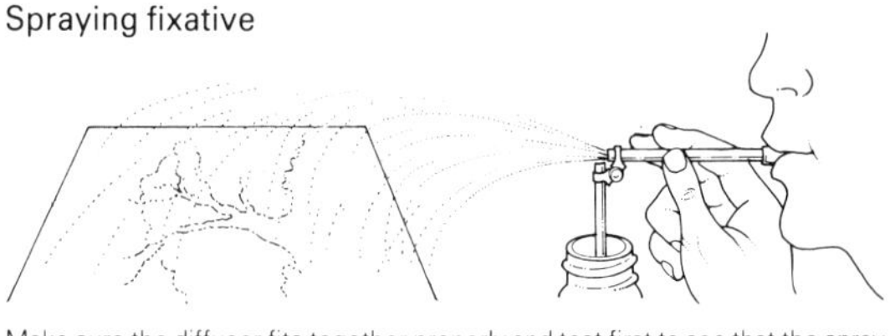

Make sure the diffuser fits together properly and test first to see that the spray is fine and that it does not drip. Lay the drawing flat and spray a fine mist above it into the air; never spray directly onto the drawing. Repeat two or three times depending on the degree of permanency required. If bubbles appear, heat paper gently over a radiator.

see also pages 12–13, 18–19, 87–88, 98–101, 136

Sketchbooks

Sketchbooks can be bought in a wide variety of size, form (in pads glued or spiral bound or in hardback books) and type of paper. A pad of, for instance, Ingres paper, may have a selection of different colours, but for a variety of different qualities that will suit different subject matter and media you will have to make your own sketchbook.

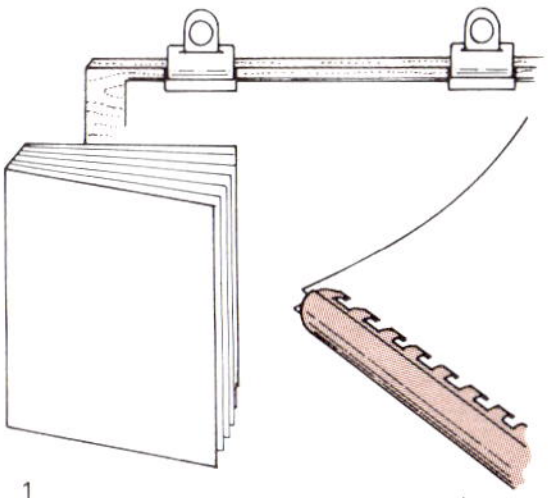

1 Cut up pieces of paper to the same size and clip them to a piece of hardboard with a bulldog clip. **2** Cut one edge of a wadge of paper quite flush and apply glue thickly to that edge. Both these methods are good temporary arrangements. **3** Your own choice of paper can be commercially spiral bound. Interleave the sheets with tissue paper if using pastel or charcoal.

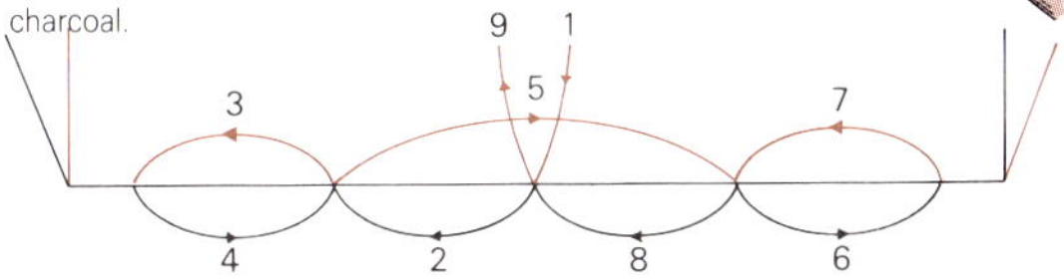

Binding is a more permanent method. Fold about ten sheets of paper with a stout piece on the outside. Stitch in the order shown. Tie a knot in the middle. Paste boards slightly larger than the paper to front and back.

Making a portfolio

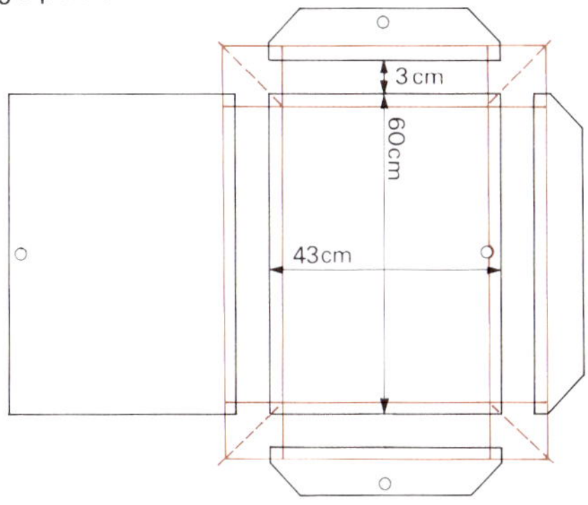

Materials needed: board (eg Millboard), paper, knife, metal ruler, bookcloth, white glue, tapes. Cut out the pattern. Measurements given will take A2 paper. Cover the front of the pieces of board with paper, folding a small flap over to the inside edge and glue down thinly all over. Make holes where shown and thread tapes through, sticking down the end on the inside with tape. Glue strips of bookcloth and stick boards together on the front with 3cm gap between them, leaving an overlap at corners where shown. Stick down with strips on the inside, trimming tape at the edges. Cut corner overlaps on front diagonally and fold in neatly. Cut pieces of paper to cover the inside pieces of board and glue down. Allow the glue to dry out completely before you store your papers and drawings in the portfolio.

Mounting and framing

A mounted, framed and glazed drawing looks impressive; it will also be protected from damp and dust. Window mounting is the best method as it does not interfere with the back of the drawing and keeps the glass away from the paper (essential for pastels and charcoal). A sandwich of glass and hardboard held together with spring clips is a simple and effective method, although not permanent. A drawing can be glued to a card mount or dry mounted, but these methods are not recommended.

Window mounting

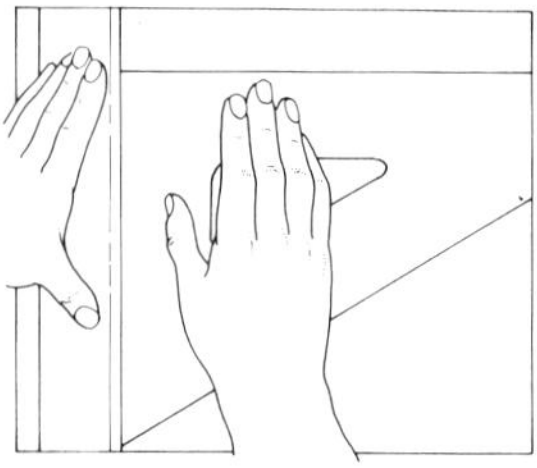

1 Trim the edges of the drawing square, masking off unwanted areas, or mark out in pencil a true rectangle. Decide on the size of the mount (don't make smaller than 6×8cm). The top and side margins should be equal widths, the bottom margin slightly deeper. Lay the card face up on some heavy cardboard. Cut the overall size of the mount, drawing the knife towards you.

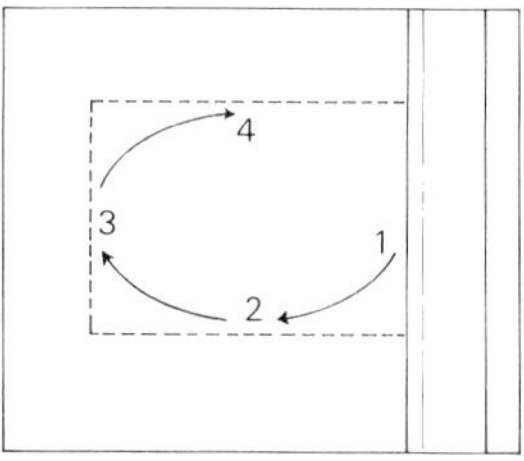

2 Mark out the window opening 3mm inwards from the corner of the drawing. If you are right-handed and are cutting on the card face up, cut in the order shown in the diagram.

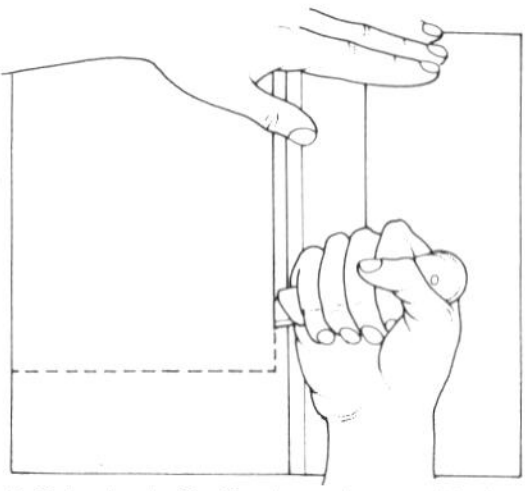

3 Grip the knife firmly and cut with the bevel of the straight edge. Neaten corner 'whiskers' by nicking with a safety-razor blade. Remove card from the centre.

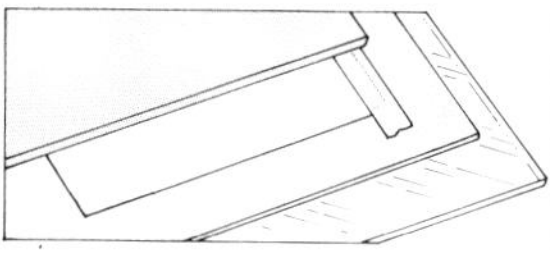

4 Stick a strip of masking tape along the top edge only of the back of the drawing. Turn face up and lay window mount on top. Cut strong backing card to the same size as the mount.

Using a ruling pen

A ruling pen can be used to decorate the mount with fine watercolour or ink lines. Test the thickness of the colour and adjust the pen to produce the required line width. Load colour with a brush to fill one third of the pen (enough to rule a whole line). Rule against the upturned bevelled edge of a steel ruler, with the curved side of the pen outwards, in an even, steady movement.

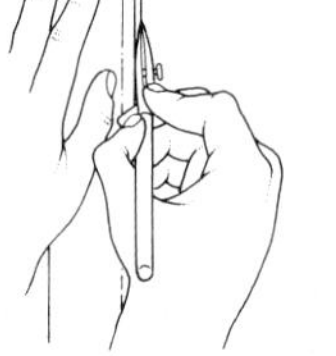

see also pages 20–21

Decorating the mount

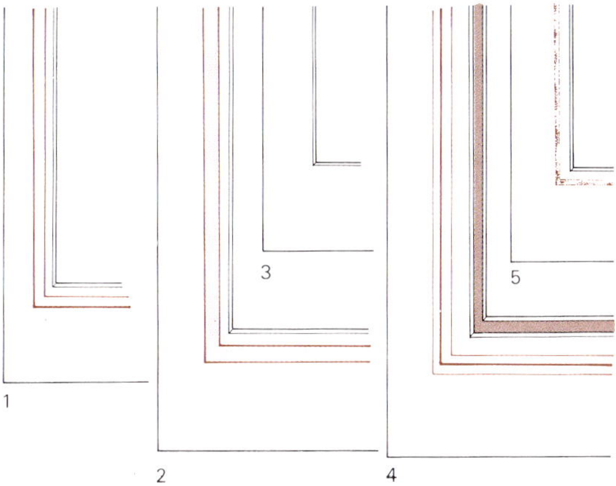

A mount will relate more closely to the drawing if you bring out some of the colours in decorative lines around the bevelled window opening. Draw them with a ruling pen as shown opposite, varying the interval, thickness and colour. **1** simple black or sepia ink lines; **2** watercolour lines, filled in with a dilute watercolour wash applied with a sable brush in the same hue; **3** gold ink lines drawn in with a ruling pen or with a thin sable brush; **4** a step mount, decorated with lines on the outer mount; **5** cut out thin strips of gold gummed paper and stick down.

Framing a mounted drawing

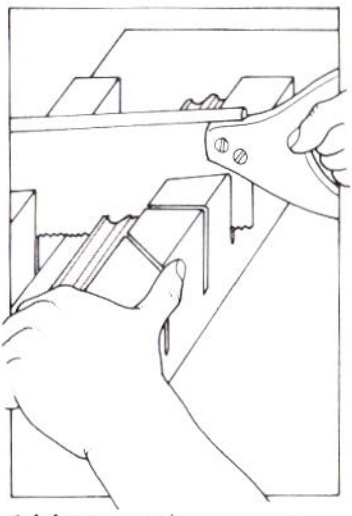

1 Measure the mount and mark out the lengths on the sight edge of the moulding. Cut each piece at an accurate 45° angle in a mitre box with a fine-tooth saw, on the outside of the mark. Assemble an L with one short and one long side; pre-drill holes for panel pins; glue sawn surfaces.

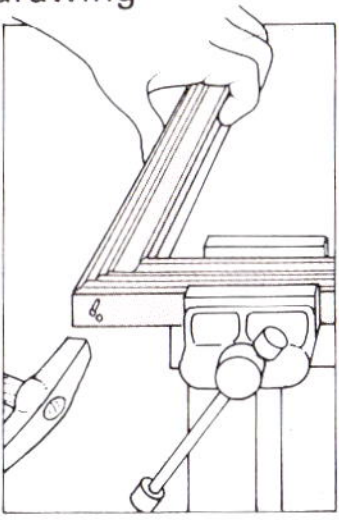

2 Clamp both pieces of the L in an inverted V in a vice, or clamp one piece and hold the other as shown. Protect the clamped moulding between cardboard. Hammer in two panel pins (to be on top or bottom of frame). Assemble opposite L. Glue two Ls together before pinning the third corner. Finish off.

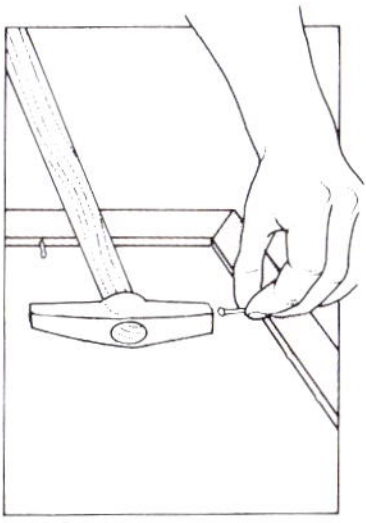

3 Check frame is a true rectangle. When glue is dry turn face down and fit glass, mounted drawing and a backing board on the rebate. Tap in panel pins to secure. Seal the join between the frame and backing board with gum strip. Fix in screw rings and hang with nylon cord or wire; don't use string – it will break.

Storage

Materials

Pens Do not leave ink or colour to dry on the nibs of dip pens; remove the nib from the pen holder and scrub well. If you allow the holder to get wet, the wood will warp and the metal fitting will rust. Fountain pens and technical pens should be rinsed out if they are not going to be used for some time. Always be sure to dry metal nibs completely. Pen-cleaning fluids should be used if ink becomes engrained.

Pencils and crayons should be treated with care since the lead is prone to shatter within the barrel if dropped. Stand them, end-up, in a pot or jar or keep them in a box.

Charcoal is brittle and should be stored in tissue paper.

Brushes should always be washed after use with soap or mild detergent. Shake out surplus water, draw sable brushes to a point with your fingers and stand them in a jar with the bristles uppermost. If you are storing brushes for a long time, make sure they are clean and dry and store them in an airtight box with a few mothballs.

Pastels are easily broken or chipped. Store them in a wooden box either in sawdust or on corrugated cardboard. Protect them with cotton wool when travelling as colours will rub off against each other, making them difficult to identify. To clean them put a handful in a jar with sawdust, close the lid and shake gently.

Paper should be stored flat in a cool, dry room, wrapped in clean paper to protect from dust and light. Paper improves with age, so if you find a good quality paper that you particularly like and have good storage facilities, it is worth considering buying in bulk (it is also more economical). Before buying large quantities test for fading. Cut out two squares of paper, leave one exposed to sunlight and cover the other one completely by closing in a book. Compare the two after a couple of weeks. A good quality non-fading paper will withstand this test. Newsprint and other poorer quality (generally woodpulp) papers will deteriorate quickly and should not be stored; take advantage of their short life and low cost to free you from inhibition when you are sketching. It will encourage you to be more prolific.

Finished drawings

Take care of all your drawings, even the smallest sketch; they may be useful in the future as reference or even as a basis for a painting. Store them loose in a portfolio (see how to make your own on p133) or in a plan chest; do not store rolled up if possible. Most ink drawings will fade if left in bright light. If you have used a medium that is likely to smudge, the drawing should be fixed or covered with tissue paper, although fixing will destroy the tender chalky quality of pastels. The best protection for soft pastel drawings, which are particularly fragile, is to frame them, taking care that the glass does not touch the surface of the drawing (see p135).

Cleaning drawings

Pen and ink drawings can be cleaned by rubbing gently over the surface of the work with pieces of fresh white bread. The bread will break up and should be removed by brushing lightly with a soft brush.

Metric conversion table

Weight		Capacity		Size	
28g	1oz	14ml	½fl oz	25mm (2.5cm)	1in
70g	2½oz	28ml	1fl oz	305mm (30.5cm)	12in (1ft)
114g	4oz	284ml	10fl oz (½ UK pt)	914mm (91.4cm)	36in (1yd)
227g	8oz	454ml	16fl oz (1 US pt)	1000mm (1m)	39in
454g	1lb	568ml	20fl oz (1 UK pt)	1524mm (1m 52.4cm)	60in (5ft)
1kg	2¼lb	1litre	1¾ UK pt (2 US pt)		

List of suppliers

Unless otherwise specified the following suppliers stock a wide range of art materials.

United Kingdom

The Arts Centre
583 Fishponds Road, Bristol

H. Band & Co Ltd (parchment & vellum)
Brent Way, High Street
Brentford, Middlesex

R. K. Burt & Co Ltd (paper)
37 Union Street, London SE1

Colyer Thorpe Ltd
31 King Street, Manchester
West 3

The Copy Shop
95 Fore Street, Exeter

Copystat (Cardiff) Ltd
9 Park Lane, Cardiff

L. Cornelison & Sons
22 Great Queen Street
London WC2

Cowling & Wilcox Ltd
26 Broadwick Street, London W1

East Anglian Art Shop
3 Great Colman Street, Ipswich

Falkiner Fine Papers Ltd (paper)
4 Mart Street, London WC2

H. D. Finch
1 University Street, Belfast

Greyfriars Art Shop
1 Greyfriars Place, Edinburgh

International Graphics (Ireland) Ltd
28 Merrion Square, Dublin

Inveresk Paper Co Ltd (paper)
19 Tudor Street, London EC4

Langford & Hill Ltd
10 Warwick Street, London W1

Miller's Drawing Materials
569 Sauchiehall Street, Glasgow

Paperchase Products Ltd (paper)
213 Tottenham Court Road,
London W1

Philip Poole & Co Ltd (pens)
182 Drury Lane, London WC2

Reeves & Sons Ltd
178 Kensington High Street
London W8

C. Roberson & Co Ltd
71 Parkway, London NW1

George Rowney & Co
121 Percy Street, London W1

Spectrum
20 Colmore Row, Birmingham 3

Wiggins Teape (paper)
Gateway House, Basing View
Basingstoke

Winsor & Newton Ltd
51 Rathbone Place, London W1

UK mail order

Artists Home Supplies, Dept 14
39–49 Roman Road, Cheltenham
Gloucester GL51 8QQ

Fine Art Mail Order Company
Artists Discount Supplies
2–4 Chatham Street
Ramsgate, Kent

Australia

Camden Art Centre
188–200 Gertrude Street
Fitzroy, Victoria

Vitrex (Aust) Pty, P.O. Box N2
Grosvenor Street P.O., Sydney

New Zealand

J. J. Caldwell
P.O. Box 38228, Petone
Lower Hutt, North Island

Republic of South Africa

Ashley & Radmore (Pty) Ltd
Van Riedbeck House, Loop Street
Capetown

Ashley & Radmore (Pty) Ltd
82 President Street, Johannesburg

Glossary

Aerial perspective See Perspective

Brushes A sable brush is best for applying watercolour washes. If well looked after the initial expense will be repaid by a long life. Other less high quality brushes, such as sabeline, can also be used.

Chiaroscuro (Italian, meaning bright-dark) The play of contrasted light and shade, usually in the depiction of movement.

Complementary colours The colour which contrasts most strongly with a given colour is its complementary, as red is to green, yellow to violet, blue to orange. The retinal after-image that occurs after staring at an intense colour is always its complementary.

Cone of vision Imaginary cone with its apex in the spectator's eye that defines the field of sight.

Conté crayon Crayon of graphite and coloured clay, named after its eighteenth-century inventor, it is slightly greasy, hard and rich in texture.

Contour Line indicating the periphery of a volume.

Cross-hatching See Hatching

Eye level In a perspective system, the height of the horizon on the paper. Anything above eye level slopes down towards the horizon, anything below it rises up to it.

Fixative Invisible coating that prevents fugitive media (such as pastels and charcoal) from coming free of the support.

Foreshortening An object seen from an oblique angle appears not in its true proportions but distorted, or foreshortened: for example, a circle seen from the side is foreshortened into an ellipse.

Gouache Watercolour made opaque by the addition of white pigment. It is fast-drying, denser and more reflective than transparent watercolour. It is also known as 'body colour' and is sometimes sold as 'Designer's colour'.

Gum strip Brown adhesive-backed tape used to attach paper when being stretched on a board.

Half-tone See Tone

Hatching Shading or filling in with lines roughly parallel; more parallel lines laid across these constitute cross-hatching.

Highlight A point of maximum light on a form often conveyed by the white paper being left blank, or by adding light tones over darker tones.

Ingres paper A soft, grainy, often flecked paper available in a range of subtle tints. Particularly suitable for conté and pastels.

Life drawing Drawing from direct observation of the model (usually nude).

Mass Volume and weight of an object, as opposed to its contour or shape.

Medium (plural, media) The material or technique in which a work of art is executed.

Mid-tone See Tone

Modelling The description of form by creating the illusion of solidity or volume.

Monochrome Strictly, in one colour; usually, in black and white or brown or grey, without colour.

Negative shape A term applied to the abstract shapes seen in the space between forms. The form may be called a positive shape.

Newsprint Paper on which newspapers are printed, also an economical drawing surface. It is absorbent, of poor quality and has a limited life, but is useful for sketches and studies.

Oil pastels See Pastels

Orthogonals In a perspective system, construction lines that create depth by converging to a vanishing point as opposed to lines parallel to the picture plane.

Pastel Soft (or true) pastels consist of chalk, gum and pigment and adhere only lightly to the paper unless held by a fixative. They have a characteristic soft, chalky texture and subtle colour. Oil pastels have a more limited colour range, they are greasier than soft pastels and adhere better to the paper.

Perspective Conveyance or suggestion of distance in a drawing or painting. Linear perspective involves the use of a grid with a vanishing point on which orthogonals converge. Aerial perspective is the suggestion of space by tone, for instance by lightening the tones as they approach the horizon.

Picture plane See Plane

Plane Face or surface, understood as being flat and of two dimensions (length and breadth but no depth). An object can be drawn as if it consisted of several planes or facets meeting at different angles. Also used to describe areas of a composition, in the same way that foreground, middle- and background are defined. The picture plane is the surface of a painting or drawing.

Plumb line Weighted string that, when held up, will hang down in a correct perpendicular, used to measure a true vertical as an aid to plotting perpendiculars.

Positive shape See Negative shape

Primary colours Red, yellow and blue are the primary colours, from which the secondary colours derive by mixing: red with yellow creates orange, yellow with blue creates green, blue with red creates violet. Mixtures of secondary with primary colours create tertiary colours.

Proportion The relation of one unit to a whole or to other units.

Scraperboard Board with a chalky surface that is coated with a layer of ink. An image is scratched through to reveal the layer below, producing a sharp, incised line.

Sepia The inky secretion of a cuttlefish, from which this cool brown coloured ink was originally made.

Sight size Size of an object as it appears to the eye, as opposed to its true size.

Still life Drawing of plants or animals with or without other objects; loosely, any scene without figures that is not landscape.

Stippling Repeated dabbing or dotting with the point of a brush, pen or other medium.

Tone Degree or quality of light or shade, hence dark tones,light tones mid- or half-tones. Colours also may be dark or light and therefore possess a tonal value.

Tooth The degree of surface texture of the paper determined during manufacture.

Vanishing point In perspective, a point on the horizon towards which lines receding into depth converge.

Volume The space that a form occupies.

Wash Dilution of ink or watercolour applied with a brush or sponge.

Index